WANDERING UNDER SAIL

The 23-foot cutter *Wanderer II*

WANDERING UNDER SAIL

BY

ERIC C. HISCOCK

Author of
Cruising Under Sail
Voyaging Under Sail
Around the World in Wanderer III
Sou'West in Wanderer IV
etc

SHERIDAN
HOUSE

Published in the United States of America 1986 by
Sheridan House Inc., 145 Palisade St, Dobbs Ferry,
New York 10522

First published in 1939
Revised and enlarged edition 1948
Published in Great Britain in hardback by
Oxford University Press 1977
Published in paperback by Adlard Coles Ltd 1986
8 Grafton Street, London W1X 3LA

ISBN 0-911378-61-8

Printed and bound in Great Britain by
Mackays of Chatham Ltd, Kent

PREFACE TO THE THIRD EDITION

IN PREPARING the third edition of this book I have made no alterations to the text, but I have added a new chapter containing an account of the first ocean voyage my wife and I ever made—a happy affair which gave us a taste for further voyaging. As my views on some matters have changed over the years, and with the hope of bringing the reader up to date a little, I have included a few notes at the end of the book, references to which appear in the appropriate places in the text; however, notes can be an irritation, and as these have little bearing on the cruises described, there is no need for the reader to bother with them unless he so wishes.

E. C. H.

Tahiti
June, 1976

PREFACE TO THE SECOND EDITION

THE FIRST edition of this book was published in 1939, and early in the war such copies as remained in stock were destroyed by enemy action. But the kindly reception accorded to it during its short life appeared to justify a reprint, and as the type had to be re-set, I have taken the opportunity to revise the entire book in the light of more mature experience and I have added much new material.

Some of the more ambitious cruises described here were made single-handed, and may therefore appear to be in the nature of stunts, though they were never intended as such. I sailed alone simply because I was seldom able to find a suitable companion with whom to share the somewhat cramped space in my small boat. Although single-handed sailing is more arduous and requires more careful preparation beforehand, it is not necessarily hazardous, and I cannot remember ever having got into a dangerous situation which could have been avoided if I had possessed a crew. I was often frightened and occasionally lonely ; but although there is a certain satisfaction and a feeling of real achievement on reaching the desired destination by one's own unaided efforts, I realise, now that I have married the perfect crew, what a lot of pleasure I missed by sailing alone ; and I find that cruising with the right companion who understands small boats and appreciates the sea in all its moods, is a very much simpler and infinitely more delightful business.

A well conducted cruise should be a pleasant progress and not a succession of exciting incidents, and on that account I like to think that I have had no more than my fair share of adventures. But the peaceful summer cruises or quiet week-ends which constitute the greater proportion of one's sailing experiences, are apt to make dull reading unless described by a far more able pen than mine, so I have selected for this book those of my cruises which contained some elements of excitement or which extended to the less frequented places. In a few instances—mostly concerned with passages which lasted for more than twenty-four hours—I have given extracts from my log-books, for although they are often inelegant and usually brief, they do sometimes give a clearer and more graphic account of what actually happened at the time, and leave the reader in no doubt as to which day of the week is being described.

I have been very fortunate in making a number of cruises in various yachts belonging to my friends, and I would like to take this opportunity of thanking them not only for taking me with them, but for lending me their log-books and leaving me free to use what material I needed for this book.

E. C. H.

Yarmouth, I.O.W.
January, 1948.

CONTENTS

ILLUSTRATIONS

FROM PHOTOGRAPHS

ILLUSTRATIONS

FROM LINE DRAWINGS

WANDERING UNDER SAIL

CHAPTER I

FIRST ADVENTURES

IT SEEMS a little odd that the bankruptcy of a firm trading under the name of Waste Food Products, Ltd., should have been the means of enabling me to go sailing. What that firm made of "the crumbs from the rich man's table" I never discovered; but my father, who had invested some money of mine in the concern, very generously refunded my loss when the smash came, thus enabling me to buy my first boat. I suppose, as yachts go, she was a poor thing, but I did not know that then. I became very attached to her, and I gather from some old writings of mine in the *Yachting Monthly* that I thought she was the finest little ship afloat.

I bought her at Bembridge in the Isle of Wight. Very little was known about her, the agents did not even know what she was called, and as I wanted to sail her away immediately I had to give her a name, for I knew enough even in those days to realise that a vessel ought not to be taken to sea without one. Thinking I was being very original, I christened her *Wanderer*, having a picture in my mind of the barque immortalised by John Masefield; but I was somewhat chagrined when the painter who was scribing it on her stern pointed to a desolate and neglected motor-boat and said:

"What, another of 'em?"

It was too late then to alter it, but I was even more disgusted when I found no less than a dozen *Wanderers* in *Lloyd's Register of Yachts*, and there must have been many more not in that book.

Bit by bit I discovered something of *Wanderer's* history, the most interesting points being that she was built in 1898 by a Southampton firm, long since defunct, and was christened *Pom-Pom*—her owner, being an army man, was desirous apparently of keeping in mind the South African war. Another point of interest was that she raced at Bembridge with conspicuous success for many years. That I found a little difficult to believe, and I fancy someone must have been confusing her with another boat, for she was certainly the slowest that I have ever sailed in ; quite tiny dinghies used to pass her with ease.

She was much too fine forward to balance her very heavy quarters, and to make matters worse her mast was too near the bow. Slowly, and so far as it was possible, I improved her as I discovered her defects. First I made the cabin habitable with a pipe cot and some lockers, and then I changed her sloop rig to cutter, fitting a longer bowsprit which considerably improved the steering, and I gave her a topsail, which helped her a lot when it could be induced to set properly. With her hull I could, of course, do nothing, but it had two assets : it was sound, despite a great slab of cement in the bilge, and it was stiff ; and that I consider to be one of the most important things in any cruising yacht. Speed does not matter very much ; in fact, if you wish to remain reasonably dry it is rather to be avoided ; accommodation is a compromise at the best of times, but at least it can be altered to suit some of the owner's requirements, and so can the rig ; but nothing much can be done about a boat that sails on her side, and life aboard her is a miserable and tiring business. For day sailing it does not matter, but it is most trying when on a longish passage to have to walk about like a fly on a wall. If modern yachts have a common fault—and some people would have us believe that they are perfect—it is that they sail on their ears, and that is what comes of sacrificing other things to windward work. Trawlers, pilot cutters and quay punts do not pretend to be clever on that point of sailing, but one can at least live aboard them without being a practised gymnast.

That I bought my boat on a Wednesday, sailed her away on a Thursday, and found her wrecked on a Friday, is an unfortunate fact ; but it taught me the valuable lesson that it is a far better thing to trust to one's own anchors and chain than to lie on a mooring the condition of which is unknown. It is more bother—at least the getting under way is—and that I suppose is the reason why nearly every anchorage in the Solent is choked with so many moorings that the visitor has much difficulty in finding a clear berth. One of the exceptions was Beaulieu River, so I decided to make that my home port, and

I used it for many years, the yacht lying to her own anchors off Gins Farm.

But the day after I had bought my boat I sailed her straight from Bembridge to the Hamble River because that was a more convenient place in which to have a refit and carry out some of the alterations that were necessary. Off the village I was directed to a mooring which I was at liberty to use during the winter, for as it was already late October the owner's yacht was laid up.

That was the first time I had ever attempted to pick up a mooring, and a pretty fine mess I made of it, for although I had read quite a lot about the subject, I found that practice and theory are very different things. The wind was blowing against the strong ebb tide, so I did as the books instructed, and lowering the mainsail, tried to run up to the buoy under jib only. But either the wind was not strong enough or the tide was too strong, for we made no headway ; so I hoisted the peak of the mainsail again ; and while I was doing that we fouled one of the large iron buoys that were scattered about the river, and broke the wire bobstay. Eventually we reached the mooring, but as it had only a small loop I missed it with the boathook. So we had to beat back again—I dared not drift as there were too many craft about—and that meant hoisting the whole mainsail. Then, like an ass, I thought I would try to pick up the mooring with all sail set, and so I did, but as we were going fast I could not hold on, and consequently lost the boathook. Instead of behaving sensibly, the boathook freed its hold of the buoy and went gaily drifting down the river with *Wanderer* in hot pursuit.

Meanwhile, a crowd had collected on the shore to watch the fun and to shout advice, as again and again I made fruitless attempts to pick up that boathook, only a few inches of which were showing above water. Off Warsash I gave up the chase and returned to the attack on the mooring again. That time I got it by lying flat on my stomach, but we were still moving fast. Grimly I hung on, leaning farther and farther over the side until suddenly I lost my balance and amidst cheers from the shore plunged head first into the muddy water. But luck favoured me, and I was able to grab the broken end of the wire bobstay and hitch it to the buoy. We were moored at last.

Having dried myself and pondered for a while on the curious ways of ships on the sea, I went ashore for the night as the boat was not then habitable.

The next day, armed with pots of paint and some carpenter's tools, I returned to find a gale blowing from S.W. and my new boat gone. I called on the harbour-master to inquire what he had done with her, but he professed complete ignorance and assured me that I must be mistaken, for nothing could possibly have happened to her on that mooring as it was a very good one. However, he came along with me, and presently we discovered *Wanderer* the best part of a mile farther up the river, lying against the stone wall on the east side above the *Mercury*.[1] Commandeering a dinghy, we rowed across to see what was to be done, and we got wrecked as well. The ebb was away, a short vicious little sea was running, and we soon discovered that there were other things besides a wall there, for a double row of short piles had been planted close to it. One of these poked itself through the bottom of our boat, so we hastily landed before she sank under us.

Wanderer, with a few feet of the broken mooring chain still hanging from her bow, was chafing badly against the wall as the little waves rocked her, and she too had found some piles to sit on, judging by the splintering noise she was making. We improvised some fenders, and burying the anchor ashore, led the throat halyard to it in an attempt to steady her. The harbour-master then returned to Hamble by ferry, and I walked to a nearby house to telephone one of the yacht yards to come and salvage the wreck. But the owner of the house happened to be Major Henderson—a well-known Solent yachtsman—and he very kindly came along in his yacht *Windhover* and towed my boat away to Moody's yard at the next high water. When she had been hauled out we discovered that both her garboard strakes had been battered and torn and several other planks damaged as well. Only the cement in the bilge had saved her from foundering. The repairs, which entailed the fitting of three and a half new planks including both garboard strakes, a new stem band and a good deal of patching and re-fastening elsewhere, cost £11 15s. and took less than a week to complete.

My first boat was an 18-foot sloop built in 1898. With her lean bow, heavy quarters and mast too far forward, she was hard on the helm until I gave her a longer bowsprit and rigged her as a cutter.

Below she is seen on the beach at Bembridge for a scrub, and on the right in Studland Bay under her improved rig and with her tiny topsail set

I kept the boat in commission throughout the winter and spent every week-end in her playing about in the Solent, and a lot of time quietly on the mud. But, as I do not think my apprenticeship to the sea can possibly be of much interest to anyone, I will only mention a few of the more amusing incidents here.

. . . . .

Wanderer had been lying in Yarmouth's little harbour for several days while a winter gale blew from the south-west. On the third day, tiring of my inactivity and being desirous of getting back to my home port, I left, and with two reefs in the mainsail had an exhilarating run up the Solent, feeling a very bold mariner. All went well until we entered the Beaulieu River and began to beat up the first long reach which runs parallel to the sea.

I very soon discovered that she would not come about, so on to the mud we went. You can gather how badly the boat was found in those days when I tell you that there was no kedge warp on board. Therefore, loading the bower anchor and as much of its chain as I could get into the dinghy, I struggled out into midstream against the gale and dropped the hook. As the tide was rising we quickly came off, but no sooner had I got the boat under way again than she went aground on the other side. Once more I took the anchor out and pulled her off, and no less than six times I repeated that performance.

Then, soaked through and weak with fatigue, I sat in the cockpit. My freshly painted little boat was in a dreadful state; her deck, sides and gear were smeared with oozy black mud, while rust-coloured water dripped from the newly tanned sails to trickle out of the scuppers. All but the reeds, the mud flats, and a solitary perch leaning at a drunken angle, was blotted out by the slanting rain, as the wind shrilled through the disordered rigging. I contemplated the scene in abject misery, and was seriously considering remaining there until the wind should moderate enough to allow me to shake out the reefs, when the idea of taking a reef in the jib occurred to me. Putting a lashing round it at the head and the foot—for there was no small jib on board—I got gingerly under way for the seventh time, and found to my relief and delight that the boat would handle once again, and although our progress was slow, we reached Gins Farm without incident.

I am almost ashamed to admit this incredible ignorance now ; but I was learning, and to prove it I bought a smaller jib and a kedge warp without delay.

. . . . .

Another adventure with anchors, but of quite a different kind, occurred in Southampton Water. I had a friend with me who knew even less about sailing than I did, and we had spent the night in Ower Lake, a narrow creek just above Calshot. In the morning, with infinite labour, we managed to beat down to the entrance against a light east breeze, and my crew was steering whilst I prepared breakfast below. All of a sudden he shouted for me ; poking my head through the hatchway, I was just in time to see the dinghy, which was towing astern, catch its bow behind one of the posts that marked the edge of the fairway, and the painter, together with the cleat to which it was made fast, fly over the stern. The only thing was to swim for it, and as I dived overboard I told George to let go the anchor, as I did not think he knew enough to keep off the mud. I reached the punt just as it arrived among the reeds, and climbing into it looked round to discover *Wanderer* hard and fast ashore.

" I did as you asked," said George, as I returned on board, " but I don't think the anchor can be holding very well."

It was holding without a doubt, but in his excitement he had thrown the kedge over the side without making anything fast to it.

. . . . .

I like to think that the following little incident was not my fault, but I expect it was really, for most of the unpleasant things that happen to us are.

I had visited Hythe, and was beating down Southampton Water against a fresh S.E. wind. A good deal of water came on board as we plunged into the head-sea and some of it found its way into the cockpit ; but I did not bother to work the pump, as most of the bilge water was in the habit of running away under the lee seat, and it would be much less trouble to deal with as soon as we were running down the Solent more or less upright.

Off the Calshot Spit light-vessel I found an unpleasant little popple with the wind blowing straight up Spithead. One of the small seas lifted *Wanderer's* stern as she turned to run, and the accumulated bilge water, of which there must have been a considerable amount by then, ran into the bows and stayed there, for the weight of the water and the mast, the press of sail and her fine lines forward, would not let her lift sufficiently for it to run aft again. With the fore-deck awash she was almost out of control. Fortunately there was no fore-hatch, but more and more water was finding its way down below through the navel pipe. I dared not round her up into the wind for fear she might plunge straight under, and I could not risk adding my weight to the already overloaded bows to get sail off her. So my only hope was to attempt to beach her before she foundered.

I managed it all right, but she took a severe hammering on the shingle. However, the tide was ebbing fast and she soon dried out ; fortunately when she floated at the next high water there was no wind, and therefore no sea, so she came off undamaged.

. . . . .

Providence must have been very busy looking after me during my first year or two of sailing, for although I got into the most ridiculous scrapes through ignorance, the boat was never seriously damaged, and neither was I.

I suppose everyone looks back upon his maiden voyage with delight, no matter how short, how slow, or how terrifying it may have been. One's feeling of satisfaction is very great when the desired landfall rises out of the sea ahead ; when the first little blow has been successfully weathered ; when the first strange and delightful harbour has been made in the dark, and one wakes in the morning to find himself in a new and lovely land. But perhaps the beginner's greatest joy of all is when his little boat lies snug once more in her home port after the cruise is over, and he dreams of the places she has taken him to and the pleasures she has given. Time is a great healer, and one soon forgets the misery of rolling becalmed in a heavy swell, the panic off a lee shore and the anxiety of fog ; somehow they seem small, unimportant things compared with the exhilaration of a glorious day at sea, when the yacht dances over the little white-caps beneath a warming sun.

My first cruise was from the Solent to Cornwall, and as cruises go it was not a very spectacular one ; but I felt myself to be a veritable Columbus—after it was all over. I made a bold beginning by sailing direct from Beaulieu River to Brixham, a distance of ninety miles, and the fact that I took no less than four days and five nights to cross West Bay was no fault of mine—there was no wind at all. For the first time in my sailing career I was thoroughly bored, but my boredom rapidly changed to anxiety when the fresh-water tank ran dry, for the weather was very hot.

Night had fallen before we rounded the head of the breakwater, and as we ghosted into the harbour, where the high shore lights made pools of brightness on the still water between the black shadows of the trawlers, I inhaled a scent that I shall never forget—the mixed odour of fish, salt, drains, and drying hay, an odour I have ever since associated with the friendly port of Brixham.

Calling at most of the Devon and Cornish ports on the way, I reached Helford, and considering that was far enough for my first lone cruise, I then worked my way slowly home again. So far as I can remember there was only one excitement, and that was a very real one.

No sensible person who has studied the chart or read the sailing directions would be fool enough, one would think, to run for Salcombe in a strong onshore wind ; but that was the very thing I did. There was absolutely no excuse, even though I was in a hurry to get in out of the wet, for Dartmouth, safe to approach in any weather, was not so very much farther on.

The seas could not have been breaking properly on the bar, or I would not have survived ; but one crest broke with sufficient force to fill *Wanderer's* large, open cockpit, and bursting open the cabin doors, flooded everything below. Fortunately we were through the worst of it by then, for if another crest had come aboard I think it would have been the end of us.

A number of unpleasant things have happened to me in the neighbourhood of Salcombe. On one of the earlier trips in my second *Wanderer* I called at that port, and when I left it the wind dropped completely near the bar, and we drifted about in a stupid little swell. I ought to have anchored at once, but instead I wasted a lot of time trying to get way on the yacht with the sweep—an impossibility except in smooth water—and not until we had been set by the swell dangerously close to the rocks on the western side, did a light air arrive to take us clear.

Another occasion was when I was bound for Ireland. After an uneventful passage from the Solent I arrived off the Start in the early hours of the morning, and there with masthead spinnaker and topsail set, got caught in a sudden summer gale. Unable to gybe or heave-to, it was just a case of getting sail off the yacht before she hit the rocks, which, near though they were, had been completely blotted out by a heavy deluge of rain.

The following year I was making Salcombe once again for a comfortable night's rest. Just before reaching the bar *Wanderer* was knocked down when she had no steerage way by a brutal squall from off the land. To start with, the water lapped over the cockpit coaming, but she went over so far that the lee seat actually prevented it from going into the bilge. When that squall at length blew over and allowed her to get upright again, I went on into the harbour, thinking that there would be plenty of room in which to round up and get the headsails stowed and the anchor ready. But there was a lot of wind at the anchorage, and the place was so full of craft—it was the eve of the regatta—that we were well up past the Bag before I was able to leave the helm. However, on that first cruise I was able to get away without adventure, and had an uneventful sail back to the Solent.

The following year I sold *Wanderer*. As yachting is now apt to be an expensive business, it is worth recording that the entire cost for the three and a half years that I had her, including everything except food, and taking into consideration her original cost and the sum I got when she was sold, was £90. I had a number of expensive alterations made, she was hauled out of the water during the laid-up periods, and was kept as smartly as her age permitted.

Despite her vices, and they were many, she taught me the rudiments of seamanship together with a thorough respect for the sea ; but it was obvious even to my prejudiced eye that she was not boat enough for the sort of cruising I was contemplating and I hoped to find in the secondhand market a rather larger and more seaworthy vessel capable of reaching more distant cruising grounds with some degree of certainty.

CHAPTER II

DYARCHY

IN THESE sophisticated days it is fashionable to scoff at working boats as being unhandy and slow, but I have no hesitation in stating that some of my happiest days were spent and many of my best cruises were made in an ex-Bristol Channel pilot cutter, for a pilot cutter *Dyarchy* was before she took to yachting.

The old saying has it that "It's not the ships but the men in 'em," and everyone who has sailed in the old *Dyarchy* knows that the efficient manner in which she was handled, the commonsense arrangement of her gear and the cheerfulness which reigned aboard her was due entirely to her owner Roger Pinckney.[2] But as he insists quite firmly that he never attempts to teach, I must hold the ship responsible for all that I learnt in her.

Built by Cooper of Pill in 1901, she measured 41 feet overall, 38 feet on the waterline, had a beam of 12 feet 9 inches and drew 7 feet of water. Her decks were wide and clear, for they were not cluttered up with the usual litter of spars and gear from which so many yachts suffer ; the bulwarks were high enough to give one a real feeling of security, and the deep self-draining cockpit was very comfortable and provided good shelter.

The gaff of a Bristol Channel pilot cutter was usually as long as the boom, but Roger had shortened *Dyarchy's* gaff by 4 feet, thus reducing the area of the mainsail by 40 square feet, and he replaced the old jib-headed topsail, which was so square at the head that it never set properly, by a yard topsail that set very well, with a marked improvement both in the ship's appearance and her sailing ability. A genoa-spinnaker of 600 square feet and a yankee jib-topsail assisted her in light winds. She had a 4 cylinder Deutz auxiliary engine which was not often used.

Below decks she had, to quote her owner, a mass of congested accommodation which was the result of various people's ideas since she became a yacht, but although it certainly had its drawbacks it possessed the great advantage that each compartment was sufficiently small to allow one to get a good grip on something solid in a seaway.

Mrs. Pinckney, Roger's mother, was the youngest old lady that I had ever met. She sailed on all of *Dyarchy's* cruises, steered a steady compass course, saw to the feeding of the crew in no sketchy or uncertain manner, and was the ship's alarm clock and doctor. There are some who say that there is no room for women in small ships, or large ones either for that matter, but Mrs. Pinckney is a definite exception to any of the usual rules. She is now well over eighty years of age, and she still goes cruising.[3]

. . . . .

For several years it had been the Pinckneys' habit to sail to the Channel Islands each Easter, the excuse being that St. Peter Port was the nearest convenient place at which to scrub and paint *Dyarchy's* bottom. It was for one of those expeditions that I joined the yacht at Lymington for the first time and with some diffidence, for I was just beginning to realise how little I really knew about sailing or seamanship. That feeling is still with me when I sail for the first time in a strange yacht, for every vessel differs in some respect from another, and each owner has ideas and habits all his own which must be learnt by the new hand before he ceases to be a liability. But I need not have worried, for I soon discovered that in *Dyarchy* I could do very much as I pleased, there was a sound commonsense reason for everything, and the many mistakes I happened to make through clumsiness or lack of knowledge appeared to pass unnoticed. It was that happy ability to live and let live without any fuss that was the secret of the harmonious life aboard the ship.

Midnight saw us off the Needles, and with a fresh N.E. wind to set us on our way, I took the first watch. Nothing was known of me, my abilities or disabilities, yet I was left in sole charge on deck while all hands turned in. That was another of the pleasant things aboard *Dyarchy* ; the man on watch was assumed to *be* on watch, and suffered nothing from the interference of a nervous owner. Roger, though he was probably

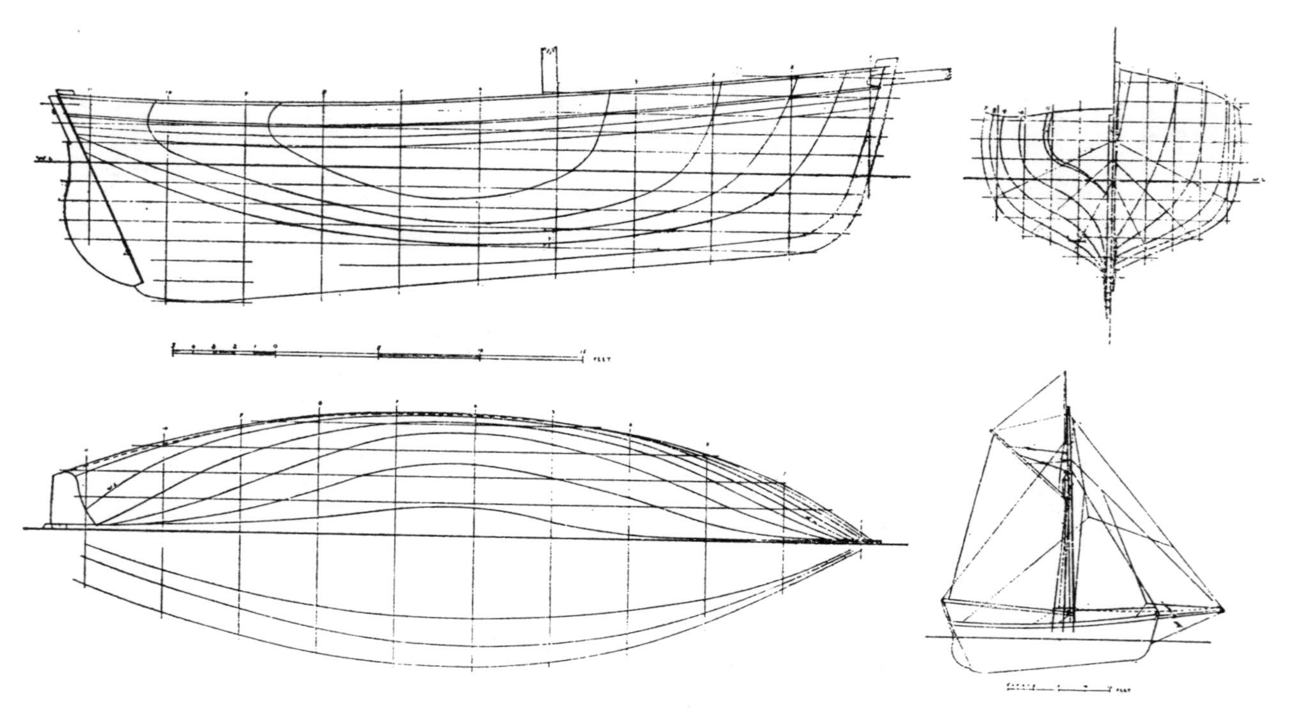

The ex-Bristol Channel Pilot Cutter *Dyarchy*.

awake and listening to every sound, remained with great self-restraint in his berth at the foot of the companionway ; but the helmsman had only to whisper his name, and he would be on deck with calm advice or reassurance within a second or two.

Some people would have us believe that pilot cutters are desperately slow, but we were at anchor in St. Peter Port harbour by noon ; year after year the old ship had made that 90 mile crossing in approximately 13 hours, and that is fast sailing.

What fun those Easters at Guernsey were ! First of all the scrubbing and painting in the inner harbour, and after that shopping expeditions in the cheerful little town ; visits to the Kinnersleys ; tea at Government House ; days spent happily among the rocks and tides surrounding Herm and Jethou, and a pause in Sark's most lovely cove, Havre Gosselin. One year we even called at St. Helier in Jersey, but the wind blew very hard while we were there making the harbour uncomfortable, and the tide had so great a range that at low water it was an acrobatic feat to get aboard from the high quay at the foot of which the ship lay, and we had to remove the crosstrees as they fouled the stonework. *Emanuel* was lying outside of us, and shortly afterwards I had the pleasure of sailing in that 7-ton cutter just before Commander Graham took her on his remarkable single-handed voyage to Newfoundland, Labrador and Bermuda, during which she successfully weathered a hurricane.

Although so keen to reach the Channel Islands, *Dyarchy* was seldom in a hurry to leave, and although—or perhaps because—she was a lucky ship, she usually managed to find a headwind to prolong our cruise awhile. But the return passages were pleasant enough, although the days were grey and cold, and the yacht steered herself so well to windward that the entire crew was able to enjoy real comfort down below gathered round the open hearth.

. . . . .

After my first cross-Channel cruise in her I was beginning to feel quite at home in *Dyarchy*, and when a month later I was asked to join her again, I was indeed delighted. She was bound on a round trip from the Solent to the Baltic, and then home north about via Scotland and the Irish Sea, and for the first stage of her cruise Roger had entered her for the Royal Ocean Racing Club's race from Burnham-on-Crouch to Heligoland.

With a fresh west wind we made a good start from the Shore End line, but that was the end of any excitement so far as the race was concerned, for the wind dropped very light and remained fair for the entire 300 miles. At times we would have been completely becalmed had it not been for the jib-topsail which we had set as a kind of mizen staysail from part way up one of the preventer backstays to the foot of the mast, and which remained bunted out to a very faint air. It was a delightful passage, and nothing like our conception of ocean racing. Most of our meals were eaten on deck in the sunshine ; a small amount of sail trimming was necessary ; there was a little navigation to be attended to, and of course someone had to steer ; but with a crew of seven, no one remained at the helm for longer than an hour as that was considered to be the limit of anybody's real concentration on a compass course. A lot of time was spent bathing and sun bathing ; we smoked a lot and ate a lot, and qualified for membership of the R.O.R.C., though I do not believe that anyone actually joined the club because of that. For three perfect days we lived a life of luxury and leisure, and when on arrival at Heligoland we learnt that on corrected time we had finished eighth out of fourteen, and had beaten those of our type without our allowance, we felt reasonably pleased with ourselves.

The weather then degenerated, and we rolled so much in the roadstead that it was decided to seek shelter in the little harbour. We were almost the last to make that decision, and the place, when we approached it under power, appeared to be completely choked with craft. Not only were there the ocean racers, but scores of small German yachts which had raced out to the island from the Elbe, row upon row of them, all with swastikas flying. However, after some complicated manœuvres with anchors and warps, we got tied up in a vacant berth and remained there for two days.

It was amusing to watch the small fry going out in the morning to race round the island, for the majority of them had no engines and just grabbed hold of those that had, the procession getting longer and longer until the whole affair came to a standstill.

The island was a strange little place of red sandstone all held together with concrete, and the town, which was on two levels, had pleasant narrow cobbled streets and no vehicles. Gun emplacements with concrete tunnels leading to magazines, occupied much of the available space, and on the remainder grazed some curious creatures which—if it is possible, and I suppose it must be—were a cross between goats and sheep. Now there is nothing but rubble and bomb craters.

I suppose that the majority of sailing people suffer in some degree from sea-sickness, but I am certain that the trouble is often a matter of nerves, not stomachs. Consider, for example, our case in *Dyarchy* when we left Heligoland bound for the Baltic by way of Lim Fjord. No sooner had we cleared the island than we encountered a fresh headwind ; the motion was not very bad, but the prospect of having to beat, probably for several days, with the covers on skylights and hatches, was so depressing that most of us felt squeamish. Mrs. Pinckney soon succumbed, I felt I would be unable to keep my breakfast down much longer, another had retired to his bunk, and generally the outlook was gloomy. Then Roger, being a sensible fellow, said, " After all, we are supposed to be out for pleasure, let's go the other way."

So the helm was put up, the yard topsail and spinnaker were set, and then the motion really was bad ; a screwing rolling, sick-making movement. But instead of lying on our bunks we all went up on deck to enjoy the sail, sickness forgotten in the happy knowledge that we would be in smooth water in a matter of hours instead of days.

We tore up the Elbe, an uncomfortable place even in the moderate weather we were fortunate enough to have, and at dusk slipped into the sea lock of the Kiel Canal at Brunsbüttel. There I had to leave the ship to continue to the Baltic without me, and returned home overland.

. . . . .

It was at Inverness that next I joined *Dyarchy*. Her wanderings in the Baltic finished for the time being, she had crossed the North Sea and was then waiting in the basin of the Caledonian Canal to be taken home.

Under power we made our way up the first flight of locks and then spent most of two days turning to windward in grim and eerie Loch Ness. Although that loch is from 80 to 100 fathoms deep in most places, we managed to run aground when seeking a berth for the night in a little bay on the south side near Foynes, with 3 feet of water forward and 3 fathoms aft. There is, of course, no rise of tide up there above sea-level, and the kedge was not of much use, for its warp led down at too steep an angle. But in *Dyarchy* little difficulties like that were soon solved, and it was only necessary to unshackle the mainsheet and swing the boom and gaff together with the stowed sail from side to side for a little while, to make her loosen her hold on the gravel, for she had not run on hard.

The canal is about 50 miles long, but only 19 miles of it are canalised, the remainder being made up of Lochs Ness, Oich, and Lochy. We took five days to get through owing to strong head-winds, and a Sunday, when the locks were kept firmly closed. The best time we could make in any of the 29 locks, even with two of the crew ashore to help the keeper, was twenty minutes. We met very few other craft, and it was difficult to believe that the canal could be a paying proposition ; but perhaps it is used more during the winter months to avoid the stormy passage through the Pentland Firth.

We left the canal at Corpach, paid a brief visit to Loch Eil, and then made our way down lovely Loch Linnhe to Oban for provisions, and to visit the new R.C. Cathedral there, with the building of which Roger was concerned. There are few professions that can be successfully combined with yachting, but architecture appears to be one of them, to a moderate degree, at least.

Continuing south, past the Isles of the Sea we swept through Scaba Sound, and beat down the ever-widening Sound of Jura against a slowly freshening head-wind. The glass was falling, and as we had no wish to beat to Holyhead, which was intended to be our next stopping-place, we slipped into Lowlandman Bay on the east side of the island of Jura to wait for a slant. It was just as well that we did so, for the wind increased to a gale from S. by W., a direction from which we were only just sheltered ; but although we rolled considerably there was no cause for anxiety as there was plenty of room in which to beat out should the wind back farther. However, it did not, and we remained there for two days.

Calling at the farm for milk, and that was the only visible habitation other than the dwelling of the lighthouse keepers, we found the " wife " most friendly ; not only did she supply us with milk and scones, but she flatly refused to accept any form of payment. The more remote a place is the more hospitable do the inhabitants seem to be, and because they are generally so poor one feels it is almost stealing to accept their gifts. The farm house was spotlessly clean and well cared for, and the folk appeared to be happy and content though Jura is a wild and lonely island with a population of little more than 300, which is scanty for its size.

The Paps of Jura were outlined black against the sunset as we left. Outside the bay, finding some swell and no wind, we kept the engine running until midnight. Then there came a light air, just sufficient to put the sails to sleep and give us steerage way ; so the engine was stopped, and by 4 a.m. we were between the Mull of Cantyre and Rathlin Island.

The system of watch-keeping aboard *Dyarchy* was simple. None was kept during the day, anyone who wished to steer could do so for as long as he pleased, and if nobody wanted to be bothered the ship could often be persuaded to do it for herself. But at 10 p.m. night watches of two hours each began, and as there were four of us (not including Mrs. Pinckney, who did not take a watch) we had only one each during the dark hours. A two-hour watch is a delight, four hours a bore, and six hours—for me at least—almost a hardship ; so I enjoyed myself, and I think everyone else liked that arrangement too.

At dawn, the wind having freed a little, we were moving along well on our course. To starboard lay the green coast of Ireland, its little villages tucked away in clefts between the hills, all lighted up by the rising sun. Swiftly we passed inside the Maidens, a group of rocks bearing one lighthouse in commission and a disused one, and continued down the coast past Larne and Belfast Lough to the Skulmartin light-vessel. There the coast receded as we stood on our course for Holyhead ; the sun vanished, sea and sky turned a uniform dark grey and the wind freshened so that the topsail had to come down. The indistinct grey lump of the Isle of Man loomed up to port during the afternoon, and we toyed with the idea of putting in at Douglas for the night. But as we could still lay the course for Holyhead it was decided to carry on, and we came-to there at 3 a.m.

We remained at anchor that day, sailed about in the dinghy and provisioned the ship. The harbour—as artificial harbours go—is a good one, and there is plenty of room ; but apart from the excellent shops ashore the place had few other attractions for the cruising man.

After our day's rest we got away at 4 a.m. in order to catch the tide off the South Stack, and had an indolent sail all day and night with light airs and calms to Fishguard, where we remained for a day in order to visit St. David's cathedral, which is situated in a hollow with the little town clustered round the edge looking down upon it.

Once more, the tide compelling, we made an early start. The wind was light S.E., fair for Land's End, the sunrise looked fine and settled and the glass was high and steady. We kept close inshore down to St. David's Head and then passed inside Ramsey Island. But as we left the Sound the wind came ahead and we stood away on the port tack to clear Grassholm. There was a S.W. swell, which very quickly turned into a heavy sea as the wind increased in strength, and it was magnificent sailing ; if only the sun had been shining we might have enjoyed it—but the sky had become overcast and visibility poor, while some water had found its way below through the skylight.

Beating to Land's End under such conditions would have been a slow and tiring business ; so, after handing the topsail, we went about and stood close-hauled for Milford Haven. Wind and sea continued to increase, the lee deck was frequently awash and the gear in the dinghy—which in those days used to be carried right side up on the port deck—had to be removed, as there was some risk of it being washed out.

The ship was moving fast with a roaring white bow-wave curling away from her stem, and several steam trawlers, also making for Milford Haven, only overhauled her slowly. Two of them came close enough to be photographed, fortunately to leeward, for I would not have cared to expose the camera in the wind's eye with so much spray flying about. It was not so much the trawlers that I wished to have a picture of as the sea ; but waves are generally disappointing in a photograph no matter how large or steep they may be, unless they are breaking, and fortunately they do not do that in the open sea. A rock or a vessel is necessary to give some idea of perspective.

Clearing Skokham Island with very little to spare, we rounded St. Ann's Head, where the seas were considerably steeper, and ran into the Haven ; on we sped past Milford with its trawlers and Pembroke with its warships, up the narrowing river, looking for a snug anchorage. Mrs. Pinckney and Hermione Cree, the other lady member of the crew, meanwhile straightened out the mess below and had a hot meal ready by the time we finally checked our headlong career among the woods and castles in a little creek near Lawrenny. There we remained for five days.

On a calm September evening we left our berth with all sail set and the engine running. We just saved our tide at Milford, and there, finding a moderate S.E. wind, the engine was stopped, the navigation lights were lit and we were soon out in the open, pitching into the swell and laying the course for Land's End. The topsail soon had to come down as the wind freshened, and during my watch (12 to 2 a.m.) it increased still more and the ship was rushing along in fine style ; but by 1 a.m. it was obvious that she was being hard pressed, for she was carrying a lot of water on the lee deck, so I called the others. The staysail was lowered, three rolls were put in the mainsail and the large jib was changed for a smaller one, the helmsman running her off as dead before the wind as he could while that was being done, for although it may be cowardly it is the easiest and driest way of dealing with headsails. Even so we were all thoroughly soaked by the time the work on deck was finished, but the ship was very comfortable under reduced sail and took nothing more than an occasional shower of spray on board. All night the wind blew hard and veered slowly until by 10 a.m. it had headed us off to W. As that was not much use we put her about, and she headed somewhere between S. and S.S.E., so we hoped that we might fetch Trevose Head. We re-set the staysail and got her going properly again, for in common with all cutters she was crippled without it. It was magnificent sailing throughout the day, the sun shone brilliantly on the heavy, white-capped seas, and we were happy to be in a ship capable of dealing with them in such an able manner.

In the evening there was a cry from forward where the side-lights were being attended to :

" Flashing light away off the port bow."

" Ah ! " we all thought, " that must be Trevose Head, and we have actually weathered it after all." But, on looking it up in the light list we learnt that it was nothing of the kind but was Lundy Island's north light. The heavy sea and the Bristol Channel inset, which is said to be strong during fresh W. and S.W. winds, must have combined to drive us so far to leeward.

We had all had quite enough of windward work for the moment, and as none of us had ever visited Lundy, we bore away for that island, and having taken a very long time rounding its north end against the 4 knot ebb, we brought up at 1 a.m. as close under its lee as we dared to go in the dark. But the wind tore down off the land in savage squalls, causing the old ship to sheer restlessly, her anchor chain rasping against the bobstay ; so as soon as it was light enough to see, we shifted to the anchorage off the landing place in the bay at the S.E. corner of the island, and there in company with several trawlers found good shelter though we rolled a little.

The bailiff of the island and some of his friends swam out to us and told us that very few yachts called there, which is not surprising considering the strong tides and overfalls with which the island is encircled ; there is no other safe landing except that which lay opposite our anchorage, and even that would be impossible in fresh E. winds. We made the most of our visit and explored the island, which is of granite and rises to a height of 440 feet. Its resident population comprised six keepers in charge of the two lighthouses and about a dozen others connected with the hotel and farm, and in between the visits of the tripping steamers from Ilfracombe and other Bristol Channel places, which call for an hour or so in settled weather, it was a wild and pleasing place. The cottages of the quarrymen, fishermen and smugglers who once inhabited the island, lie in ruins in the S.E. corner, and there are some walls and tracks still in existence built by the convicts which one owner had been paid to ship overseas but brought to work on Lundy instead. There was plenty of bird and animal life there, puffins, cormorants and gulls, ponies, goats and deer.

For a second night we remained at anchor and then sailed across to the Devon shore and brought up for a few hours off Clovelly ; from our anchorage it looked very attractive with its cobbled street of steps flanked by pink and white cottages, the ground floor windows of one looking over the roof of the next below, and so on right down to the little boat harbour. But ashore it was very crowded with holiday makers, and in the evening we left with the wind still ahead, and ahead it remained the whole way to Helford, persistently backing as we rounded each corner—Pendeen, Longships, Runnelstone, and Lizard.

Although I have been round Land's End several times since then, I have never yet seen that rugged toe of England properly ; it has either been dark or foggy, and frequently both. It is a well-lighted corner and the fog signals are cleverly arranged so that there is no risk of one being mistaken for another, but owing to the rapidity with which the weather changes in that vicinity, and the great number of steamers which use the lane between the Longships and the Seven Stones, it is not a corner to be treated in a light-hearted manner by sailing men. But on that occasion the wind was light, there was little sea and no fog, so we rounded it and arrived at Helford without incident, and there I had to leave *Dyarchy*. She concluded her fine cruise by calling at Lezardrieux in Brittany and at the Channel Islands on her way back to her home port of Lymington, whence she had set out for Heligoland and beyond four and a half months previously.

. . . . .

My last cruise in *Dyarchy* was a good example of what every cruise should be. There were no gales and no rough seas, so one might almost say that there was no excitement at all, but that would hardly be true, for there is always a thrill in making a strange port for the first time, especially when that port has never been visited by any British yacht before ; we had that honour at the Ile de Sein. We also hit a rock, settled a dog-fight, and were chased by irate fishermen who thought we had fouled their lobster-pots with our damaged keel-band just for the fun of the thing. But they were mere incidents.

Helford was our last English port ; we left it one July evening in a fine drizzle with a moderate west wind, and as we took our departure from the Manacles the sun set behind the hills in a daub of angry red ; it looked most threatening, but like so many of its kind, nothing came of it, and we made Le Palais Harbour in Belle Ile forty hours later.

During the passage I was taught the rudiments of navigation and how to handle and read a sextant. The finding of a ship's position at sea from observations of the heavenly bodies is usually wrapped up in mystery by those who can do it. That is a pity, for although pilotage is generally all that is required by the yachtsman in home waters, it is both reassuring and interesting during a slow passage out of sight of land, to be able to fix the ship's position by means of the sun, a sextant, a clock, and a book of tables. After a little practice the majority of one's results are surprisingly accurate.

I had read several textbooks on navigation, and was still in the dark, for they all set out with the idea of teaching the why and the wherefore, and as I am lazy and no mathematician I could not be bothered. I wanted results, not a lecture on why and how the world spins round, and judging by the wry faces they make when one mentions the words " meridian altitude " or " position line," most yachtsmen are in a similar plight.

Roger Pinckney knew little more of the theory of navigation than I did, but he was able and willing to show me how to take a sight and find the position from it. Although I am sure the more advanced navigators will disagree with me entirely, I do not consider that there is any need to understand why you do certain queer things with the apparently meaningless figures in a book of nautical tables. What you do need to know is where and how to find the figures you require, and how to add or subtract degrees, minutes, and seconds.

To beginners I would say just this : get someone who does

not know too much about the subject to show you what tables to use and how to handle the sextant, for he will be more likely to understand your little difficulties than will one who is in possession of his "ticket," and has had to learn everything the Board of Trade way. As a textbook nothing, I think, could be better than Worth's *Yacht Navigation and Voyaging*, for if you wish to do no more than work the sums out parrot-fashion, all the information with plenty of clear examples is there; but those who wish to know more of the fascinating subject will find sufficient theory in the book as well. Every term used is explained in simple language.

There are, of course, several methods of working out and making use of sights, and each man uses those which he finds to be the easiest or most convenient. Personally I prefer the longitude by chronometer method to the position line, as it entails no drawing on the chart and the answer is in degrees, minutes, and seconds of longitude. But unless you are pretty sure of your latitude at the time, it is necessary to take this sight when the sun bears true east or west; if the sun does not show himself at the required moment and the latitude is uncertain, one has to work the sight as a position line, and for that I use Hall's *Appendix to Raper*.[4]

Time is another of the little troubles connected with celestial navigation. For all sights, except the meridian altitude, accurate Greenwich time is needed, and the only way of knowing that in the days before reliable radio sets, was to have a chronometer. One of the chief disadvantages of that instrument is its high price, but even if you can afford to buy one there is no guarantee that it will keep a steady rate in a small yacht at sea. Chronometer watches having a lever movement are more reliable when the motion is violent, but they are by no means cheap, either.

Excellent little radio sets, able to endure the heat, cold, damp, and general knocking about that they get in small yachts, are made by Schooner Marine Sets of Bridgwater. With one of these and a cheap but reasonably reliable timepiece (I use the cabin clock) there is no excuse for being more than a quarter of a minute wrong, provided that the time signals are received once or twice a day.[5] In the latitude of the

English Channel a difference of a quarter of a minute only puts one about three miles out, and that is not much of an error. For the noon latitude only the sextant and the nautical almanac are required, and the little sum is very easy to work out.

Having got as far south-east on the Brittany coast as we wished to go in one hop, we were able to devote the rest of our time to wandering slowly home, calling on the way at every place that took our fancy. Day after day the sun shone on the incredibly blue sea, and on the multi-coloured sails of the tunnymen that flitted here and there like gigantic butterflies with their slender fishing rods guyed out each side. We visited the Morbihan which, with its sluicing tides and many islands, is almost a cruising ground in itself; Auray with its steep and cobbled streets, and its swarms of small children who swept all the dirt off the quay on to our deck before we could lift a finger to stop them; La Trinité, with its fine topsail schooners; Loc Maria, choked with sardine boats; Port Tudy, crammed with a glorious gathering of tunnymen; Concarneau, with its ancient Ville Close; and Audierne with its rows of crabbers lined up on legs, with their steeved-up bowsprits overhanging the road.

My memories of that cruise are now just a pleasant haze of luxurious sailing in perfect summer weather, always with the genoa set; I have almost forgotten what other places we visited, and only a few small incidents stand boldly out from the rest.

One was the night we left Loc Maria, bound north. The light breeze slowly died away to leave us completely becalmed by midnight; so, as the tide was against us, we anchored in 15 fathoms with the kedge. The phosphorescence was amazing, the whole of the ship's bottom and the kedge warp were bathed in silvery light. For a while we lay on the deck watching it, and then stripped off our clothes and dived in. It is quite beyond my powers to describe the effect; the slightest movement produced a Milky Way of light, and even when rubbing down on deck afterwards little flakes of silver fell off one. But we paid a heavy price for our night's pleasure—in the morning we lost our kedge; possibly it fouled a rock, for the warp parted when we put it on the winch.

Another incident occurred the morning that we made the

Ile de Groix. The scene was full of life, the sparkling sea was dotted with the sails of fishing boats, and as we approached the island a little black lugger closed with us, her crew shouting and gesticulating wildly at our stern. We looked over and discovered that we were towing some lobster pots, their corks and lines tangled up and held by our keel-band which had got broken on a rock in the Morbihan. The lugger's crew were shouting what we took to be Breton curses, and it was obvious that they thought we were stealing their pots. Twice they tried to ram our dinghy—which, as the weather was so fine, we had omitted to get on deck—but we were able to out-manœuvre them, and finally got the pots clear with the boathook, but not before the furious Frenchmen had made an attempt to rip our genoa with a knife. The lugger then sheered off still boiling with indignation, and we were able to make Port Tudy harbour without further incident.

But the day that stands out above all others was the day we visited Ile de Sein. Our cruise on that delightful coast nearly at an end, we had left Audierne and were bound north and east for the Channel Isles, and were approaching the Raz de Sein when the idea of calling at the tiny rock encircled island occurred to us.

With good visibility to let us pick out the leading marks, and a fair wind, there was nothing very exciting or spectacular about our approach, but our anchorage in the roadstead, surrounded as it was by jagged rocks of the most fantastic shapes, amongst which sailed little black cutters strangely resembling bats with their dark brown sails, was an eerie one indeed.

Ashore we were met with the usual kindly Breton welcome, and were told that ours was the first British yacht ever to have called there, so it almost seemed as though we had *discovered* an island. Unlike their brothers on the mainland, there was something lean and grim about those toilers of the sea, as though they had warred too long with the elements. The women, too, had a distant look on their weather-beaten faces, and the black caps they wore instead of the usual white embroidered head-dresses, were much in keeping with their grey and bleak surroundings.

We found the island to be little more than a flat rock just over a mile long ; a few patches of coarse grass, on each of which was tethered an undersized cow, appeared to be the only vegetation, and even if there had been some soil there was but little room for anything to grow, for the greater part of the rock was covered with the stone dwellings of the inhabitants, closely packed as though for mutual protection. Seven hundred souls there wrest a living from the rocks and the sea in the form of crabs and lobsters, their huge wooden pots littering the foreshore and the quay of the little harbour, all of which dries. There is no spring on the island, and fresh water has to be brought over from Audierne ; even in summer food is scarce, and it is difficult to understand how so many people can live there in the winter when it is no uncommon thing for the island to be cut off from the mainland by bad weather for two or three weeks at a time. We walked across to the west end of the island to look at the Chaussée de Sein (or Saints) a tapering ridge of rocks and shoals extending for ten miles straight out into the Atlantic. There were several towers marking channels through the reefs which were used by the local boats, but although the weather was fine and the sea was almost calm, it looked a really dreadful place, and we could easily imagine what it must be like in an onshore gale.

After a quiet night in our strange anchorage we sailed away, and having passed through the Chenal du Four, got becalmed near the Porsal Rocks ; there we spent six peaceful hours lying quite securely in thirty fathoms to the little dinghy anchor. A partly foggy passage to Guernsey and a delightful crossing to the Solent concluded that perfect summer cruise, the last I ever made in the ship.

. . . . .

After 25,000 miles of cruising in her, Roger Pinckney decided that he needed something a little larger, faster, and more modern than his pilot cutter, so a new *Dyarchy* was built, a 28-tonner designed by Laurent Giles. The old ship was sold to be used as a house-boat, and for the first and last time in her life was being sailed towards her new home port by a professional yacht skipper, when she ran aground on the Mixon off Selsea Bill in broad daylight with an offshore wind and a rising tide. Her crew abandoned her immediately, and a little while later she sailed off to sink in deep water. A clear case of suicide.

CHAPTER III

TERN II OFF THE NEEDLES

" North-east by north," said the owner as he came up the companionway after looking at the chart. I repeated the course and steadied the yacht on it, then when we had got properly settled down on the fresh point of sailing with sheets well eased to the west wind on the quarter, I had leisure to look about me once more.

The jagged Casquets on the beam, with the swell churning white against them, stood out clearly in the September sunshine ; the deep blue sea was dotted with the tiny white flashes of wind-blown crests, while to starboard lay the round, grey hump of Alderney with the thin, pencilled line of the French coast in the distance beyond.

Perfect conditions, one might think, for a fast and comfortable run to the Needles, were it not for those long white streamers radiating from the south-west across the sky and a narrow grey line on the horizon to windward. At the back of our minds, too, was the weather forecast to which, in a weak moment, we had listened that morning aboard a friendly yacht in St. Peter Port harbour. " Winds backing and freshening," it had said, and had concluded with a gale warning.

There were only two of us aboard, Clive Wright and myself, and neither of us had very much faith in weather forecasts ; conditions did not appear to be at all unfavourable, and time was short at the end of our three weeks' cruise along the north coast of Brittany, so we had started. If we had listened to all the gale warnings that had been broadcast during those three weeks we would not have got far, for in September, 1935, a series of deep depressions had crossed the British Isles, bringing with them strong winds including the great gale of September 16th, which wrought such havoc among yachts and shipping generally. We had ridden that out safely but anxiously at St. Peter Port to 40 fathoms of chain, while the wind howled through the rigging and spray rattled on the deck and sides like hail, and we were now trying to get home to the Solent between two of those fast-moving depressions.

All that afternoon we ran happily on our course, the 9-ton yawl *Tern II* (who had once belonged to Claud Worth) was revelling in the breeze ; with mainsail, topsail, mizen and squaresail bellying out in firm curves, she logged 6 knots hour after hour, lifting her shapely counter gently to the following sea, and running steady and true with a light helm.

The wind was certainly backing ; by 4 p.m. it was dead astern, and freshening, too, but as yet no reduction of canvas was necessary. The scene had changed since leaving the Casquets ; the sky had become overcast and the sea a uniform grey to match it ; even the wind-whipped crests were no longer pure white.

At dusk the squaresail had to come in, for that large area of canvas was rather more than *Tern* required, and she ran on just as fast without it ; but we hung on to the topsail, for having rigged a leader to it recently we were confident of being able to get it and its yard down in the dark without much difficulty should the occasion arise. A single leader through a thimble seized to the foot of a topsail yard makes control of the sail easy, and prevents it from taking charge and blowing away to leeward like a kite. Sidelights were lit, and after a hot dinner we felt fit to deal with any kind of weather.

At about 10 p.m. we picked up the loom of St. Catherine's powerful light and the flash every 10 seconds of Anvil Point, and as the wind suddenly became stronger we handed the topsail and staysail. Suddenly Anvil light went dim, and before we could get a bearing of it, vanished completely in driving rain. The Needles light, which had just begun to show its weak self, went as well, but we knew the bearing of that and quickly got a rough one of St. Catherine's before that was swallowed up too. Wright went below to plot our position and have a look at the chart, and came up with the news that we would be off the Needles at about a third of the ebb.

On a fine summer's day the Needles Channel may be harmless enough, but with a fresh wind blowing against the spring ebb at night and in thick weather it needs the careful consideration that we duly gave it. For a time we debated whether we should beat up for Studland Bay, anchor there for another meal, and await the turn of the tide ; but by the time we would arrive there it would be almost time to start again. So it was decided to stand on with this reservation : if we did not sight the Needles or one of the light buoys in half an hour's time we would heave-to on the offshore tack. The ebb would then keep us clear of all dangers until daylight.

The first quarter of an hour dragged slowly by, and presently Wright consulted the cabin clock.

" Twenty minutes gone," he said, as he slammed the hatch against a shower of spray, and once more we sat huddled in the cockpit against the cold, he straining his eyes into the darkness, while mine were fixed on the dimly lighted compass card.

" Time must be nearly up," I said. The seas, beginning to feel the bottom and the stronger tide, were getting steeper and their crests were breaking more readily.

" Another four minutes to go," said the quiet voice.

Still we sailed on through the night, the wind moaning in the rigging and the crests breaking in our wake. I do not believe that Wright was ever nervous except when strange dinghies came alongside without proper regard for his paint, but I was getting very worried. It was true that we ought to fetch the Bridge buoy on that course, but the course might so easily be wrong, for a position got from cross bearings of two indistinct lights is always liable to be inaccurate. There was also the tide to consider ; it might not have set us so far to the westward as we had expected, and then. . . .

" There she is ! "

I looked up from the swinging compass and saw it sure enough, a yellow blur on the starboard bow, and a few seconds later discovered a rapidly flashing light almost in line with it—the Bridge or the S.W. Shingles, it did not matter which ; the rain was lifting.

" Can't fetch in on this gybe," I shouted, having put the yacht as dead before the wind as I could.

" All right, we'll gybe her now. Stand by."

I handed over the tiller and started rounding in the mainsheet. Up to then I had been too busy trying to steer an accurate compass course to take much notice of the sea, but sitting on deck with my feet braced against the bulwarks, hauling in that stiff rope, I had ample opportunity for seeing the ghostly crests rushing up astern.

"That'll do."

I took a turn round the cleat. "All fast!"

The helm was put up; for a moment, the mainsail hung uncertain as it emptied of wind, then the boom came over and I let the sheet render until it was squared off on the other gybe.

We were a little too far north and feeling the effect of the tail-end of the Dolphin Bank, which has a depth of only four fathoms. The yacht was hurrying forward on the crests, and her desire to turn round and face the seas was evident from the amount of weather helm she was carrying. But Wright showed no anxiety; he understood his ship in all her moods and nursed her along cleverly.

We surged between the winking buoys which were now perched on the top of a sea, then lost in the trough, and picking up the Warden buoy away to the right of Hurst lights, found we were just able to lay it before it and everything else, except the Needles light showing mistily red, vanished in another rain squall.

I went below to consult the chart, for although we both knew the channel quite well, it is unwise to rely too much on one's memory when conditions are bad. With the companion hatch closed it was wonderfully snug and peaceful down there, the gimballed lamp casting dancing shadows on the polished teak and lace-wood panelling; the only noises were a slight creak from the mast, the gentle swish of water running past the sides, and the ticking of the clock. I looked at the chart and ruled off a course from the Warden to the Hurst narrows, and then glanced at the barometer; it had fallen two-tenths in as many hours. I tapped it and it fell still farther. "Well," I thought, "it doesn't matter now, we shall be in the shelter of the Solent within the hour." With a last look at that snug retreat I went out into the wind and rain and turmoil again.

All along the yacht had kept her deck fairly dry, the little water she did take on board came over near the main rigging when she was running forward on the crests, and it was a constant source of wonder to me how she managed to lift her stern so cleverly always just in time, for the seas were steep.

Presently the Warden buoy loomed out of the murk away on the port bow ; we were heading inside it, and fine on the port bow could also be seen once more the lights of Hurst, so again we had to gybe. Bit by bit I got the boom in and the sheet made fast ; up went the helm, the boom, after its customary hesitation, came over with rather more of a jar than usual, and then there was another sound—the ripping noise of heavy canvas tearing. At the same moment the yacht failed to lift to a particularly steep crest, and it broke aboard over the stern, sweeping the deck fore and aft and filling the self-draining cockpit. Dashing the water from our eyes we could dimly see the mainsail in ribbons ; it had split from luff to leach, and the top half of the sail was flogging violently in the wind, shaking the mast.

" Set up the topping lift and get the boom inboard, old chap," said Wright.

I jumped to it, Wright lending his weight when he could, which was not often, for we dared not risk another gybe, or the uncontrolled gaff might do some serious damage up aloft, and we could not deal with that just yet ; first we must get more sail on the yacht, for the ebb tide was setting her across to the N.E. Shingles. So I hastily set the staysail and the mizen, and under those small sails and the jib she once more forged ahead, but whether or not she would be able to stem the six knot tide in the narrows remained to be seen.

Then I started to clear up the mess, and the first job was to get the gaff down. I let go the peak halyard, but when nothing happened I realised the hopelessness of getting it down without first going aloft to cut away the sail. So I pulled the throat down until the jaws jammed, and had to leave it at that for the time being, as we slowly crept up past Hurst.

It was difficult to know just how far we were from the shore, for the high light blinded us and there was only a black smudge —not much blacker than the night itself—to show where the Isle of Wight shore lay. At last the light bore N. by W., and altering course we brought up in Hurst Roads, dropped the headsails and mizen, and paying out plenty of chain, went below for a tot of rum and a change of clothes. Only then did I discover a lump the size of an egg on my head, and two cut and bleeding fingers ; strangely enough I could not remember when or how I had come by any of my injuries.

I think we might have stayed below in comfort longer and possibly have dropped off to sleep, had it not been for the slatting and cracking of torn canvas overhead reminding us of what there was yet to do.

Laboriously I hauled myself aloft, and standing on the cross-trees proceeded to unravel the tangle—no easy job in the dark with so strong a wind—while Wright stood by to tend the ropes as necessary. I had to cut away the canvas piecemeal as long streamers of it had wrapped themselves tightly round the mast and gear, but at last we got the gaff down, and lashing the remains of the sail to it, we turned in at 4 a.m. and slept heavily until the relentless alarm, a repeater, called us at daybreak to sail on to the Hamble.

. . . . .

There was a fresh W.S.W. wind blowing when one evening in late October, *Tern II* beat swiftly down the Solent on the ebb bound for Poole where arrangements had been made for Newmans to install a new auxiliary engine ; the old one which *Tern* had carried for many years had a number of almost incurable defects and was quite unreliable. The crew consisted of Clive Wright and myself.

About 6 p.m., just before reaching Hurst narrows, we hung up the sidelights and put the riding light in the cockpit, where not only would it be handy if needed, but would keep the man on watch warm if he covered it and his knees with a sail bag.[6] The glass was inclined to fall and the wind was definitely on the increase, so we handed the mizen. It might, too, have been a good thing to have changed the working jib for a smaller one, but *Tern*, having her mast rather far forward and only a small staysail in consequence, liked a big jib when going to windward.

In the Needles Channel we found the usual short, steep sea, for the tide was running against the wind and the old S.W. swell. The yacht made remarkably good going of it ; her old-fashioned, lean, straight stem rose smoothly just far enough each time to prevent solid water from coming aboard, and in spite of her long, straight keel, she came about surely at the end of each tack without the slightest hesitation. There was certainly some water on the lee deck, for we were driving her, but none of it came anywhere near the cockpit. Her bowsprit, however, some ten feet of it outboard, was burying itself more often than seemed desirable, and when she rose on a sea, a torrent of water poured out of the big jib ; a great strain was being put on all the head gear.

Night was upon us by the time we had passed the Needles ; out in the open the seas were larger but more regular, and the yacht was going well. We had sailed between the Bridge and the S.W. Shingles buoys on the starboard tack, and were considering remaining on that leg for some time and getting a tin of soup heated up, when a larger sea than the others came rearing its white cap out of the darkness on the starboard bow. The yacht lifted to it, but was not quite fast enough, and some solid water came on to the fore-deck. In the succeeding trough she dived deep, burying her bowsprit and filling a large area of the jib with water. As she shook herself clear there was a sudden thunder of flapping canvas, and it was just possible to see the dark shape of the jib, still tethered by sheet and halyard, flogging furiously from side to side.

I was very scared at the thought of muzzling that sail single-handed while Wright did his best with the helm to prevent heavy water coming aboard while I was on the fore-deck. But it had to be done, so scrambling forward I took a turn with a rope's end round my waist before starting operations, and then sat on deck with my feet wedged against the bulwarks and my shoulders against the mast. I remember feeling surprised and very thankful that it was so safe there ; I had expected to be up to my neck in water, but there was nothing more solid than spray flying about. I think it is more the noise than anything else that is so frightening on such occasions.

Carefully I started the jib halyard, and, inch by inch, got the thrashing canvas down on deck without a single tear, thanks to the good, stout flax of which the sail was made, cursing the while all jib outhauls, for I was convinced that ours had carried away ; how else could the tack have got free?

Bundling the sodden canvas up as best I could, I dragged it along the weather deck and stowed it in the cockpit.

Without her jib, and without backing the staysail, the yacht had almost stopped and was riding fairly comfortably ; but there was too much sea to permit me to go to the bowsprit end to reeve a new outhaul. So we reluctantly decided to give up our attempt to reach Poole that week-end and to run back into the Solent.

That should have been easy enough, for all we had to do was to back the staysail, let out some mainsheet, put the helm up and round we would go. We did all those things—and remained hove-to. We gave her all the sheet, and still she stayed quietly hove-to. We thought it very odd, for one of the most talked about advantages of the yawl is that she will manœuvre under either jib and mizen or main and staysail. Well, if she would not, we must lower the mainsail, pay off under staysail and then re-set the mainsail running; but it might be worth while to try the engine first. Wright wrestled with it for a little while and then much to our surprise it started.

Slowly, as though loath the give up her objective, the yacht turned round under power and headed back between the buoys for the flash of the Warden. In a little while the cabin was full of blue smoke and the engine was found to be so hot that it had to be stopped. But it had done what was necessary, and with the wind aft *Tern* seemed to be under control again, though she was curiously heavy on the helm and sluggish.

Wright then went below to light the galley stove, but quickly reappeared saying that there was a harsh, grinding noise going on somewhere forward, and crawled along the deck to investigate. He did not take long, and returned with the startling information that the bowsprit had broken off and was hanging below the waterline still held by the outhaul and bobstay.

That just shows how unobservant one can become when busy, and that one ought never to take anything for granted. I suppose I had been on the fore-deck dealing with the jib for about ten minutes, and yet I had not noticed that obvious damage only a few feet away.

It was serious news, for apart from the damage the bowsprit itself might do, a few feet along it was clamped a heavy iron lead through which the chain passed when at anchor, and if that once got fairly up against our planking it might do untold harm. It was probably doing so even then, for every time we dropped into the trough between the seas, that grinding noise could not only be heard but felt right through the ship.

The first thing was to reduce our wild rush to a more sedate speed, for we were by then back once more in the steep seas of the Needles Channel and the wind was blowing hard—force 7 on the Beaufort scale I discovered later from the Calshot weather station. Wright took the helm again, for steering was tricky with a press of sail aloft and those awkward seas coming up astern ; he was a first-class helmsman, while I was the more powerful of the two.

I started by putting a few rolls in the mainsail, and although I had never used one before, I found the Worth's reefing gear very easy to use even in the dark. Then up forward I found real chaos.

The bowsprit shrouds were painted, and only the previous week they had been scraped before repainting so that they could be inspected. They appeared to be in good condition but unfortunately the serving over the splices had not been removed and it was there that the weather one had rusted ; presumably the sudden weight of water in the jib had done the rest.

The spar itself had snapped at the gammon iron where it was protected against chafe by a piece of copper sheeting, and it is interesting to note that the break had occurred exactly on the line of tacks that kept it in position ; the wood, however, was perfectly sound. The other shroud had stood, but its large gun-metal rigging screw had broken clean across. The wire jib-outhaul had an eye spliced in at each end ; one of these, apparently, had jammed in the bowsprit sheave, and the other in a fairlead on the port rail, while from its fitting on the stem the metal bobstay led away on the starboard side.

For a time I was completely mystified by a wire, taut as a towing hawser, leading from somewhere up aloft down over the rail into the sea amidships ; not until I discovered its other end leading over the opposite rail and made fast to the bitts, did I realise that it was the topmast stay which passed through a block on the bowsprit end.

It was hardly surprising that the yacht had refused to turn round with all that gear hanging down beneath her. It seemed an almost hopeless task to sort it out then, for owing to our speed through the water there was a great strain on everything. I suggested going either into Yarmouth or Lymington, and had to be reminded : (*a*) that the yacht was almost unmanageable except with the wind aft ; (*b*) that the engine was hardly likely to function again until it had been attended to ; and (*c*) what did I think was happening to the ship's bottom while I was wasting time talking? So I returned to the fore-deck and thought out a plan of campaign.

First I hooked the lower block of the jib halyard into the end of the outhaul and hoisted away, but nothing happened. I swigged with all my weight on it, and suddenly, jerking itself out of the fairlead, the topmast stay slid round the bow and, scraping along the rail, brought up with a clang against the main shrouds, nearly decapitating me as it went. Then once more I hoisted away until the cranse iron on the bowsprit was level with the rail, and there I lashed it securely ; I next passed a strop round the spar, pushed it as far as I could reach, and once more using the jib halyard hoisted the thing up. We were by then in the Solent where there was not much sea, otherwise I am sure I could never have got it up and lashed alongside above the channels. It was quite beyond me then to get it on deck, for, in the perverse way that inanimate things have, it came up with the great chain lead next to the side.

I took off the topmast stay and the remains of the shrouds, and having unshackled the anchor, passed the chain clear of the wreckage and shackled it on again all clear for running. Then I staggered aft and we had our much-needed soup just two hours after we had first thought about it.

The Solent Banks buoy was well astern and the simplest thing then seemed to be to go up Southampton Water, and there, as near to the weather shore as we could get just below Fawley Beacon, we anchored at midnight.

. . . . .

I made many passages in *Tern II* with " Skipper " Wright, as all his friends called him, and as the above mentioned incidents may give the impression that the yacht was ill found or badly managed, I must say that they were the only incidents—other than pleasant ones—that I ever experienced in her, for she was as well found and superbly handled as any vessel could be.[7]

During all the years I knew him Skipper was a chronic invalid, and the only tonic that did him any good was sailing in his beloved *Tern.* Often he would arrive from London, where he worked, so short of breath and so exhausted that he was incapable of climbing aboard from the dinghy, and I had to lift him over the rail and carry him to the cockpit. I would hoist the dinghy aboard, for he would never allow it to be towed, lash it down over the skylight, make sail and slip the mooring. He would take the helm, and as we slipped down the Solent, rounded the Needles and settled on a course for the Channel Isles or the Britanny coast, which were his only cruising grounds, a little colour would come into his sallow cheeks and a twinkle would appear behind his tinted spectacles. Lighting a cigarette, he would say :

" Now we're off," and casting his eye aloft, would add, " the little old box could do with the squaresail, please."

So I would set that sail and trim its sheets and braces until it set to his satisfaction. Skipper was feeling better.

. . . . .

He died in 1946, and was cremated.

It was a grey afternoon in April of that year when my wife and I in our own boat sped down the Solent with a fresh, squally N.E. wind and a strong spring ebb. Quickly we passed through the narrows of Hurst, left the Warden buoy astern, and at 3.30 were off the Needles. There we altered course to S.W. by S. for the Casquets, and taking a small casket from its locker we scattered in our hissing wake all that remained of Skipper Wright. As we streamed the log and pulled our coats more closely round us, the clouds parted and for a moment the Needles and the high cliffs of Scratchels Bay were picked out in a shaft of brilliant sunshine.

The yawl *Tern II* running with her squaresail set. The crosstrees were hinged to the mast so that the yard could push the lee topmast shroud out of the way when the sail was braced up to a beam wind.

CHAPTER IV

THE BUILDING OF WANDERER II

FOR MORE than a year I had been without a boat of my own, and although I had perused the advertisement columns in the yachting magazines and had travelled up and down the coast looking at all manner of yachts which were offered for sale, I had been unable to find one to meet my requirements at a price I could afford. Some, in spite of the glowing advertisements, were rotten, while those that were in reasonable condition needed much to be done to them to bring their rig and accommodation up to the standard I required for extensive single-handed cruising.

After many disappointments I decided that it might in the long run be no more expensive to build the kind of yacht I wanted than to buy one which would be only a makeshift. So, as I liked the boats that Laurent Giles & Partners designed, I went one day to Lymington and talked the matter over with Jack Giles. He agreed that just then second-hand vessels were fetching very high prices, and said he thought it might cost no more to build what I wanted—a comfortable, seaworthy and easily handled 4–5-tonner—than to buy what I did not want and have to spend money on extensive alterations.

I paid many visits to his office, and bit by bit after much discussion my ship took form—on paper. The exact size and design of even such a minor article as a cabin table required considerable thought, for, unlike a house, where if a little more room is required, it is a comparatively easy matter to add a wing, a room or even a lean-to in the garden, a boat, once she has started building, cannot well be enlarged and every care must therefore be taken to utilize the available space in her to the best advantage. So it was not until about Christmas time that the completed plans and specifications of a 4½-ton sea-going gaff cutter were sent out for tender to all the local boat-builders.

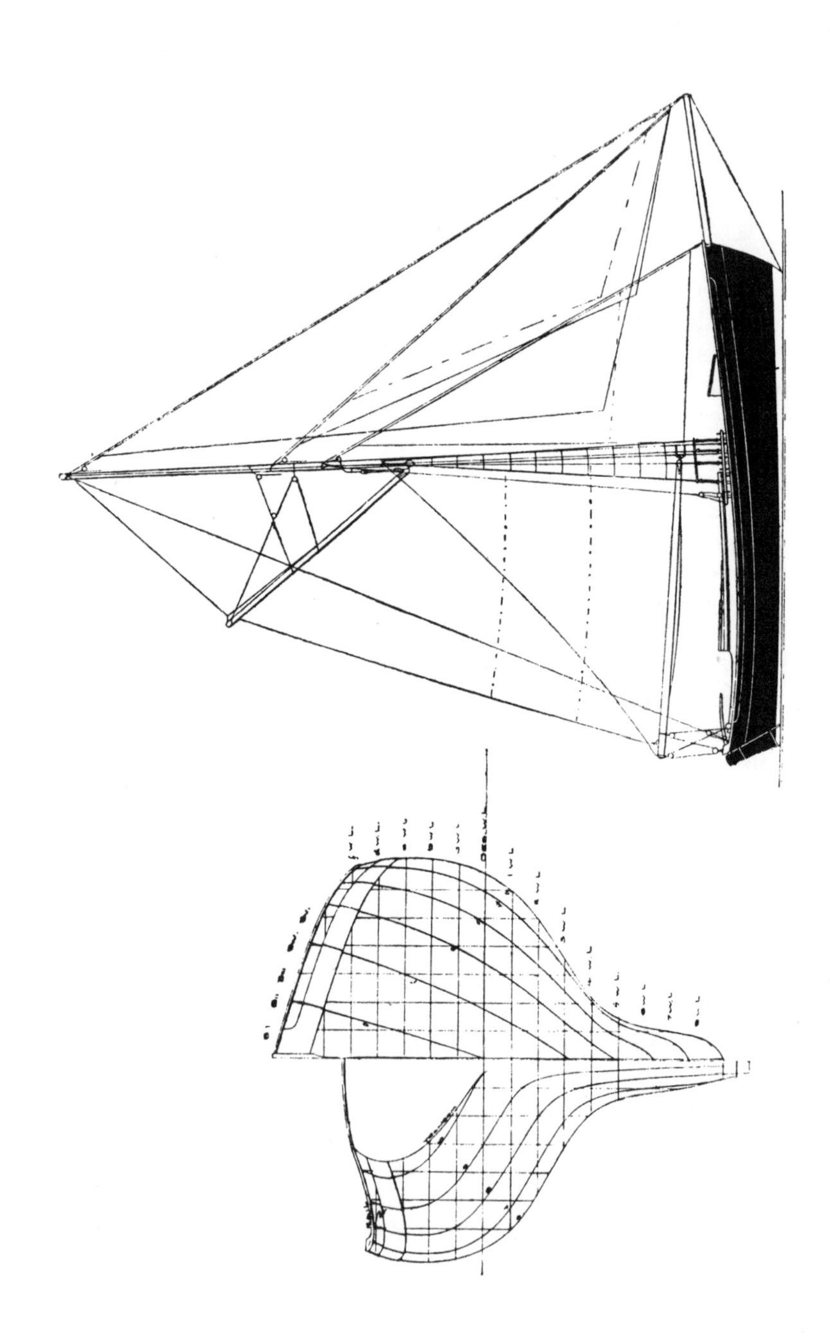

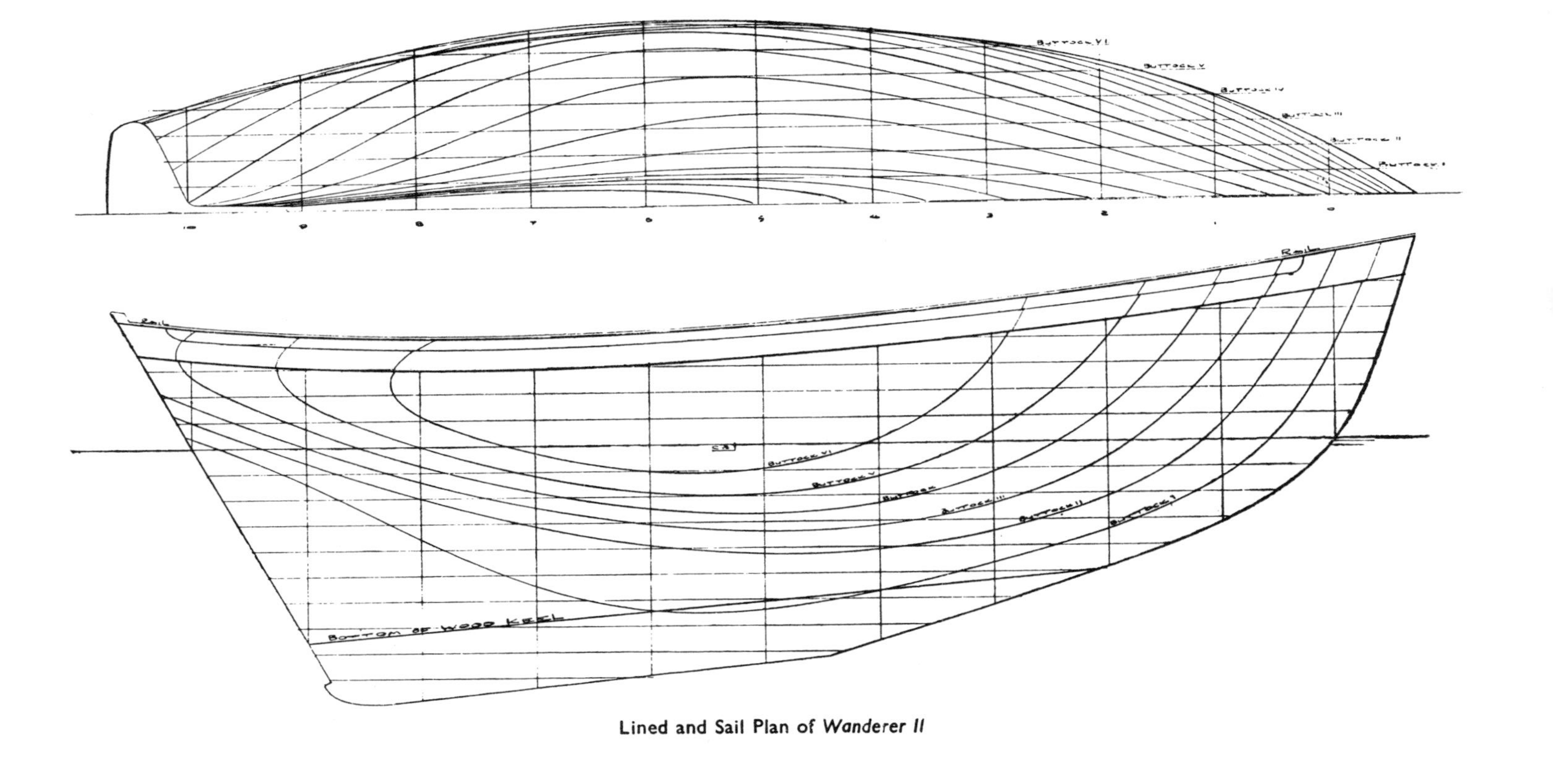

Lined and Sail Plan of *Wanderer II*

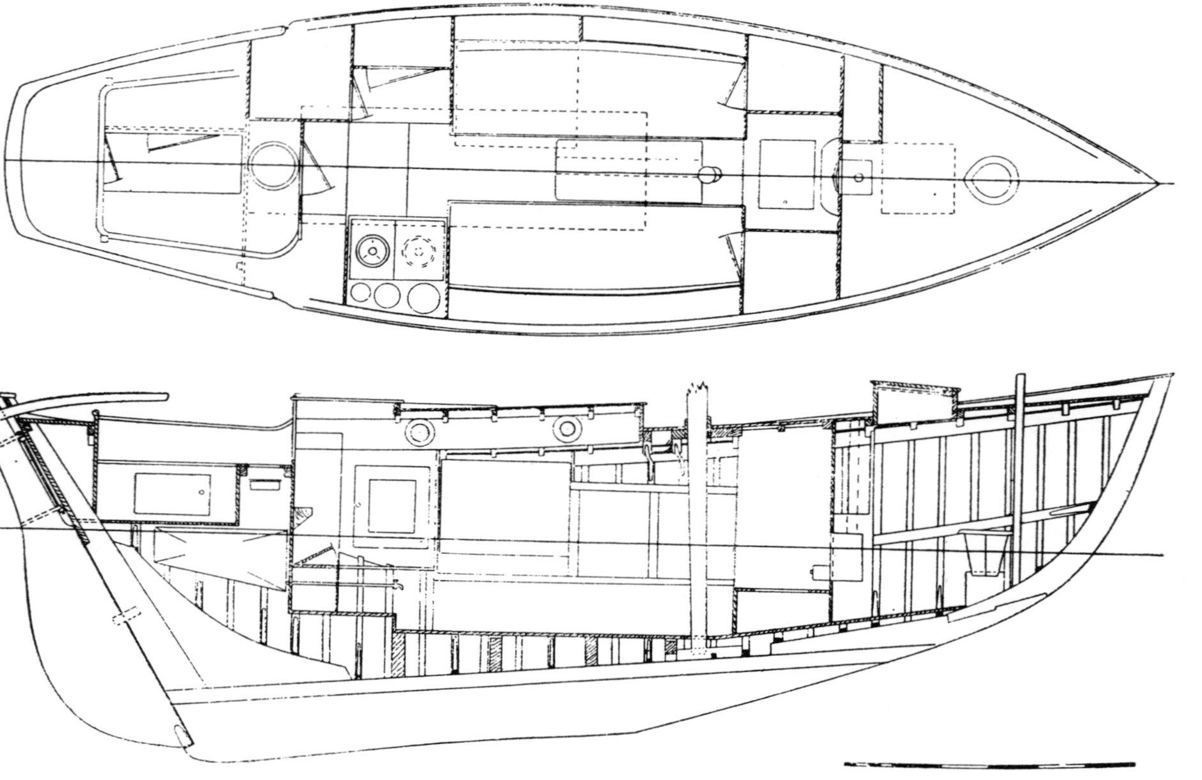

Wanderer II General Arrangement.

The first quotation to come in was most depressing, a figure I could not hope to face even in my wildest dreams ; so with the second, and the third, and . . . My visions began to fade, as they usually do when confronted with the hard facts of pounds shillings and pence.

Then, just when I had abandoned all hope, a new firm of builders at Poole, a firm all ready to build and only waiting for a job, cut prices in order to get it, and within the week the contract was signed ; they on their part agreeing to build the vessel of best materials and workmanship by the end of May, and I on mine agreeing to pay the sum of £350. Such an opportunity may come but once in a lifetime, and when I discovered that my friend John Tew, who had assisted in the designing of the yacht, had joined up with the yard and was to supervise the building, I was delighted.

Having got that far I was naturally eager to see my ship take form ; but there was much to be done first. On a large, black-painted floor—the mould loft—she was drawn out in chalk full size from measurements called offsets which were supplied by the designer. Pieces of three-ply wood were then cut to the exact shape of the frames, keel, stem, sternpost, etc., and taken to the saw-mill, where, laid on oak to the best advantage as regards the grain, the pieces were cut out to shape with a band saw—a machine which cuts through wood like butter and is capable of going round quite sharp corners. Oak, elm, pitchpine, mahogany, teak, oregon, silver spruce, red cedar, and ash had to be ordered in the quantity and approximate sizes required, and a wooden mould the size and shape of the 1½-ton iron keel had to be made and dispatched to the foundry.

The boat was to be 24 feet over all ; not that I consider that anything like long enough, for it seems that 30 feet overall and 25 feet on the waterline is the smallest size into which one can fit the necessary accommodation for a real cruiser, and nothing shorter than that is much good at sea when it comes to windward work. But I had only a very limited amount of capital, and adding even one foot to her overall length would have increased the Thames tonnage on which the estimate had been based ; so, although I would have preferred more overhang to the bow, I had to be satisfied with the above length, and I had left the other dimensions entirely to the designer, not limiting the draught in any way as the boat was not intended for ditch-crawling, and draught has no effect upon Thames tonnage.

Jack Giles produced the lovely set of lines which appear on pages 42 and 43, with a beam of 7 feet 2 inches, a draught of 5 feet, and plenty of sheer, for a vessel without any looks very commonplace and rather depressed. The waterlines were very fine each end, and that is probably the reason why the boat proved to be exceptionally fast in light airs. But she also proved to be somewhat tender, and as the draught is considerable for such a small vessel and the midship section is a firm one, the fine lines at each end must be held mainly responsible for that defect, though I have no doubt that the weight and windage of the gear aloft also had something to do with it.[8]

The bermuda rig is so obviously the correct one for a yacht of under 10 tons, that many people wondered why I wanted to be bothered with all the extra gear and complications of the gaff. My argument was that in a bermuda-rigged vessel if the mainsail is to be of much use in light winds it has to be a reasonable size, which means that as soon as the wind starts to blow it must be reefed. I preferred to have the first reef in the topsail, which, if it is a jib-header and correctly rigged, can be got down and stowed away in its bag in a few seconds. The gaff rig also has the advantage that a greater area of sail can be set for a given height of mast.

The mainsail had two deep reefs in it, and I did not have roller gear as I wanted to try out a loose-footed sail. The second reef unfortunately reduced it to a trysail of an inefficient shape with the gaff jaws only four feet above the boom. In a small boat I believed that reefing in the old-fashioned way would be no more trouble than reefing with roller gear, provided that the tackles and pendants were always kept rove as they should be ; and, except for the sake of tidiness, there is no need to tie the points with a loose-footed sail. For the tack I used quick-release gun-metal hooks shackled to the gooseneck, instead of the usual tack lashing, in order to save time, and with the luff of the sail laced to the mast with a 1¼-inch rope, I avoided the necessity for cutting adrift any mast-hoops when taking in a deep reef. During the first few cruises I began to think I had been mistaken in having the old style reefing arrangements, but I soon became accustomed to them, and having sailed since in a number of yachts with roller gear, I am satisfied that in a yacht smaller than 10-tons the old way of reefing is just as quick and easy, less likely to go wrong on a dark night and is kinder to the sail.[9]

As regards headsails she had the ordinary working jib and staysail, and for light weather a large yankee jib-topsail setting from the mast head to the bowsprit end. That is a wonderful sail for windward work, but it needs preventer backstays to make it set properly, for a headsail does no good unless its luff is straight ; and backstays that have to be let go and set up afresh every time one goes about are hard on the single-hander, while the business of getting that sail in when the wind starts to blow, entailing as it does a journey to the bowsprit end to undo the hanks, has often proved to be a difficult undertaking. With the bermuda rig and no bowsprit these difficulties are overcome, for a permanent backstay holds the mast straight and the sail can be comfortably dealt with from the fore-deck. The yankee is, however, such a fine pulling sail that in spite of its many drawbacks it has proved to be one of the hardest worked sails in the yacht, and I suppose that when I get too old and fat to sit on the bowsprit end I shall set it on a running stay which can be hauled inboard, and put up with the extra complications of gear.

Once upon a time I used to laugh at the jib-headed rig on account of the necessary tall mast, but I can do so no longer, for the new boat's mast was also very tall to enable a good sized topsail to be set, and therein lies the main disadvantage of the gaff rig. When the topsail is handed there is a great length of naked mast waving about, and the leading edge—which does most of the work to windward—is almost halved. But as I consider windward work at sea in a small vessel to be a vanity, the above disadvantages are not so serious as they at first appear, and when running or reaching I think the gaff rig has the advantage every time ; besides, I much prefer the appearance of it.[10]

Accommodation is a personal matter, and even at the best of times—except perhaps in a large vessel—the whole affair is a compromise. Fortunately I never worry about full headroom, for if I wish to stand upright and walk about I can always go on deck. The cabin-top was therefore kept low and narrow ; low so that a 7-foot dinghy could be carried comfortably upside down over it, and narrow to allow a wide deck each side under which there was sitting headroom. A clear deck is such a joy that I almost dispensed with a cabin-top ; but that meant having a skylight, and skylights generally leak unless they are covered up, and then they provide neither light nor ventilation.

The cockpit is not self-draining, for if a sea were to come aboard, I would much rather that it distributed itself fore-and-aft at once instead of remaining for a while in the cockpit, where it would put the boat down by the stern and possibly cause the next one to come aboard as well ; also, in a small vessel, a self-draining cockpit must be very shallow. I was later to discover that the boat was so buoyant that it would be almost impossible to ship heavy water unless she were to continue running too long in a gale of wind.

One of the few advantages of having no auxiliary engine is that the steering compass may be placed in a position where it can be seen ; so, under the bridge deck between the cockpit and the companionway, protected by a deadlight of unbreakable glass, was fitted a Husun dead-beat compass with an 8-inch card, which at night could be lit from below by a small electric bulb driven off a dry battery. Beneath the cockpit was a 15-gallon fresh-water tank, and I have since fitted two more emergency tanks holding another 12 gallons under the cabin sole.

It was indeed a red-letter day, and one worthy of being entered in the logbook which I had started keeping even at that early date, when, arriving at the yard one frosty morning, I found the keel laid and the stem, sternpost and most of the frames in position. I could see at last what my ship was going to look like, and very fine I thought her.

From that day she progressed apace, and in a short while ribbands—long bendy pieces of pine—were temporarily fastened in a fore-and-aft direction outside the frames, and American elm timbers, having been heated in a steam chest, were bent into position against them, two between each pair of frames. In my mind there is little doubt that the best construction is of all sawn frames, but oak with the grain running the right way is difficult to come by and is very expensive. So I had what was then considered to be the next best thing, sawn frames every two feet, which were strong enough to keep the hull in shape, and steam-bent elm timbers between them. Today, of course, most boats are built without any grown frames, and are perfectly satisfactory.

In order that the boat should not lose her shape during construction, every frame and timber was firmly shored down from the roof of the shed before planking was begun. As each plank was forced into position by screw clamps, a great squeezing pressure was put on the middle frames, and only after the deck beams had been fitted were the shores removed. It is probably through lack of these precautions that so many boats which are designed with a noble sheer turn out to be so disappointingly flat.

Planking was started at the bottom and was of inch-thick pitchpine, all except the garboard strakes—the lowest planks next to the keel on each side—for they had two awkward twists in them and many fastenings, and so were made of elm. A plank would be roughly fashioned to shape on the bench, forced into position, marked with a piece of chalk, and then taken back to the bench to be finished. When bent into position for the second time it seldom needed any alteration and touched its neighbour fairly for its whole length. The planking having been fitted half-way up the hull each side, a start was made at the top working downwards, the last plank to go in—the shutter—having to fit exactly to the ones above and below it. A difficult job, one might have thought, but the shipwrights did it in an hour and it fitted beautifully.

Each plank was fastened to the frames and timbers by some eighty odd copper spikes, and as there were 16 planks each side, that made the astonishing total of 2,500 fastenings. When the last one had been driven, Bob, the master-shipwright, climbed gingerly into the hull, cut each spike off short and hammered the stump over a copper roove making a neat and effective rivet.

After that I was able to go aboard and walk about on the keel, admiring my fine ship, and trying to make up my mind where everything was to be fitted. That was no easy matter, for there was not a straight line anywhere from which to measure, and she looked much smaller then than she did after the deck had been laid.

When the shelves and stringers—heavy pine planks binding all the frames and timbers together—had been put in, the shipwrights made a start with the deck by fitting the oak beams to support it, each one dovetailed into the shelf, and then they laid the deck itself. I had always wanted to have a real teak deck with each narrow plank tapering fore-and-aft and separated from its neighbours by neat lines of marine glue. But weight and cost were against it, and I had to be content with red cedar tongued and grooved, the whole thing painted, covered with tightly stretched canvas, and painted again. That at least has the advantage that it is light and waterproof, but should there be a leak it would be difficult to trace, for water getting beneath the canvas might creep several feet before percolating through. Red cedar was used because it is less liable to rot than are most other light woods.

Whilst the shipwrights were planing the sides and caulking them, the inside of the vessel was given over to the blacksmith and his mate. Wrought-iron floors had to be made and fitted to bind the frames and timbers to the keel and to their opposite numbers ; strengthening knees had to be fitted in the neighbourhood of the mast and shroud plates, and the shroud plates had to be made too. That was a most entertaining business, for the smithy was some little distance from the building shed, and the smith's mate had to run with the redhot iron in a pair of pincers and pass it to the smith who was on board ; he, rapidly fitting it into place, shaped it with a few deft blows with a hammer before it cooled.

Although I had found time to watch those things happening, I had not been entirely idle myself. Because I like to know that beneath its parcelling and serving every splice has at least four tucks, and that all the eyes are properly protected against damp, I undertook the rigging myself.[11] I believe there were 90 splices all told, and I became quite proficient at turning them in, but I found that it was no easy matter to get the length of the shrouds exactly right so that the deadeyes were level. Instead of the usual strips of tarred canvas I used insulating tape for the parcellings and found it easier to put on ; it is quite impervious to water, and because each turn sticks to its neighbour, the splice can be used either way up without risk of water getting in.

Meanwhile Terence North was busy in his loft making the sails. He was a romantic figure with his thin gold earrings, and flaming red beard, and he knew his business. The mainsail, staysail, No. 1 jib and topsail totalled 365 square feet, and were all made from canvas tanned a rich red-brown in the bolt, mildew and dirt proof. The No. 2 jib and the storm staysail were also made from that material. All were fitted with large gunmetal cringles capable of taking stout lashings or shackles. For such a little vessel the sails were somewhat heavy, but as a result they have survived 11,000 miles of cruising which included countless days spent crashing becalmed in a swell. In addition to these there was a mast-head spinnaker of 350 square feet and a yankee jib-topsail of 170 square feet, both made from very light untanned canvas so that they would bunt out to the faintest air.

In my store a large pile of gear was accumulating : sails, rigging, cooking stoves, mattresses and bedding, navigation instruments, tinned food and a lot of other apparently necessary but bulky articles. Where they were all going to be stowed I had no idea, for a 24-foot yacht has not unlimited capacity if any room is to be left for living in, and a man takes up just as much space in a 4-tonner as he does in a 40-tonner. But they did all stow away when the time came, along with many other things, and still there was room for more.

One day I noticed a shipwright hacking away with an adze at a balk of timber perched on a couple of trestles. On inquiry he told me that he was making my mast, and I was not at all impressed. But, to my utter amazement, the very next day on those same trestles I found a slender, tapering, silver spruce spar receiving a final rub down before its first coat of varnish, and it had not a single crack or blemish on it anywhere. Though it was a solid stick with a maximum diameter of 5 inches and a total length of 37-feet, I found that I could pick it up quite easily and walk about with it on my shoulder, but it whipped to such an extent that its ends touched the ground. I thought that such a flimsy thing would be dangerous, and I said so, but John Tew assured me that it is only those spars which will not bend that break, and time has proved him to be right, for that mast has since had to put up with a good deal of stress and strain.

It was well into May before my boat was moved out of the building shed to have her iron keel bolted on. Three joiners then went aboard, and the speed with which bulkheads, berths, lockers, and lining took shape was astonishing. I had to be on the spot all the while, for little details kept cropping up, and several alterations from the original plans had to be made, but the final arrangement was as shown in the accommodation plan on page 44, and is as follows.

Immediately inside the companionway is the galley, rather an elaborate one for so small a boat, a two burner Para-Fin stove with oven and saucepan rack behind it being to starboard and a Primus stove in gimballs with pantry locker behind it to port. Abaft the galley on the port side is a large blanket locker extending partly under the cockpit seat, and on the starboard side is stowage space for oilskins. The cabin has two berths with Dunlopillo mattresses and canvas leeboards to keep one snug at night;[12] there are lockers with a shelf above them behind the berths, and on the port side flush with the panelling (all of which is of Masonite wood fibre) is a hinged chart case which holds 100 Admiralty charts quite flat, and when let down is held by rope lanyards to form a chart table.

The cabin table is fitted with removable fiddles and has one leg at its aft end, its forward end being attached to the mast; the gimballed cabin lamp is also attached to the mast. At the forward end of each berth is a large locker for clothes, etc., and between them, sunk flush into the bulkhead between the cabin and the forepeak, is an open fireplace with a locker to hold half a hundredweight of coal in front of it. With this arrangement it is, of course, impossible to have a door through into the forepeak, but that is a disadvantage more apparent on paper than it is in fact, and because there never has been a door there I have never noticed the lack of it.

The forepeak contains a chain locker, a bucket w.c. and ample stowage space for sails and navigation lamps, and as the body of the coal fireplace projects through the bulkhead, that compartment makes an excellent drying cupboard for wet gear and clothes which therefore need not clutter up the cabin.

On the fateful day the bottle was broken by my mother with all due ceremony, and the crowd cheered as *Wanderer II*, gleaming in her coat of brand new white enamel, slid down the ways into the water where, to everyone's relief, she floated just above her designed waterline, as every good ship should. But between the launching of a vessel and her completion much time elapses. A hundred things require doing, and no sooner are they dealt with than a fresh lot of equal importance appear, and so it goes on ; shipwrights, plumbers, joiners, and riggers swarm all over her getting hopelessly in each other's way.

Sheet leads and cleats had to be made and fitted ; anchor chocks had to be altered, for someone arranged the bower where the kedge should be ; the pram dinghy had to be placed on deck and fittings made to keep her there, and then it was discovered that the sliding hatch would no longer slide, so a new one had to be made. Various items of equipment had to be returned to their makers as they were either the wrong size or the wrong shape, and when the main water tank arrived nearly a fortnight late, almost the entire cockpit had to be dismantled and rebuilt to take the thing. While the "chippie" was doing that the plumber trod on his hand ; he, of course, was wearing the kind of boots that plumbers affect, and the injured man in his agony leapt wildly on deck upsetting a pot of varnish the painter was using. Turning to watch the fun the rigger's mate by chance let slip the topsail halyard ; an unfortunate business because the rigger happened to be sitting in a bo'sun's chair attached to the other end of it, and was nearly at the masthead at the time ; the port crosstree broke his fall, but he broke the crosstree, so that was just one more item to be added to the list of things to do and see to on the morrow.

For ten days *Wanderer II* lay alongside her builders' pier while the finishing touches were completed, and when the shore parties had knocked off for the night I set to and generally worked until the early hours of the morning. But only those who have had their own ships built and have watched them building, can have any idea of the vast number of little things that need to be done before a new yacht is completed, and it was not until the end of August that, at last being in all respects ready for sea, I got canvas on *Wanderer II* for the first time, and dipping my ensign to the knot of men who had collected on the pier to see me off, sailed away on the trial cruise.

CHAPTER V

THE TRIAL CRUISE

TAKING to sea for the first time a new and untried vessel whose speed, leeway, turning circle and general behaviour are unknown quantities, is apt to be an exciting business, especially for a lone hand. But I very soon discovered that my new boat had good manners ; her steadiness on the helm, the sure manner in which she came about even when I had been pinching her in order to clear one or other of the yachts lying on moorings off Poole, and the speed with which she gathered way and slipped through the water without any fuss, combined to give me a feeling of real confidence.

All went well until we had cleared the harbour entrance and were in the mile long channel of approach which is bounded on one side by a sandbank and on the other by a stone training wall, placed there to compel the tides to sweep more strongly through the channel in order to scour the silting sand away. There the wind left us to wallow in the short ground-swell, and the tide, which does not run fairly down the channel, set us slowly towards the wall. At once I set the yankee jib-topsail, but even that large light sail only flapped uselessly from side to side as we rolled without steerage way. Instead of an auxiliary engine *Wanderer II* carries a 12-foot sweep, and by sculling with it over the stern, using the large rowlock fitted in the taffrail for that purpose, she can be made to move at about 1½ knots in a calm provided the sea is smooth. I wasted several valuable minutes sculling before I realised that we were making no progress because of the swell, so I did then what I ought to have done earlier, and let go the bower anchor, which brought us up with our stern only a few yards away from the training wall which was just beginning to show its ragged top above the receding tide.

I rather think that refusing to have an auxiliary engine aboard is an admission of weak-mindedness, for there is no need to use it except in times of emergency ; but I know perfectly well that if I had one I would seldom attempt to enter or leave harbour without its assistance, to the ruination of such seamanship as I may have acquired. I once believed that the solution of that problem would be to have an engine of such low power that it would be useless in anything except a calm ; but that will not do for it is then useless in a swell also, and the sea is seldom smooth. Although I could well have done with an engine on my first and subsequent cruises, I am still glad after many miles of sailing in her that *Wanderer II* has not got one, for the technique of cruising under sail alone is very different from, and much more interesting than, cruising under sail with the knowledge that beneath the cockpit floor is a power unit which, to a touch on the self-starter knob, will spring to life and whisk one away from dangerous or difficult situations. Without the help of an auxiliary one has to study carefully the tidal streams and insets, just as our grandfathers used to, and jockey for position so that should the wind fail at a vital moment the yacht is not endangered ; one has to learn to keep on the windward side of a river and to steer a course to windward of the destination so as to have something always in hand should the wind head. Above all one has to learn to be patient, but although it may be trying to have to spend a windless night within sight of the desired harbour, that is compensated for by the delight of ghosting up some glorious loch or estuary with only a gossamer breeze in the stillness of a summer's evening—a pleasure which only the strongest-minded owners of auxiliary engines enjoy, for the temptation to start the machine and get to an anchorage in good time for dinner is a powerful one.

The internal combustion engine has done much to popularise yachting by encouraging newcomers, who do not feel sure of their ability under sail, to take up the sport. It allows the owner who has but limited time to get much farther afield with the certainty of being able to return when he wants to, and it has opened up some of the more difficult creeks and anchorages which he might not have attempted to reach under sail alone. But to cover a big mileage and to visit many places does not necessarily give one the greatest satisfaction ; much more can often be had by making use of the winds and tides and one's own skill and cunning, while those who go about under "Solent rig"—jib, mizen and engine—miss much of the fun that could be theirs for the taking.

It was late in the afternoon when a light air made and enabled me to leave my unpleasant anchorage, and I sailed on down the channel with the intention of bringing up for the night in Studland Bay ; but near the bar the wind freshened to such purpose from N.E. that I decided to make the most of it in a summer of almost incessant west winds, so at 8 p.m. off Anvil Point I streamed the patent log and set a course S.W. for the Casquets, leaving the choice of a definite destination until later.

With the wind aft the yankee was no longer of any help, so I handed it, but kept the topsail aloft as there was not too much wind for it. I have sailed in yachts whose owners insist on stowing all light weather canvas at sundown, no matter what the weather is like, with the result that the poor things dawdle half crippled through the night. Every man, of course, must do whatever he thinks fit in his own craft, but he has no just cause for complaint when he finds himself a second night at sea instead of in the haven where he would be, simply because he has "snugged her down." If sails are carried which cannot be handed safely in the dark, surely it is a sign that their rigging requires revision, or that the owner and his crew are not familiar with their working. One possible exception is a large spinnaker, and that is usually something of a problem even in broad daylight if one happens to be short-handed.

Supper was just a picnic snatched between hurried dashes to the helm, for *Wanderer*, I found, would not hold her course before the wind for more than a few moments. Of course I could have hove her to and had my meal in comfort, but I did not wish to waste a breath of that fair wind.

It was a lovely starlit night and the compass was necessary only to select a suitable star to steer by ; also, for a night passage, it was reasonably warm. The result was that at about 2 a.m. I discovered we were many points off our course and realised I had been dozing. I did heave-to then, made myself some strong coffee, ate some biscuits and plotted the position on the chart, then bearing away once more on the course I kept a lookout for lights, and an hour later sighted the group flash of Alderney.

That vicinity is an easy landfall at night with its three powerful lights in 17 miles—Cap la Hague, Alderney and the Casquets. Soon the other two lights appeared ; I got a fix by bearings of them, and looked up the tides which run strongly among the Channel Islands. I found that I had missed the ebb through the Race of Alderney, which was unfortunate, for if one is bound for Guernsey, and I had finally decided to go there, it gives one a powerful push in the right direction. I therefore had to go round outside the Casquets after all, and had them bearing E. at breakfast time.

As is usually the case there the sea was lumpy and confused, and the wind had moderated, though there was still sufficient of it to keep us going at about 3 knots with a crashing boom, for I was finding my new boat quite slippery in light winds. Deciding that it was time to get properly awake, I did what I usually do in similar circumstances, stripped off the layers of clothing which had accumulated during the night, and went over the stern to tow along on the end of the mainsheet. That is always an exhilarating way of bathing, for one is whipped through the crests and down into the troughs at what appears to be great speed ; but that morning it was more fun than usual for I was seeing my new boat under full sail for the first time, and she looked most attractive. After a rub down I set up the boom guy (a single rope from the end of the boom to the forward bitts and tautened by hauling in some of the mainsheet) and then was ready for breakfast. *Wanderer* steered herself while I cooked and ate it, and afterwards I sat in the cockpit to wait for land to appear. But it was a long time coming, for visibility was indifferent, there was a strong tide against us and we were not sailing very fast, so it was 4 p.m. when I slipped into St. Peter Port harbour, glad to be at anchor after twenty-two hours at sea.

From Guernsey to the north coast of Brittany I had a crew of two. George and Peter Kinnersley were going over to collect a Morlaix pilot boat which Peter had bought, and the journey by steamer and rail being particularly tedious, they were pleased to get a passage, and I was delighted to have them especially as I wanted to show off my new boat's paces.

We left in sunshine with all sail to topsail and yankee set to a light N.E. breeze, and having rounded St. Martin's Point (the S.E. corner of Guernsey) we set a course for Tréguier. The masthead spinnaker was hoisted up to starboard, rather to the crew's disgust for it kept the sun off them and I had quickly occupied the only sunny spot on the fore-deck. It was a grand run ; the wind had freshened enough to drive the yacht at 5½ knots, which at that time I thought must be the maximum speed for a boat with a waterline length of less than 21 feet, and while my crew took turns at steering a somewhat laborious compass course, for the sea was getting up, I just lay on my back admiring my lovely new sails which were bellied out in firm curves, the rich red-brown of the working sails, the almost gold of the spinnaker ; and I watched the masthead sweep its graceful arcs against the sky.

Then a thought came to trouble me. Hurrying along as we were it was likely that we would reach Tréguier at 11 p.m. ; only the entrance to that river was lighted ; in the dark it would be impossible to go far beyond the lighthouse, and with the onshore wind that berth would be an uncomfortable, if not dangerous, one. I therefore decided that we would do better to make for the Pontrieux River which was well lighted right up to the snuggest of berths ; so when we had brought the great lighthouse on the Roches Douvres abeam, we handed the spinnaker, gybed, and altered course accordingly.

Shortly after sunset Les Heaux appeared surprisingly close ahead, which showed that we were farther to the west than we should be, due either to the tide or indifferent steering, and we had to put *Wanderer* on the wind for Horaine, one of the light buoys near the mouth of the Pontrieux River. At once there was a change in the motion as we plunged along with the lee rail awash and a steep sea on the bow ; the buoyant lift and surge of a vessel running free had changed for the pitch and lurch of one closehauled. As wind, tide and sea were setting us towards a ragged coast, I took a series of cross-bearings with the hand-bearing compass which was one of the many gifts *Wanderer* had received when she was launched. It was a beautifully made little thing and I had thought a lot of it, but I soon found that it did not agree with the steering compass (which had been checked and proved reliable), for in so small a yacht it is almost impossible to get sufficiently far away from the influence of ironwork. On deck one is too close to the wire rigging, and in the cockpit or companionway too close to the steering compass. I have since tried the hand-bearing compass in many positions, but except in settled weather when one can stand on deck amidships well clear of anything that might disturb it, I find it is far more satisfactory to put the yacht's head or stern on the object of which a bearing is required and then read the bearing from the steering compass.

But when I saw how rapidly we were moving along the coast and bringing the leading lights into line, I put my toy away and took the helm, for it would be a dead run up the river, and if it was necessary to gybe with a press of canvas aloft, I preferred to do that myself. The lights were quickly brought into line, and turning we kept them so. The tide was setting athwart the course and care was necessary, for the leading lights took us very close to some rocks on the port side, which were only just visible in the darkness with the grey of breaking seas on them.

As soon as the low light obscured the high one we altered course a little and brought the second pair, red ones, into line, and they soon led us between cliffs which blanketed the wind to a light air. The river, as calm as a pond there, then widened, and sailing silently up to the green Perdrix light, we anchored at midnight in 7 fathoms just below the little town of Lezardrieux. That may seem a great depth for a small boat to bring up in, but it was near high water, and the tides at springs along that part of the coast rise thirty-four feet.

My friends left me in the morning to find their way to Morlaix, and I spent several very pleasant days dodging rocks in the neighbourhood. I had with me only the Royal Cruising Club chart, a large portion of which was bounded by a dotted line ; there was a notice in one corner stating that as the French survey (from which the chart was taken) was of an incomplete nature, great caution should be used when navigating inside the dotted line. A glance at any chart of that locality is rather disconcerting because of the many dangers shown, and *The Channel Pilot Part II* is not encouraging. Perhaps those are the reasons why so few British yachts visit the place, although it is only about 50 miles from Guernsey. But when one has become accustomed to a strong tide with great range, pilotage is quite simple in the main channels, for they are well marked with stone towers, buoys and lighthouses. Many of these were destroyed during the German occupation but they are now (1947) rapidly being re-built, and at the same time the system of marking, which used to be one of the simplest and clearest in the world, is being changed. The Compass System is now used for those coasts which are surrounded by rocks, and for isolated dangers, while the Channel System is used elsewhere, an arrangement which is apt to be confusing to the stranger.[13]

I spent a day at Loguivi, a fishing boat harbour which dries, examining the local crabbers with their powerful bows, raking sterns and great sheer, and had the good fortune to find two killicks, genuine ones of wood and stone, still in daily use. Then I sailed round to Tréguier, and did not choose an ideal day, for visibility was poor. There are two ways of getting there from the Pontrieux River, either inside or outside Les Heaux ; the first is considerably shorter but is among rocks. I started off for that passage with a fresh E. wind, and got the first pair of leading marks in line over the stern. Wind and tide hurried us along, and it was soon time to alter course for the second set of marks which lead one through a passage between rocks which were just covered at that state of the tide. I was unable to find them in the haze, so I had to go round outside Les Heaux after all, and therefore I did not bring up off Tréguier until sunset.

Tréguier with its crooked grey houses, its market, its fine cathedral and its friendly inhabitants, is a charming place, and I found it very difficult to leave after a stay of several days, but by 11 o'clock one fine morning I had cleared the approaches to the river and was bound back for Guernsey with a light N.W. wind, which died completely when the Roches Douvres were abeam. The tide set *Wanderer* so close to the rocks that I got the kedge and warp ready, but fortunately a light breeze made just before it was necessary to anchor, and by 8 p.m. we were near St. Martin's Point. I had hoped to spend that night at

St. Peter Port, but the tide was setting south out of the Little Russel and we made no progress against it.

I listened to the last gramophone record of dance music and heard the B.B.C. announcer say " Good night, everybody. Good night ! " and I thought I might as well go to bed too, for there was by then not a breath of wind. So I stowed the headsails, lashed the riding light in the rigging, had some soup and turned in.

This practice of going to sleep at sea horrifies my sailing friends, but I think that there is little real risk on a fine night clear of the steamer lanes, for I have developed the useful habit of waking every hour to have a look round, and then going off to sleep again. Also, the burgee, being mounted by wire on its stick, makes a slight rattling noise in the lightest breeze, and that always wakes me up. But sleep is certainly something of a problem for the single-hander, and many is the night that, owing to stress of weather, proximity of the land or the presence of other craft, it is impossible. The greatest danger arises the second or third night out, when owing to lack of proper sleep during the previous night, one is really tired, and then the freshening of the wind, the altering of the course, or the muffled beat of a steamer's propeller may fail to wake one from heavy slumber. But after all it is possible to heave-to under snug canvas on the offshore tack and sleep all day when one reaches that state of fatigue.

During the night we drifted several miles to the E.S.E., and at 6 a.m. I turned out thoroughly refreshed, and was having breakfast when a light breeze sprang up from S.E. I went on deck to set the headsails and saw a bank of thick grey fog rolling down upon us. Quickly I got bearings of Little Sark and Jethou, fixing our position at 1½ miles S.W. of the former. Then I hardened in the sheets and stood close-hauled to the southward, for although the security of St. Peter Port harbour lay only 6 miles away, I did not care to attempt to make it in such a smother.

The fog was soon upon us, cold and clammy, and visibility was reduced to a few yards. When I had been out in fog before I had usually been able to see some sort of dividing line between sea and sky ; here there was nothing but swirling blinding fog, my only friend was the compass, my only aid the breeze. The air was raw and damp. Great drops of moisture ran down the rigging and dripped from the sheer-poles and spider-band on to the deck. The sails soon became sodden and stiff as cardboard, and flapped sullenly from side to side with a faint protesting groan from the swinging spars, as *Wanderer* rolled on the swell to which the fog had lent a deceptive size and swiftness. There were no other sounds ; no foghorns, no steamers' sirens. The feeling of isolation was profound.

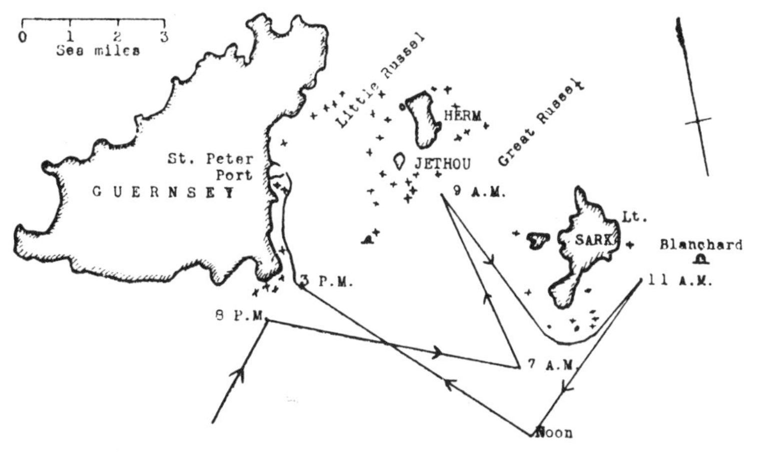

Wanderer's track in the fog.

The wind soon fell very light and veered to S. To the north of us lay Sark, Herm and Jethou with their surrounding rocks, and by then the tide would be setting us towards them ; with enough wind to give a speed of only about one knot, I did not feel confident of being able to sail blindfold through the Great Russel with any degree of safety, for the tide would have more effect on us than the wind and might set us into danger. So I persisted in my attempt to sail south and hoped at least to hold my own against the tide.

At 9 a.m. the fog thinned for a moment, and through an almost clear lane I got a glimpse of what I thought, to judge by its shape, was Jethou. It bore N.W. and looked to be less than a mile away. Then the lane closed and the fog was as thick as ever. Soon afterwards I heard the three blasts of the foghorn on Sark. That, as near as I could judge it, bore E.N.E. ; so it seemed that we had actually lost ground and were by then well into the Great Russel.

Two hours later Sark foghorn bore N. and somewhere near-by I could hear the irregular groaning noise that could only be made by the Blanchard whistle buoy east of Sark. I found it difficult to believe that we had actually been set south out of the Great Russel, east past Little Sark and north up Sark's eastern side, and when shortly afterwards I lost the sound of both the Blanchard buoy and Sark siren, I felt utterly bewildered and lost and I would have anchored, but with no bottom at 30 fathoms the depth of water was too great.

It must have been about noon when I first heard the long hoot of a steamer under way to which I replied. Steadily the hoots drew nearer and very soon I could hear distinctly the churning beat of a ship's propeller and the hiss of her bow-wave. It was a desperately anxious moment ; *Wanderer* barely had steerage way and I could not guess which side the ship would pass. Then, right over my head, so it seemed, came the deep-throated roar of her siren again, and close on the beam I could dimly see the red anti-fouling and white boot-top line of a Southern Railway mail boat. As she swept by I could just discern her blurred white superstructure and the outline of two funnels. She was quickly past and her siren soon faded away in the distance. Unpleasant though our meeting had been she had given me a position line which passed clear of all dangers, if she was bound from St. Peter Port to Jersey, as I concluded she must be. So when her wash had rolled by I steered W.N.W. with a slightly better breeze and an hour later I picked up the sound of the diaphone on St. Martin's Point ahead. The noise from such a contrivance is supposed to carry farther in fog than anything else, but although I had been within a few miles of it for many hours that day, that was the first time I had heard it.

At 3 p.m., just when the diaphone was getting unpleasantly close and I was thinking of standing out to sea once more, the fog lifted and I found myself close to the point very near to the position I had occupied the previous evening. The sun then came out to dry the sails and ate up what little wind there was, and only by using the sweep was I able to round the point and get into the north-going eddy close inshore. I had to scull all the way to St. Peter Port and brought up in the harbour there at 8 p.m.

Wanderer and I had taken no less than 24 hours to make good a distance of 4 miles. Where we had been to in the meantime is rather uncertain, and opinions at Guernsey differed, but it seems that we had drifted up the Great Russel and out again, then partly up the east side of Sark, and out from there to the steamer track, for all of which the tide must be held responsible.

I remained for one night only in harbour, and the following afternoon sailed for Alderney by way of the Race, with a light S.E. breeze. I ought to have gone there through the Swinge, and then the tide would have carried me to Braye Harbour which is on the north side of the island. But I reckoned on getting there when the tide was slack to the north, and so I did, but the wind died and I was unable to edge out of the Alderney Race stream which was running very hard just then. The division between it and the slack water was only a hundred yards or so away, and was very clearly defined, but we were rapidly swept away to the N.E., and when presently a good beam wind sprang up, it was too late to be of use. So I reluctantly had to give up the idea of visiting Alderney on that occasion, and with everything including the yankee full and drawing we romped across the Channel.

The crossing was fast but uneventful, and although I kept a good lookout for steamers I spent very little time on deck. Conditions suiting her perfectly, my little boat was showing me what she could do in the way of steering herself, and not until the Needles were close aboard did I take over and pilot her up the Solent.

CHAPTER VI

TWIN SPINNAKERS

MY FIRST season with her had shown me that *Wanderer II* was able to steer herself reasonably well with the wind abeam or forward of the beam, when she usually kept a steady course, but with the wind aft of the beam she needed a hand at the helm all the time. As it is very inconvenient for the single-hander to have to heave-to or alter course every time he wishes to eat or sleep or attend to the navigation, I decided to try out twin spinnakers.

There is, of course, nothing at all original about that rig; the Atlantic and other oceans have been crossed on several occasions with its assistance, but at that time there was very little published information about its use and behaviour at sea from the single-hander's point of view. So, with the assistance of Jack Giles, a rig was designed under which it was considered that *Wanderer* would run safely with the wind aft of the beam and without the need for a helmsman.

The theory of the rig is simple. Two sails of equal area are set on booms one each side forward of the mast, with guys leading aft to the quarters to keep the booms at the correct angle to the fore-and-aft line; I found that about forty-five degrees was the best angle. Suppose, then, the yacht is running with the wind aft, and for some reason, perhaps a larger or more irregular sea than usual, she takes a sheer to port, the port sail then gets more wind than the other and pushes her back on to the course again. Even with the wind on the quarter it should be possible to make her steer herself in the desired direction by hauling in on one guy and slacking off the other until the sails balance one another again.

The sails were cut without much belly, the canvas being of the same weight as that of which the working sails were made, and small headboards were fitted to give a better spread. Quite unnecessarily I had reef cringles and points put in them, for I had not then realised that the easiest way of reducing the effective area of such sails would be to let the booms go farther forward as the wind increased, thus spilling more and more wind out of them. With no fore-and-aft canvas to steady her I knew that the yacht would roll heavily, so I had the sails cut with their clews 7 feet above the waterline. But that was not a sufficient clearance, and many times the booms have dipped their ends in the sea. The tacks were shackled to eye-bolts in the deck near the mast, and the halyards—single parts of 1½-inch manilla—passed through side sheaves on the mast just below the jib halyard block. That was the only point in the rig where chafe could occur, and chain or wire would, I think, be necessary on a long voyage.

The booms were 11 feet long and had open, leather-covered jaws, which could be pushed up the mast to any desired height, where they were held from slipping by a turn of one of the idle main halyards. With their inboard ends slightly higher than their outer ends the booms showed no tendency to lift, and in moderate weather I did not bother to push them up the mast at all as their own weight kept them from lifting. To start with I used outhauls and topping lifts, but soon realised that such complications were not necessary for sails of only 110 square feet each.

I experimented with the new rig in the smooth water of the Solent where it did everything I had hoped for and the yacht performed like a model, but the opportunity for trying it out properly in the open sea did not occur until *Wanderer* was making a passage from the Isles of Scilly to the south-west coast of Ireland.

She had left the anchorage at New Grimsby under all lower sail with a fresh S.E. wind, almost dead astern as the course for the Fastnet was N.W.½N., so as soon as the islands had been cleared I stowed all fore-and-aft canvas and set the twins. That may sound simple enough, but it took a long time and required a great deal of effort as I was not then familiar with the best way of doing it, and the S.W. swell, crossed by a sea running from S.E., threw the little vessel wildly about.

Eventually I got her away dead before the wind, and sat for a while in the cockpit to see how she behaved. In spite of much adjustment of the guys she would only hold her course for a few minutes at a time, and then, on an extra steep sea, would sheer away to starboard until the lee sail was shaking, and took a long time to pay off again. That would not have mattered much if she had done it to both sides of the course, but unfortunately she always sheered in the same direction, something east of north.

When single-handed on a long passage I do not usually waste much time and energy adjusting sheets and helm in what is frequently an abortive attempt to make the yacht steer herself on the right course. I let her please herself, and when she has settled on a course that suits her, I rule that on the chart, provided it is in approximately the right direction. That may seem a strange way of going about the sea, but it seldom adds more than a mile or two to the distance sailed, and there is always the chance that the wind may become more favourable later.

But to head east of north when I wanted to go north-west was quite absurd, and as I did not wish to steer, for heavy rain had set in, I tried out an arrangement used in model yachts whose sails are made to control the helm. I lashed a block to each of the aftermost samson posts, of which *Wanderer* has two each side of her cockpit, and leading the spinnaker boom guys through them, clove-hitched their ends to the tiller. That scheme was a great success, and for the next 8 hours the yacht steered herself N.W., while I kept warm and dry down below. It was fascinating to watch through the companionway the helm being pulled firmly up to windward every time she began to sheer, and to learn from the compass that although she was sheering a point or more off her course she was doing so each side of it, and every hour was making good 5 miles in the right direction.

But with no steadying canvas set she rolled her rails under in the beam swell. I tried to improve matters by setting the storm staysail abaft the mast on the peak halyard, but that upset the balance and she came up until the wind was abeam and the lee spinnaker shaking. So I took the staysail in again and then made myself as comfortable as possible on the cabin floor, wedged between the bunks with cushions and pillows, and that was the only time I have ever been glad of a narrow cabin floor.

At 8 o'clock that evening the wind backed a couple of points and it was necessary to readjust the length of the boom guys to keep *Wanderer* sailing on her course. But she was then no longer entirely self-steering, and although I did not have to remain at the helm I had to keep on the alert, for every now and again as a larger sea raised her stern she would round up with the wind abeam and would not pay off again without assistance.

I was both surprised and disappointed and did not understand why she should behave like that. Later that year I corresponded with Sherman Hoyt of the New York Yacht Club who had used twin spinnakers successfully in his *Barnswallow*. He assured me that the sails would behave properly and make the boat steer herself if their tacks were secured to sheets leading through fairleads near the stem-head, and that the trimming of the sails should be done by means of these sheets ; the booms to be regarded as more or less permanent. Such an arrangement, he said, would also tend to minimise rolling. So I tried them rigged like that, but finding them even less efficient, I soon reverted to the original arrangement which did at least work properly when the wind was right aft. The fact that in smooth water the rig did all that one might ask of it and only failed in a seaway, has led me to conclude that my boat is too small and that she gets tossed about to such an extent that the seas have more effect on her than a pair of balanced sails.

If at that time I had known about Marin Marie's twin staysails I would have tried them out, for they appear to have several advantages over spinnakers, one of the most important being the ease with which they can be set and stowed, and being farther forward they might have more control over the yacht. But I did not read his book, *Wind Aloft, Wind Alow*, until after I had married an efficient crew who liked steering, and by that time *Wanderer* had become more orthodox, carrying only one spinnaker boom, though she still had in her sail locker one of the twins as well as her masthead spinnaker, for use in fresh winds when it helps to ease the helm.

I consider, however, that twin spinnakers, if they can be made to work properly, are a great boon to the single-hander on a passage of fifty miles or more, given the right conditions; but for shorter distances they are hardly worth while as one needs ordinary working sails for getting out of harbour, and they have to be set again before closing with the land. On short passages it is far less bother to sit and steer and by carrying a great area of canvas get to the destination more quickly. Of course, in a really fresh wind and a heavy sea, the fact that spinnakers eliminate any possibility of gybing is a big consideration, spoilt only by the knowledge that there will be much sail shifting to do before it is safe to make harbour.[14]

Under snug canvas *Wanderer II* leaves Mounts Bay with a fresh wind bound round the Lizard

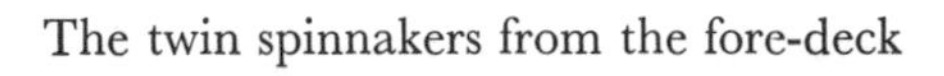

The twin spinnakers from the fore-deck

CHAPTER VII

ON THE SOUTH-WEST COAST OF IRELAND

THE REST of the passage across to the Irish coast was not very interesting, for the wind became light and variable and eventually settled at N.W. So I altered my plans, and instead of beating to the Fastnet, decided to sail close-hauled on the port tack until I reached the coast, and I hoped that would not be farther eastward than Kinsale. After two nights at sea, one spent almost becalmed, and the other jilling along under mainsail and staysail only in a fresh wind while I slept, I was feeling very fit and cheerful when a landfall was made at the Old Head of Kinsale. In the sunshine the coastline looked friendly and inviting, and as Eire was a new land to me, I was excited at the prospect of getting ashore, so I eased sheets a little and headed for the nearest harbour, which was Kinsale. There, off the town, I anchored in the evening, 52 hours out from New Grimsby ; it had been a slow but very easy passage as *Wanderer* had steered herself nearly all the way.

Ashore I received very great kindness from everyone ; I was entertained and taken round the countryside, much interest was shown in my passage and many visitors came out to inspect the yacht. I was a little surprised at so much attention as it did not seem to me that my single-handed crossing was particularly venturesome or outstanding ; but I realised later that it was simply the inborn hospitality of the Irish showing itself, for all the people I met in the smaller towns and villages along the coast were just as kind, whether they knew anything about sailing or not, and I was never treated as a traveller but as a guest.

My intention was to explore the coast to the west and north as far as might be possible in the time at my disposal, but first I sailed to Oyster Haven, a most delightful little anchorage only two miles east of Kinsale. In the evening I rowed in the dinghy out of the Haven to the Big Sovereign, a rock 90 feet high which lies about half a mile to seaward of the entrance. The wind was offshore and light, and there was only a slight swell, otherwise such an expedition would not have been possible in my 7-foot pram. The Big Sovereign is split by a deep and narrow cleft, and as I rowed through it a cloud of gulls rose into the air wheeling and swooping above me, their wild cries echoing from side to side between the vertical walls. The rock appeared to be inaccessible and I made no attempt to land on it for I could find no safe place at which to leave the dinghy unmolested by the swell.

The next morning the wind was still N. but was fresh with some very strong squalls, as *Wanderer*, under lower sail and small jib, ran out of the Haven in brilliant sunshine bound to the westward. We passed very close in round the Old Head of Kinsale, and for a few moments were quite becalmed under its lee, but the west-going tide soon took us clear, and hardening in the sheets I fetched into Courtmacsherry Bay and beat into the estuary at its head, not to stop, but just to have a look at it. It is one of the few places on that coast where there is any appreciable tidal stream at the anchorage and where large areas of the harbour dry at low water. Because of the unmarked dangers which lie in Courtmacsherry Bay, it would be unwise for the stranger to approach it without the large scale chart. I had on board the complete set of Admiralty charts for that coast, and found them excellent in every way, many of them being on a large scale, 7 or 12 inches to the mile.

Turning just below the village, I ran out of the harbour, rounded the Seven Heads and was halfway across Clonakilty Bay before the wind showed any signs of easing. I set the topsail and changed the small jib for the large one, but soon had to replace that sail with the yankee as the wind fell very light. While at the Isles of Scilly I had rigged a bowsprit net. It was nothing very elaborate, just a few lengths of hambro line seized to the bowsprit shrouds and knotted to another piece running fore-and-aft, but I found it of the greatest assistance in keeping the yankee dry while that large light sail was being hanked on or unhanked, and I could leave it there securely when it had to be handed for a short-lived squall.

At 5 p.m. we were approaching the channel between Galley

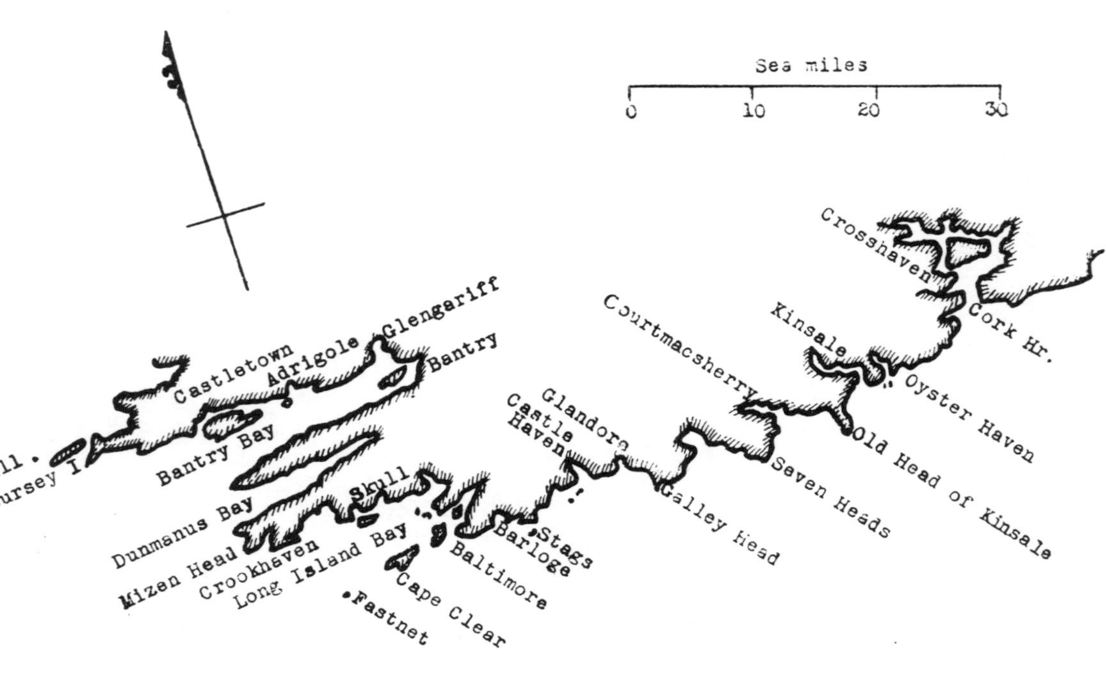

Sketch Map of South-West Ireland.

Head and Dhulic Rock. The long easy swell running from the west was spouting on the rock, but I was for a moment somewhat disconcerted to see between it and the Head what looked like another rock but which was visible only when we were on top of the swell. That, however, proved to be a small rowing boat whose crew were attending to their lobster pots. They stood up waving their arms and caps as *Wanderer*, heeled to a sudden squall and with lee rail awash, went storming past, only to be almost becalmed again as soon as the Head had been dropped astern.

The tide should long since have turned against us, but we ghosted over what little stream there may have been, for along the S.W. coast of Ireland the tide does not run hard except off the more prominent headlands and through some inshore passages. The coast looked perfect with its background of purple mountains, over which the evening shadows were creeping as we slipped past the islands and rocks in the entrance, which are well marked, and brought up in the harbour of Glandore after a lovely sail of 35 miles.

I had met only a few people who had cruised on the Irish coast and they all complained that there was no book of sailing directions written from the yachtsman's point of view available. That was not entirely true, for members of the Irish Cruising Club had compiled such a book, but at that time very few copies had been produced, they could only be had by members and associate members of that club, and I had been unable to borrow one.[15] My own view was that well written accounts of cruises under sail, such as those published in the journals of the Royal Cruising Club and the Little Ship Club, comprised the best and most interesting form of sailing directions for any coast. But such a library is apt to be bulky for a small yacht, and I could see the advantages of having in one compact volume information on every harbour and anchorage along one stretch of coast, together with small charts of the lesser known places to amplify the details given on the Admiralty charts. I therefore decided that I would try my hand at writing such a book, provided that the weather remained suitable for a thorough collection of the necessary information. The undertaking would make an object for the cruise, and the resulting book might possibly be of some assistance to other visitors, more especially as the coast between Bantry and Cork appeared from the charts to be a very jolly cruising ground with a great many more natural harbours than one could possibly make use of, as I was to discover the next day when, on making good a distance of only 8 miles, I called at no fewer than 4 little inlets, each quite perfect in its way.

The wind was still at N. and squally at times, but after some rain in the early morning, the sun came out and the scene was enlivened by an army of magnificent white cumulus clouds marching in stately procession from the distant mountains out to the open sea, their shadows pursuing one another across the fields and bays, but they never seemed to obscure the sun overhead for very long.

Although I had set the topsail I used only the small jib, for the topsail, as I have already explained, is quickly handled, while to change jibs takes much longer and with the land close aboard is not always possible. We ran swiftly out of the harbour, leaving Adam and Eve Islands to port, reached in behind Rabbit Island and beat into Carrigillihy Cove, a snug little place, and protected as it is by the rocks east of Rabbit Island, should, I think, offer secure anchorage except in S.E. winds. We then sailed on to Squince Harbour, out again, and reaching a mile down the coast, brought up in Blind Harbour for lunch. These last two coves are open to the S., but a few small boats lay on moorings in the E. corner of Blind Harbour.

In a very fresh squall which lay *Wanderer* well over, we left in the afternoon, skirted the shore closely and anchored for the night in Castle Haven. The gardens in the village of Castletownsend were a blaze of colour, and the little cobbled lanes quite charming and unspoilt.

Halfway between Castle Haven and the fine big harbour of Baltimore lies a romantic little cove known as Barloge ; close inland, and connected to it by a narrow channel which is only navigable by dinghy from half flood to half ebb, is deep Lough Hyne which has a tiny island with a castle on it. I had read about that wild little place in *Yacht Cruising*, and wished to spend a night there if possible.

Once again the day was fine, but there was no wind until 11 o'clock, when I left Castle Haven under all sail to topsail and yankee and beat pleasantly out against a light southerly air. But outside there was a better breeze from the west, and owing to our late start we found the tide running too strongly to the east in Stag Sound, so that we failed to beat through and had to go round outside the Stags, a group of remarkably pointed rocks ; having weathered them we were able to tack and fetch into Barloge. I had anchored and stowed the sails and was just about to row up to Lough Hyne when the wind suddenly piped up from east of south, blowing straight into the cove ; the sky began to veil over and the glass to drop. I thought it might be wise to get away immediately, so I made sail, beat out, and an hour later entered Baltimore Harbour and came-to in 8 feet of water close to the little quay by the town on the east side. The wind died right away in the evening, so we would have been quite comfortable at Barloge after all, and the barometer, having dropped only a little, was rising again. But from my anchorage at Baltimore I had a fine view of the beacon fires which were blazing on all the surrounding hills, that being mid-summer night. The evening was perfectly still and grey with a low pall of clouds, on the under side of which were reflected the red glow of the fires. I sat on deck watching them and turned in late.

At 4 a.m. I was awakened by a harsh rasping noise along the yacht's bottom. I hurried on deck where it was sufficiently light for me to see some large creature swimming backwards and forwards across our bows, rubbing its body against the anchor chain. Then it swam away, described a circle, and approached from astern, rubbing itself along the bilge and heeling the yacht over to an alarming angle. I estimated its length at about 15 feet, and I was scared lest it might do some serious damage. As it rubbed along just below the waterline for the second time, I jabbed at it with the boathook ; it felt very hard and solid, almost like striking a rock. After it had passed I continued splashing with the boathook in an attempt to scare it off, and it did not return.

When I landed at Baltimore after breakfast I mentioned my early morning adventure with some hesitation to the post-mistress, for I hardly expected to be believed. But she showed not the slightest surprise, and told me that the creature was known as Albert, a small whale which had made Baltimore Harbour its headquarters for the past two years and had a fondness for anchor chains, particularly new or brightly galvanised ones.

Most people have heard of Pelorous Jack, a pilot whale protected by Act of Parliament, and presumably Albert had the same ideas ; he was known to escort vessels from and to the harbour mouth. Later I met several cruising men who had had similar experiences to mine. That was in 1937, and Albert is still in Baltimore. In 1946, when John Morris visited that port in *Mercy Jane*, Albert contrived in one visit to put two turns of the chain round the fluke of the anchor, a 36-lb. C.Q.R., so that the yacht dragged rapidly towards the quay. I think that Morris had anchored in almost the same place as I had occupied in *Wanderer*.

With such a creature in the harbour I did not care to spend a second night there, so in the afternoon, with a fresh offshore wind, I left under lower sail and second jib, being escorted by Albert whose upper tail fin could be seen cutting through the water a short distance ahead. He left me at the entrance and I sailed on alone past the majestic coast of Sherkin Island and across the mouth of Gascanane Sound through which I had a lovely view of Long Island Bay. The precipitous heights of Cape Clear Island towered dark and forbidding above us as in calms and squalls we coasted along its S.E. side as far as Ineer (or South Harbour), and beating into it came-to in 3 fathoms near its head where the water was so clear that I could see the anchor biting into the sand.

That was the best adventure of the whole cruise. Ineer is seldom used by visitors as it is only safe in settled weather, being entirely open to the south. I was told that hookers used to lie in safety there throughout the year with anchors in the middle of the cove and stern lines out to ring-bolts ashore, but that is not in agreement with a paragraph in *The Irish Coast Pilot*, which reads ; " In boisterous weather . . . the reflux of the sea is so powerful as to draw vessels to sea, however well secured they may be." Such few yachts as call at the island generally use North Harbour, but that is a difficult place to make without the assistance of an engine, for it is narrow with a high cliff on the east side and the wind usually blows straight in or straight out. In the days of sail, boats using North Harbour would sail right up to the rocks where their heads were pushed round with an oar on to the other tack.

Many of the Capers, delighted at seeing a sailing vessel beat into Ineer, came to the wall on the east side to meet me when I landed there. At once someone took my punt and put her on an outhaul, for there was a slight scend which might have damaged her if left against the wall, and then I was escorted along the track which leads through a valley, where most of the dwellings are, to North Harbour. On the way I parted with a half-a-crown to a very charming beggar with perfect manners and a twinkle in his bright blue eye. At once he invited me to the inn to drink whisky as his guest, and he told me many stories of that island and its race of bearded seamen. I also met Tim Regan who had sailed with Conor O'Brien and had skippered the post boat for many years, but I was unable to discover from him or from anyone else what the Capers lived on since they no longer did any large scale fishing.

During the night the wind blew hard from N., but the holding ground there is good and we lay securely.

I left in the morning and sailed about among the many islands in Long Island Bay, which place would, I think, be an almost perfect playground for a man with a centreboard half-decked boat, as it has countless snug anchorages and backwaters to explore, and the tidal streams, except in Long Island Sound where they run at 1½ knots, are so weak that one can ignore them. I anchored for lunch off the little quay on the N. side of Long Island and had a walk ashore. It was from that and the other islands in the bay that most of the lobster fishermen I met up and down the coast came. During the summer they lived for from two weeks to three months at a time in their open boats, which varied in length from 18 to 25 feet and were rigged with a small lug and jib ; they had no engines. At night the oars were placed athwart the gunwales forward of the mast, and the sails were spread over them to form a rough shelter beneath which the crew of three slept and cooked their meals on an open stone hearth, even baking their own doughy bread.

I spent the night at Skull. From the offing that place looked attractive crouched at the feet of Mount Gabriel, but on approaching it closely the mountain appeared to recede into the background and became almost insignificant. The holding ground there is good, but southerly winds send in a heavy sea.

The fine weather still continued, so, having collected my mail, I sailed again in Long Island Bay the following morning and then went out to look at the Fastnet and ended the day's sail in the fine harbour of Crookhaven. The only vessels to call there, other than occasional yachts, were steamers to load stone from the quarry on the north shore and Breton crabbers who brought their catches to the lobster pond on Rock Island, there to await the vivier which would carry them off to France. Some years ago there used to be a trade in lobsters between Crookhaven and Warsash on the Hamble River, and it is on record that *Gem*, one of the ketches engaged in that trade, once made the passage in 44 hours, an average speed of more than 8 knots.

I was astir early in the morning, for I wished to catch the first of the west going stream outside as I was bound round the Mizen for Berehaven. It was fine and warm, but there was no breath of wind until 11 o'clock, so I had all my belongings out on deck for an airing and hastily stowed them away again as soon as the breeze made from W. Carrying all sail to yankee I beat down the coast, and rounding the Mizen with the last drain of fair tide, looked forward to a fast reach across the mouths of Dunmanus and Bantry Bays ; but the wind soon veered to N.W., and we could only just lay for the W. entrance to Berehaven close-hauled. However, it was good sailing, and *Wanderer* steered herself well while I studied the chart and read the sailing directions. As Bantry Bay opened up to starboard a fine panorama of mountain scenery presented itself, with Hungry Hill dominating the other heights, and the scene had the same friendly air on which I had remarked when making a landfall off Kinsale. Mountains can be very forbidding at times, as they often are in Scotland, but those Irish hills, purple with heather and haze, looked softer, and their lower slopes were green and mostly cultivated.

By 4.30 p.m. we had reached the W. entrance to Berehaven. The wind came ahead, blowing straight out as it so often does in a sound where the land each side is high, and it freshened so that both the yankee and the topsail had to come in, and even under the snug rig of lower sail and small jib the yacht was hard pressed in the squalls. Perched on the weather coaming of the cockpit with the chart in one hand, the tiller in the other and a pair of binoculars slung round my neck, I beat up that lovely waterway between Bere Island and the mainland, standing close in towards the shore on each tack. The wind was squally and uncertain, and I acted on the advice given in the old doggerel :

In a puff spring a luff,
In a lull keep her full.

To work one's way under sail in a weatherly little vessel right into some new and lovely haven, using to the full one's skill in seamanship and ability to read a chart, is surely the most thrilling and satisfying part of the whole business of cruising, and when eventually the cruising man finds himself, as I soon did, in a little landlocked pool with scarcely a ripple on it, the feeling of achievement and content is very great. Fortunately a lucky fluke of wind enabled me to fetch through the channel into Castletown Harbour, which lies in the N.W. corner of Berehaven, for it is almost too narrow to beat through, and at 5 p.m. I let the anchor go close to the ferry pier.

I found the little town a friendly place with good shops. It had steamer and bus connections with Bantry, but for popular amusements it relied on a circus in the summer and an occasional travelling film show.

The next day I sailed up Bantry Bay to Glengariff, the rough glen, where I met *North Star*, the first yacht I had encountered since arriving on the Irish coast. There was a very fresh W. wind, so I brought up W. of Pot Rock, for that anchorage offered better shelter than the more usual one to the eastward. I could well understand why most visiting yachts made direct for Glengariff ; it is a lovely place and offers a secure berth no matter from which direction the wind may blow, but as a recognised beauty spot it has been somewhat spoilt

The weather which had been so perfect then deteriorated, and for several days winds of gale force blustered down the glens between the hills and a great deal of rain fell. A basin 5 inches deep left in the cockpit was filled in 4 hours, and so much rain water running into the harbour produced a slight seaward stream ; the water was coloured dark brown and stained the white paint near the waterline. However, I had much work to do on the book I was preparing, and I was entertained aboard H.M.S. *Wolverine*, who was on a visit from Cork, and at Roches Hotel each evening, so the time passed quickly.

As soon as the weather moderated sufficiently, I put the typewriter away in its locker and continued my explorations, calling first at Bantry and Whiddy Island, and then at Adrigole on the north shore of Bantry Bay. It is difficult to select any one of so many peerless havens as being better than the rest, but I think that Adrigole was the most beautiful, or perhaps it was that I chanced to see it under ideal conditions.

The 10-mile sail from Whiddy Island, at the head of the bay, had been particularly tedious. The wind was variable in strength and direction, and it always seemed to head us no matter which tack we were on, so that much time and effort was wasted in putting about in the hope of pointing better, but always with the same irritating result. There was some swell running up the bay, but that was round and easy so that it did not interfere with our progress, but on top of it was a short, confused little popple which was very hindering, and we had to carry every possible square inch of canvas in order to advance against it. But every few minutes a squall would come up the bay with a darkening of the sea beneath it and a spatter of rain. Then the yankee would have to come in, and possibly the topsail as well, while the yacht buried her lee deck and wallowed. In a moment the squall would pass and all the kites would have to be set once more.

I was therefore very thankful when at last we had worked our way up to Adrigole, and there as the last of the squalls passed away, rounded up and anchored behind the little island which occupies the centre of that harbour. The sky cleared, and at sundown a small golden cloud materialised from nowhere and paused above the purple mass of Hungry Hill, the rugged side of which was streaked with the silver thread of a waterfall. As night came on, the mountain, with its dark reflection in the still water, seemed to advance more closely on the little lagoon as though to protect it, and except for the sucking of the swell on the entrance points, the silence was profound.

In the morning I visited Mrs. Power's shop in the village where I bought some butter. There were two kinds of butter, one was really excellent, the other was rancid ; both were unsalted and the price was the same. I then returned to Berehaven and spent several days exploring all the little coves and anchorages in which that place abounds, Lawrence, Lonehort, Dunboy, and the rest, before returning to my old anchorage at Castletown.

CHAPTER VIII

RELIEF OF THE BULL ROCK LIGHTHOUSE

THE RELIEF was many days overdue. Strong west and north-west winds had prevented the motor-tender *Nabro* from making the trip to the Bull which is in a very exposed position west of Dursey Island. But early one morning a message—semaphored to Dursey and thence telegraphed to Castletown—came through reporting that the north landing was possible and that there was an injured man on the rock who needed to be taken ashore.

Within a quarter of an hour of receiving the message *Nabro's* cutter came alongside *Wanderer II*, and Captain Busher, whose acquaintance I had made on my first visit to Castletown, invited me to go out with him to see how a rock lighthouse is relieved. A few minutes later, with the cutter aboard, the tender slipped from her buoy and proceeded out of the west entrance at a steady eight knots.

That sturdy little vessel's job was to wait on the lighthouses from the Fastnet to Valencia, an area open to the full drift of the Atlantic, yet she was the smallest craft in the Irish service. Built at Arklow in 1926, the 56-ton *Nabro* was strongly built entirely of wood, her grown oak frames being double throughout and so closely spaced that there would not be room for extra ones between them. Her twin screws were driven by two Petter paraffin engines controlled from the wheelhouse. Having two masts she set mainsail, staysail, and mizen, and although they were only intended to steady her in a seaway, she once successfully carried out a relief under them and one engine only, the other having broken down.

Forward she had a large fo'c'sle for her crew and the captain's cabin, abaft of that was the hold, then the engine-room containing an electric lighting plant and pumps besides the main engines, and right at the stern a bosun's store. Her enclosed wheelhouse was well aft, leaving good deck space for the carrying of water-casks and other stores.

We were soon out in the open heading west and feeling the ocean swell. The wind, still at N.W., had fortunately moderated, but the skipper cast many anxious glances towards Sheep Head which lay 5 miles away, for when the swell can be seen breaking there landing at the Bull is usually impossible, and although occasional flashes of white could be seen in that direction he carried on, for with a sick man to bring ashore an attempt at least must be made.

Rolling slowly but heavily we passed close to Blackball Head, and half an hour later, rounding Cod Head, stopped in smooth water under the lee of Dursey Island, while the cutter was launched and pulled in to the shore to take aboard the relief keeper from the station on the mainland there.

The 18-foot boat was clinker built and entirely open, and she it was who did all the ferrying between shore and tender, and tender and lighthouse. She had four thwarts, but the third one from forward was generally removed so that a load of provisions or gear could be stowed there, and then she only rowed three oars. In the stern sheets sat the mate who was in command, and although he had no rudder or steering-oar, he handled her beautifully by giving quiet orders to the crew in his sing-song Irish voice.

She was soon back alongside, bearing as well as a load of provisions and the keeper, a workman to take the place of the injured man. Several weeks previously there had been a landslide at the Bull, and it was one of the ten men engaged on repairs who had been hurt.

With the cutter once more up in davits and a strong tide under us, we swept through Dursey Sound, which divides the island of that name from the mainland. With the wind at N.W. the island afforded no shelter that side, and although the steadying sails were sheeted flat amidships *Nabro* rolled her scuppers under at times.

The Bull is only 6 miles from Dursey Sound with the Cow a little nearer, and very grand they looked in the sunshine as we approached, with the swell breaking round them. From a distance the Bull looks remarkably like a ruined cathedral, and the great cavern which pierces it through adds to the delusion. From its summit flew the answering pennant, " You have been sighted," and alongside of it a black cone point up, "North landing is possible." It seemed strange that with a N.W. wind the north landing should be the better of the two, but Captain Busher explained that a tidal eddy offers it some measure of protection. So we steered towards the north side and stopped about a hundred yards from the rock.

The cutter in the meantime had been prepared, the thwart removed and a cargo net spread out in her, and into this had been passed the first load of provisions while farther forward two water-casks had been stowed.

As soon as *Nabro* had lost way the cutter was launched, and seizing our opportunity as she lifted on the swell, the seven of us dropped in to her one by one over the rail, the falls and bow-line were cast off and we pulled in towards the mouth of the cavern.

A grey pall of cloud had by then obscured the sun, and down in the cove at the foot of the towering cliffs it was almost twilight. Although so deeply laden the cutter made slow but good going of it, lifting easily on the swell and dropping down in the trough until only the masts of the tender were visible. Probably the swell was not more than five feet high, but thundering on the rocks each side of the cove and sending fountains of spray up the vertical cliffs, it seemed much higher from that small open boat.

The cutter was pulled to the mouth of the cavern, which is a vast tunnel running right through the rock from its north to its south side ; it is nearly square and the smooth sides are thickly encrusted with small black barnacles. I was told that there is not less than five fathoms of water in it, and in very settled weather it is possible to row through.

At a word from the mate the men stopped rowing and lay on their oars, just pulling or backing as necessary to keep out of reach of the breakers on each side, while from high overhead a weighted hook on the end of a wire dropped slowly towards us from a derrick whose jib could be seen projecting from a platform cut in the face of the rock a hundred feet above.

The boat dropped in the trough, and one of her crew grabbed the hook and made it fast to the four corners of the cargo net.

"All fast, sir."

" Stand clear," cried the mate, and turning his face to the platform high overhead with his hands cupped round his mouth, he shouted " Hoist away."

" Hoist away, away, away . . ." echoed the cavern.

The wire tautened and slowly, twisting and turning as it went, the load lifted out of the boat which was at once pulled from under, lest a swell higher than the rest should lift and dash her against it before it was clear. Craning our necks we watched it getting smaller and smaller, while the gulls wheeled around sending their wild and raucous cries echoing from side to side of the cove in which we lay, and the sea swirled against the smooth sides of the cavern with a sinister sucking and gurgling, which was almost drowned in the noise of the breakers outside.

While we waited to send up the water casks the mate told me of an exciting incident which had happened there. A sling of provisions was being sent up and the hand making the hook fast did not notice that one corner of the net was foul of a thwart. As soon as the men above started their winch the boat was heeled over suddenly, and having a large fly-wheel for the foghorn engine stowed across her gunwales, was all but capsized before they could get the net clear. But, considering the risks taken of necessity by the men of that fine service, accidents are very rare indeed.

The two casks of water were soon sent up, for the derrick winch was motor-driven, and then the business of landing the keeper, the workman, and myself was started. In very bad weather, when the relief has been long overdue, men are sometimes hauled up by derrick, but whenever it is possible the safer way is to jump ashore and walk up by the steps cut in the rock for that purpose.

The cutter was backed in towards the landing-place and then kept a few yards away while a succession of heavy seas expended their force over it. Then again she was backed in until her stern almost touched the barnacle-encrusted rock, and seizing his chance when she was on the top of a sea, the keeper—with his dispatch-case slung around his neck—leapt and made a perfect landing. Then came my turn, and standing on the stern seat of the boat while I waited, hanging on to the arm of the mate to steady myself, I began to wish I had not come. It would not be far to jump, I knew, but I was scared of missing my footing on the wet steps and getting crushed between them and the cutter. A few moments later we lifted on a swell and for a second the cutter's stern grazed the rock. "Jump," shouted someone, and I jumped as far and as hard as I could, landed, slipped, and was at once caught by the keeper, and turning looked with some surprise at the boat now quite a distance away. Last of all came the workman, and he nearly ended his lighthouse career there and then by jumping at the wrong moment, but we grabbed him before he could slip and the three of us then began the ascent, which was easy enough as the steps though steep were good, while the cutter returned to *Nabro* for another load of stores and water.

Halfway up I stopped for a while on the derrick platform and watched some water-casks being hoisted up, emptied, and returned to the cutter which looked a very tiny thing away down in the shadows amongst the surf and rocks. There I met the other keepers and the man we had come to fetch, and it appeared that he was not so very badly injured after all, which was fortunate for it would have been no easy matter to get a cripple into the cutter from the steps. A fall of loose rock had crushed his arm, which was in a sling, but he was able to walk and generally fend for himself.

Continuing my climb I reached the lighthouse, which, together with the dwelling-house and the hut erected to shelter men working on the landslide, was about two-thirds of the way up, the lantern itself being 270 feet above the sea. The higher the light the farther it can be seen, but in a locality prone to much fog like that one, it had been found better to place it lower down, although that made it invisible for a small part of its arc where the higher rock masked it. The old lights at Beachy Head, St. Catherine's, and Cape Clear were examples of high lights and had eventually to be replaced by lighthouses lower down. The foghorn engine-house was also on the same level but the horn itself was right at the summit, 300 feet above the sea, from which point it could be heard all round.

It was from the very top of the rock that the landslide had started, and crashing down through part of the dwelling-house roof, had buried the bed in which a fitter had been sleeping only the night before it occurred under several tons of rock. It was thought that the slide had undermined the siren-house, in which case that might have to be dismantled and re-erected somewhere else ; a big undertaking, as a site would first have to be blasted out of the rock and levelled. But the immediate job in hand was to repair the dwelling-house, for until its roof and guttering were complete once more rain with which to fill the fresh-water tanks could not be caught, and ferrying off water for thirteen men is no light undertaking in the summer, and an utter impossibility in the winter.

There were four keepers attached to the Bull, three on and one ashore. Weather permitting, reliefs were effected fortnightly, so that in ordinary circumstances a keeper would do a term of six weeks on the rock and two ashore. But bad weather frequently interferes with the regular relief of such exposed rock lighthouses as that on the Bull and the Fastnet ; one of the keepers of the latter was once marooned on the rock for 85 days. The rota is not altered when a relief is overdue, and the man who chances to be ashore then is fortunate and only has to do a six-week spell of duty at the lighthouse on his return, unless of course bad weather comes again when he is due to leave. But over a period of years a fair average works out.

The men order and buy their own food and there always has to be a reserve supply for three months at the lighthouse, tinned of course, so there is seldom any shortage ; but being unable to afford to buy a large stock at one time, tobacco is often scarce.

As it was relief day everyone was very busy, but they all found time to make me welcome, and in the intervals of filling up forms, hoisting the provisions, and reading their mail, they gave me tea in the lighthouse kitchen, a temporary one, for the other had been wrecked by the landslide. Then they suggested that I might like to go up and have a look round the lighthouse, so I made my way up the spiral stairs and arrived in the lamp room. The blinds were drawn to protect the delicate apparatus from the rays of the sun, and in the half-light it was very quiet after the roaring of the breakers outside, with only the muffled drumming of the wind against the plate-glass windows to remind one that this was not some peaceful inland laboratory, with its shining prisms, its gleaming brass and gun-metal.

The source of light was an incandescent gas mantle lit by vaporised paraffin which was pumped up from the tanks below, and it owed its power and character to the prismatic lens. That complicated glass structure—floating in a trough of mercury to reduce friction to a minimum—was revolved about the light on much the same principle as a grandfather clock, a weight working in a tunnel in the tower having to be wound up every forty minutes, and so that this necessary attention should not be overlooked, the weight automatically rang an electric bell in the tower as well as one close to the bedrooms of the men off watch when nearing the bottom of its journey unless it was re-wound in time.

The Bull light is visible for 23 miles and by the arrangement of the prisms it gives one flash of concentrated light every 15 seconds. It seemed remarkable that such a fragile thing could have been landed and brought to its final resting place without damage, but I was told that the builders of the Fastnet lighthouse were not so fortunate. When the tower was ready to receive it, the lantern was landed on the rock and put in what was considered to be a safe position for the night ; then a gale sprang up, and some days later when the fitters were able to land on the rock to continue operations, they found that the lantern had been swept away by the sea.

The fog siren on the Bull gives two blasts close together every two minutes, and is worked by compressed air, the engines and compressors being housed in a building near the dwelling house. Although only one engine would be used at a time, there were two others of the same power in reserve in case of a breakdown, and lest there should ever be any dispute as to whether the siren was working or not—for fog is a queer thing and often blankets sound—every single blast made is recorded in indelible ink against the time on a revolving clockwork driven chart.

By the time I had finished my investigations the afternoon was well advanced, and I returned to the derrick platform in time to see the last boatload of empty casks being taken off. The wind had veered a little with the flood, increasing in strength, and the seas were breaking heavily over the steps at which we had landed. But while I watched, someone came out of *Nabro's* wheelhouse and began to semaphore. A keeper standing near me answered with a pair of white " ping-pong bats " such as have since come into use aboard aircraft carriers, and he spelt the message out for my benefit.

" Will take party off at south landing." I was glad to be reminded that there was another landing place, novel experience though it would have been to remain marooned on a rock lighthouse.

So the relieved keeper, the injured man and I made our way down some two hundred steps to the landing, and there, strangely enough, I discovered that leaping into a small moving boat is no more difficult than jumping out of one on to firm but slippery rock. Without a hitch we were all taken off and were soon back aboard *Nabro*, whose wide decks and high bulwarks felt very secure.

The cutter was hoisted aboard, and with a long farewell blast from her siren, the tender turned, circled the rock and headed back for Dursey where the keeper was landed to be welcomed by his wife ; but the injured man went round to Castletown with us for medical attention, and there at dusk we moored to our buoy.

CHAPTER IX

RETURN FROM IRELAND

WITH Castletown as my headquarters I made several short cruises so that I could add to my knowledge of the coast, and I was much struck by the beauty and able appearance of the open seine boats which fished for mackerel during August, September and October between Berehaven and Valencia. Apart from these and the lobster boats, I saw no other fishing vessels. I was told that fish were scarce and that when any were caught there was some difficulty in marketing them.

Mr. J. Sheekin of Castletown, besides giving me information about seine fishing and the method of curing the fish, kindly allowed me to measure and photograph his boat, No. S375, which is typical of her class, although rather larger than most as she often had to face heavy seas at the entrance to Berehaven. She measured 33 feet 6 inches overall, had a beam of 7 feet and depth amidships to top of keel of 2 feet 6 inches, and in common with her sisters had good sheer, 9 inches forward and 8 inches aft. A tiny bottle of holy water was lashed to her stem. The 6 thwarts left a space in the stern 12 feet long with a seat at its after end, and it was in that space that the seine net was carried.

The boat was built at Bantry in 1922, and few boats have been built since them for the fishing has gone into a decline. Her carvel planking of pine was ½ in. thick (many of the boats were clinker built) on steamed 1-inch oak timbers spaced 1 foot apart and bound to the elm keel by oak floors. The stem was of oak, the built-up transom of elm, and the thwarts of 1½ inch pine. The workmanship generally was high class, all the knees and breasthooks fitting accurately, while the stringer beneath the thwarts lay fairly against all the timbers.

The method of fishing was interesting and, I believe, unique. The seine boat carried a crew of 10, 8 being at the six 19-foot oars, the middle two being double banked ; one man stood in the bows with a heap of stones taken from the beach at his feet, and the other sat aft to steer. The seine boat was always accompanied by the "follower"; she was manned by a crew of 7, usually carried 5 oars, and also had a man in the bows and a steersman. The follower assisted in the casting of the net, and took aboard part of the catch, which would usually be too large for the seine boat to cope with alone.

A dark and preferably calm night would be chosen when the two boats set out in company for the open sea. Close under the cliffs they waited in places which experience had shown to be best, seldom going far from the shore. Presently a glowing patch of phosphorescence would be seen, not bright enough to be the breaking crest of a sea; the fish were rising. The follower would then take one end of the net, and as both boats approached the shoal of mackerel they would separate and row round in a circle, the man in the stern of the seine boat throwing out armfuls of the net while both bowmen threw a barrage of stones ahead of the fish, the streaks of light so caused heading them back into the net which was steadily closing round them. When the two boats met, the ends of the net were drawn together and half-hundredweights were let down on snatch blocks attached to the line running through rings at the foot of the net, drawing it together in the form of a bag. Oars were then cock-billed with their handles jammed beneath the stringer, and all hands turned to to haul in the catch. The net was pulled in over the gunwale, which was thus pressed down level with the water, and the fish were scooped aboard in their hundreds, filling the seine boat—which could carry about 5,000—up to the thwarts until she had only a few inches of freeboard. The rest were taken into the follower which, as she was not hampered by the net, could carry about 8,000.

When the catch was very heavy—and more than 32,000 fish have been caught at one cast—there was a danger that the fish at the bottom of the net would suffocate, in which case it might have to be cut adrift to save the boats. To avoid that, if the coast permitted it, the two boats carrying the net slung between them would head in for the shore until it grounded, and wait there while additional boats were summoned from the harbour.

During the 1914–18 war a night's fishing would often bring

in as much as £100, but now the market is a limited one. The coves and harbours from which the seine boats put out were provided with stone curing sheds and stores where the fish were gutted and put in salt for six days, after which they were packed in brine for shipment abroad, mostly to America. The fish were sorted and packed according to size, but on an average a barrel held about 260. Many of the curing and packing stations which I saw were in ruins, and most of the boats lay neglected with gaping seams.

It was towards the end of July that at last I said goodbye to the many friends I had made at Castletown and sailed for Crookhaven, the first step of my homeward journey. From there, where I was completely becalmed for three days, I made short sails along the coast, re-visiting some of my previous anchorages and making acquaintance with new ones, and finally arrived in the Carrigaliane River, just within the entrance to Cork Harbour, where I brought up off the Royal Munster Yacht Club at Crosshaven. That concluded my exploration of the coast, though I hoped one day to return and continue it farther to the north, for I believe the south and west coasts of Ireland to be one of the very best of cruising grounds.[16] I filled the water tanks, took aboard some fresh provisions, re-rove the twin spinnaker halyards and generally prepared for the passage to Cornwall.

Monday, 9th August. At 11 a.m. under a leaden sky and with a moderate to fresh W.S.W. wind in which *Wanderer* could just carry her topsail, I left Crosshaven on the ebb. There was a very confused sea in the entrance of Cork Harbour where a southerly swell was running in against the strong ebb, and at 11.35 a.m., with Roche Point abeam, I set the patent log and course S.E. by S.½S. The correct course to clear the Longships by two miles (I always like to head a little to windward of my objective) was a quarter point more southerly, but in Ireland I had been told by several experienced sailing men that there was a westerly set between Land's End and the Irish coast, for which, on an average passage, one should allow 10 miles. I had allowed nothing for that set when outward bound, but the sights I had been able to get had placed the yacht each time a little to the westward of the dead reckoning; that appeared to confirm what my Irish friends had told me, so I made the 10 mile allowance.

Although the wind was abeam *Wanderer* seemed to be incapable of steering herself unless I eased the mainsheet until the topsail was lifting. This I think was due to the fact that I had set only the small jib. She did not require the larger jib, but was just able to carry the topsail without being unduly pressed, so in order to make the most of such a fine fair wind, I sat steering until 8 p.m. By then we had averaged 5½ knots since leaving Cork Harbour, but the wind fell light, and after I had set the No. 1 jib, the yacht steered herself without attention while I prepared and ate the evening meal. By midnight we were almost becalmed in a drizzle of rain with very poor visibility. P.L. 57.

Tuesday, 10th August. As we only just had steerage way at 1 a.m. I backed the headsails and turned in, dozing fitfully and looking out every hour or so. It remained calm with gentle rain until 11.30 a.m., when the sun shone wanly, encircled by a halo, and there was a light S.W. breeze to which I set the yankee; the barometer had fallen one-tenth since leaving port. At noon I got a meridian altitude, but as that placed us 12 miles back on our course, and as the log invariably under-registered to a small extent, especially at slow speeds, I assumed that there must be abnormal refraction and ignored the sight. The light breeze held throughout the afternoon, but there was very little of it and I was able to get a few hours' sleep. At 10 p.m. the wind had a little more weight in it; I handed the yankee and set the No. 1 jib, and *Wanderer* continued to steer herself. Because of our slow progress the westerly set would have a greater effect upon us, and I therefore altered course a quarter point more easterly, for the weather had come in thick again and I did not wish to find myself in the neighbourhood of the Seven Stones.

Wednesday, 11th August. During the night the wind died again and the fog closed down more thickly, so that the beams from the sidelights shone on it as though it were something solid and we floated in a tiny little world of our own. At 6 a.m., when the log registered only 128 miles, I could hear several foghorns, but the ceaseless slatting of the sails, stiff and heavy with moisture, prevented me from identifying any of them properly, though I thought I could distinguish the siren at Pendeen on the starboard bow, where it had no business to be ; but I could not be sufficiently certain of that to warrant an alteration of course. After breakfast visibility improved a little and several steamers crossed ahead steering about S.W., but although the fog signals had stopped by then, it was not until noon that I could see land away off the starboard bow.

It seemed either that I had allowed too much for the westerly set, or else that there was no such set, for on getting cross bearings of Godrevy and Pendeen lighthouses, I found that we were 15 miles to the east of our proper course. I therefore decided to go to St. Ives for a rest and to wait there for a worthwhile breeze as I was becoming very weary at our slow progress, and the wind was now a headwind for the Longships. It was 6.15 p.m. when I anchored off the sandy beach in St. Ives Bay close to the harbour. By contrast the water was beautifully still, the slight swell being hardly noticeable after 54 hours spent at sea. I did not enter the harbour as it dries, and I wished to be free to continue round Land's End as soon as there was sufficient wind to enable me to do so in safety.

Thursday, 12th August. Two customs officers, seeing that I was flying International " Q " at the masthead, came out to give me pratique, but in the afternoon, just as I was making sail to a fresh N.E. wind which had sprung up with great suddenness, they called again to take the form away, saying that they had no power to grant pratique and that I must clear at Falmouth.

Wanderer was snubbing at her anchor before all was ready, and although the tides were wrong with the flood making into the Bristol Channel, I had no option but to clear out of that exposed berth at once. At 4.15 we got away under all sail to topsail, and although sailing fast through the water with a fresh fair wind, we made slow progress over the ground and did not round Pendeen until 7.30 p.m. because of the strong adverse tide. At 8 p.m., with Cape Cornwall abeam, there was too much wind for the topsail, so I handed it, but a few minutes later the wind died right away, leaving us becalmed in the swell which was breaking noisily on the shore uncomfortably close to port, and I had to use the sweep to keep clear of the Brisons, which consist of two large rocks 90 and 70 feet high connected with the shore by a submerged reef. With a fair tide under us at last, we rounded them at dusk very close to, but fortunately they have no dangers on their seaward side. Presently the N.E. breeze made again, but it had so little heart in it that I did not care to risk taking the passage inside the Longships where one ought to have a commanding breeze, and we passed outside but close to that lighthouse at 11 p.m. There were many steamers also rounding the land that night, but they all passed to seaward of us.

Friday, 13th August. At 1 a.m. we were off the Runnelstone Buoy and altered course to S.E. by E. ½E. for the Lizard. With sheets just started to a light S. wind *Wanderer* steered herself while I lay comfortably on the lee bunk down below reading and looking out frequently to make sure that we were clear of all traffic. The tide had turned when we were off Cape Cornwall, and as we had the flood against us when leaving St. Ives, we of course had the ebb against us as soon as we had rounded the Runnelstone, so our progress was very slow. We were quite becalmed for a while at dawn, but then an air came from W. to which I set the masthead spinnaker.

Throughout the morning the wind freshened slowly but steadily until the spinnaker had to come in at noon, and by 3 p.m. we were running hard in a confused sea off the Lizard. The tide was against us again by then, and only slowly did the Lizard alter its bearing in spite of our speed through the water, but when we did get clear of it at last we had a fast reach in smooth water to Falmouth, with " Q " once more at the masthead and the Eire flag flying from the starboard crosstree. I anchored off the Royal Cornwall Yacht Club at 7 p.m., the Customs launch was alongside before I had stowed the sails, and the formality of clearance was completed in a very few minutes.

CHAPTER X

FIRE !

THE SUN was setting as *Wanderer II* slipped quietly out of Falmouth harbour. Although the wind was only light from the west, there were indications of more to come : the glass was low and falling slightly, while the clouds were moving fast across the sky.

The white sector of St. Anthony's light had started to occult in the gathering darkness as I rounded the point, and setting the patent log and a course E.¾S., I settled myself for a long spell at the helm on the run to the Start some fifty miles away. With the masthead spinnaker set to starboard I was hoping to make a fast passage up Channel, and I intended to reach the Solent without a stop if possible. With plenty of wind-proof clothing outside and a hot dinner inside, I was well prepared.

There is a certain magic about a night passage under sail. One's ship seems bigger and more confident as she rustles her way along ; the sails and rigging outlined black against the starlit sky, the red and green reflections from the navigation lamps and the hurrying, phosphorescent wake streaming out astern, all lend an air of urgent importance to her mission. But that is only at the start, for as dawn approaches the night turns cold, the romance vanishes, and it is only with an effort that eyes gummed up for want of sleep can be forced to watch the dimly lighted compass card, or scan the dark horizon for the lights of other ships.

Sunrise is supposed to be the most romantic moment of all, but the single-handed yachtsman seldom has much opportunity for appreciating it. The wind generally increases at daybreak, sails have to be handed from a deck slippery with spray by hands both stiff and cold after the night watch, while the steel-grey seas look steep and threatening in the chilly morning light. The hour just before sunrise is the most lonely and depressing of all. Sometimes, of course, the sea is smooth, and the sky with its slowly changing pastel shades is a joy to behold ; but the single-hander rarely sees it like that, for when such easy conditions prevail he is sleeping the deep sleep of the weary. Far more frequently the angry sun lurches above the tumbling horizon, glares redly for a short while, and is then rapidly swallowed up by an advancing army of hurrying black clouds. Tired, empty, and seasick, the lone sailorman reduces sail, makes himself a cup of scalding coffee, munches a few biscuits, plots the dead reckoning, and returns to the helm.

I have spent many a night at sea, but I am quite unable to remember a wholly enjoyable one when I have been alone. Nevertheless the thrilling magic of the early part of the night has not yet ceased to enchant me.

I was not left for long to enjoy the beginning of that particular night, for off the Dodman the wind freshened so that the spinnaker had to come in, and then it started to rain. I could have set the twin spinnakers and got *Wanderer* to sail herself, but as we would soon be in the busy waters off the Eddystone where sidelights must be seen and where the vessel should be under complete control, I wrapped myself in oilskins and hoped that the rain would blow over. But it got worse, if anything, and visibility became very poor. With the increased wind the sea was rising, too, but we were making a steady 5½ knots in the right direction, and should pass close to the Eddystone at about 3 a.m. If I got really tired or if the weather worsened I could always put into conveniently situated Salcombe at daybreak, or else bring up for a rest in Start Bay. There was nothing at all to worry about, I assured myself as we foamed along, provided that I steered a careful compass course and kept a good look-out for steamers. With my glowing pipe-bowl inverted and the rain spattering against my back and on my sou'wester, I was not unhappy ; I knew the waters, I knew the lights, and I was homeward bound with a fine fair wind.

It was at about 2 a.m. that I first saw a reddish glow away on the starboard bow. For a while I did not pay it much attention as I thought it was the blurred lights of some steamer, or the lamps of a trawler at work. A little later, however, it struck me as being too red for either, and as it was changing its bearing so rapidly it must be fairly close ; but it was nearly abeam before curiosity got the better of me, and I decided to investigate.

So I altered course directly for it, and then, as is usually the case when one ceases to run, I found that the wind was a lot stronger than I had imagined, and the yacht was rather pressed with the topsail aloft. But as I only intended to satisfy my curiosity and then bear away again, I eased the mainsheet until the topsail was shaking, and headed for the glow.

Apparently it was stationary, and we closed it with surprising rapidity. Visibility must have been very poor indeed or I would surely have seen it earlier. I steered to pass close to windward of it, and crouching down to leeward, got occasional glimpses beneath the mainsail.

As I approached I realised that there was something very wrong ; the glow was varying in size and height and could be nothing other than a fire. I tried to make out the type of ship

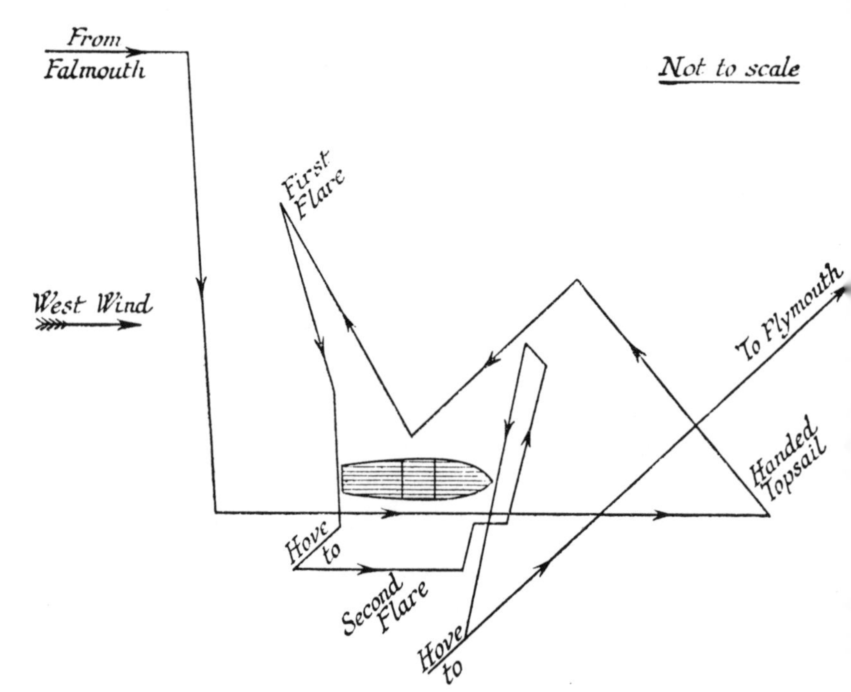

Diagram of rescue manœuvres.

as we lurched along, but there was much smoke and I was kept busy handling *Wanderer* under her press of sail.

We were soon to windward of the other craft, and, bearing away, I ran down-wind to her. With the assistance of my powerful electric torch I at last discovered that she was a white motor-cruiser with high flaring bows. I supposed her to be forty feet or so in length, but it was difficult to judge, and I had other things to consider. Amidships was a deck-house, blazing furiously, and standing on the short stern deck, silhouetted against the flames, were two dark figures.

It is not easy to give an impression of the scene. I only got a brief glimpse, and as we rushed past a faint hail came down-wind to me. Although I could not catch what was said, it was clear that I must do something about it. But I did not know what action to take and I wasted several valuable moments still running away. That I was very frightened goes without saying. An astonishing number of jumbled thoughts ran through my mind in a few seconds, and I will try to give you some idea of the situation as I saw it then. I have since thought of other things that might have been done, but as they did not occur to me at the time, they are of no interest so far as this account is concerned.

Why the crew had not taken to their boat I could not understand, but I learnt afterwards that the forward falls had burnt at the outset. My own dinghy was useless, for it was lashed bottom up on deck, and would take some time to launch, and as it was a badly shaped pram only 7 feet long, there was little hope of being able to row it in the sea then running, and even if that had been possible I could not leave *Wanderer* unattended. I was sorely tempted to tell the crew to swim for it, but in the dark the chance of being able to pick them up under sail would be remote. Therefore the only solution left was to sail close alongside so that they might be able to jump on board. The idea scared me badly, for I am never very competent at going alongside anything even in calm weather, as my poor sight makes it difficult for me to judge distances. If I got too close and had a collision, *Wanderer* would probably be holed, and then there would be little chance for any of us ; but as that was the only way I could think of just then, at least it had got to be tried.

All this takes time to write, but it, and a lot more, ran through my mind in a few moments. Hauling the staysail to port and pushing the helm down, I scrambled forward and got the topsail off as *Wanderer* rounded up and hove herself to. I bundled it up on deck, not waiting to unbend it, and leaping aft to the helm again, let draw the staysail and beat back to the motor-cruiser.

So far as I could make out she was lying fairly steadily stern to the wind—I suppose on account of her high bow, and she probably drew more water aft than she did forward—but she was rolling and pitching heavily. The fire had increased considerably even in the short time it had taken for me to manœuvre, and the dinghy on her aft cabin top was alight. Little though I knew of power craft I realised that there was not much time to waste if she was petrol-driven ; it only needed the tanks to explode and that would be the end.

On the next tack I stood in very close to her port side, and as I went about with the bowsprit a few feet from her, I shouted at the two people crouching aft : " I will sail across your stern. When I shout, jump." With the sails slatting in stays, the crackling of the flames, and the general noise of a windy night at sea, I could not hear their reply, and I wondered whether they had understood me.

I sailed well away on that tack in order to give myself time for some necessary preparations. First I fetched a tin of flares on deck, tore off the lid and jammed a blue one into the ensign-staff socket by the taffrail, for although the flames were bright the light from them was flickering and at times obscured by smoke. Then, tacking once more, I lowered the peak of the mainsail, and hauling the boom hard amidships, headed back with my heart in my mouth and a sinking feeling in my inside. Everything depended on my seamanship now ; I had got to judge my distance carefully and give the word to jump at the right moment.

Even with the scandalised mainsail we were, I knew, still going too fast. There was no time to stow any more sail, so, as we approached, I let fly the jib and staysail sheets, and lit the flare, which at once brilliantly illuminated the scene.

Fearful that our rigging might foul some part of the cruiser—

for we had a big angle of heel—I had cautiously steered to pass too far off and realised that I would have to make another attempt, when a steeper sea than the rest lifted *Wanderer* bodily to leeward, placing her for an instant within a few feet of the motor-boat's stern.

"Jump !" I yelled.

Two people landed with a simultaneous thud, one on the foredeck, the other amidships abaft the rigging. At the same moment there was a splintering crack as our topmast rigging fouled some part of the cruiser, probably her ensign staff, but it did not check our headlong career. As soon as we were well clear I hauled in the weather head-sheets and hove-to.

"Anyone else on board ?" I asked, as a man and woman came crawling aft in the searching blue light of the flare. They were gasping and panting as though they had been sprinting.

I had to ask a second time. The man said "Yes," the woman said "No."

It was no moment for standing on ceremony, so I bluntly demanded to know what they meant. The man insisted that Mary or Molly or someone was still on board, and when I inquired why she had not jumped with the rest of them, he explained that she was cut off by the flames in the bows. The woman remained silent.

My stupendous luck so far had not made me over-confident. I had seen what it was like, and I dreaded the idea of having to attempt that hazardous manœuvre a second time. But there was no alternative. Much against their will I made the man and woman go below, for there was no room in the cockpit to spare, and I did not wish to be hampered when handling the sheets and tiller. There was nothing that they could do, so I slammed the hatch on them, and hoisting the peak once more reached back to the motor-cruiser.

She was still lying more or less stern to wind, but a shower of sparks was blowing out over her bow, and flames were licking round the fore-deck. Then for the first time I saw a bare-legged figure holding on to the anchor davit, but only for a moment as the thick smoke quickly obscured it.

The actual business of passing close enough to the bows for the woman to jump on board should be easier than the previous manœuvre, for at least our rigging would be in no danger of fouling as we would be heeled away from the motor-cruiser. But it would be almost impossible to judge the distance correctly as the fore end of the vessel was obscured by smoke for the greater part of the time.

With a splutter the flare died. Hastily I replaced it with a new one.

My first attempt to get close enough was a failure ; thick smoke hid the entire boat forward of amidships, and I was compelled to bear away for fear of a collision, but I shouted that I would return. There was no reply from the cruiser, but *Wanderer's* hatch slid back and the woman poked her head out and moaned something to the effect that it was no good to try again.

"Get below and stay there," I snapped, "I've enough to do without being bothered by you." The head withdrew, and I closed the slide feeling the better for my outburst.

I tacked and made another attempt. It was better judged. For a moment the smoke cleared, and as we swept across the flaring bows in the hot lee of the fire, the cruiser pitched heavily. I told the silhouetted figure to jump.

She obeyed and fell slightly short with her chest over the rail, but with some assistance from me she was soon aboard and huddled up in the cockpit.

" Are you the last ? " I asked, dreading to hear that there was yet some other person aboard that floating inferno.

" I am," she gasped. " Thank God you came in time."

She looked to be in a dreadful state in the harsh blue light. Her face was blackened, her clothes were singed and wet, and most of the breath had been knocked out of her by her fall.

" Damaged ? " I inquired, expecting to hear that a rib at least was broken.

" I think I'm all right," she replied, " only shaken."

So I bundled her down below to her companions, and as soon as I had got *Wanderer* comfortably hove-to I went below to join them.

A curious sight met my eyes. Three nightmarish, smoke-grimed faces, grotesquely illuminated by the swinging lamp, made a strange contrast to the polished woodwork and the

Compared with most 4-tonners *Wanderer II* had wide side decks, for her cabintop was narrow. That was a great advantage when taking off the crew of the burning motor cruiser. The spars lashed in the rigging are the twin spinnaker booms.

clean blue cushions. On inquiry I learnt that no one was seriously hurt, but some burn dressings from the medicine chest were of use for their hands were scorched, and the girl's legs—she was wearing shorts—were severely blistered.

There was a good deal of hysterical talk, which I suppose is inevitable in such circumstances, and I was shaking miserably and could not stop my teeth from chattering for quite a while. The fact is I am no hero ; that night's work had shaken me badly. I know of many people who would have done the job without turning a hair, and done it far more quickly and efficiently, too. I got out the bottle of rum and we all had a tot. The heartening spirit took effect at once, and we were soon talking and behaving like rational human beings again.

I decided that Plymouth was the best place to make for, and to that they agreed. I ruled off the course, got out some blankets and gave the girl the pick of my scanty wardrobe. Then I went on deck into the wind and rain again, and discovered that the motor-cruiser had vanished. No doubt the fire had reached the petrol tanks at last, and it was only by the grace of God that it had not done so earlier, but we heard no explosion. It seemed as though hours must have elapsed since first I sighted the fire, but when I looked at the watch in the helmsman's locker I found that it was barely 3 o'clock.

Putting *Wanderer* on her course for Plymouth I sat in the cockpit steering, and thought about the curious affair and the strange folk I had picked up—so strange that they did not seem to know how many there were on board. Then the hatch was slid back and the girl handed out a mug of soup, and followed with one for herself. As she wormed her way into the cockpit I got a glimpse of the dimly lit cabin, and could not help smiling at what I saw : the bunks were occupied by two very seasick people, and a communal bowl was wedged conveniently on the floor between them.

That girl was apparently used to small boats ; in spite of the motion she had managed to light the Primus stove and warm up the soup which was ready in the saucepan, and she was able to relieve me at the helm. I tried to draw her into conversation, but naturally enough she was unwilling to talk of her recent terrifying experience, and I was unable to get any names, times, or facts from her. But I cannot say that I tried very hard, for reaction was setting in and I felt sleepy.

Dawn found us tumbling about in the confused sea off Rame Head. The rain stopped, and about an hour later we were comfortably at anchor in the Cattewater. Only then did the other passengers come to life. Having washed their faces they consumed a hearty breakfast, and then requested the loan of the dinghy as they wished to telephone. I launched it for them, and they all tumbled in and paddled ashore.

That was the last I saw or heard of any of them. The fair wind continued blowing, and by teatime I was impatient to be off, but there was still no sign of the returning dinghy. So at last I got a passing boatman to put me ashore ; I found my punt lying deserted at the Barbican steps, and as there was no longer any reason for me to wait, I sailed at once. I did not wish for an effusion of thanks ; it was only by chance that I happened to be passing close enough to see the burning motor-cruiser and take off her crew, but they might at least have returned the dinghy, and a pair of burnt shorts was a poor exchange for some excellent flannels. I cannot help thinking that there was something very strange about the whole affair.

CHAPTER XI

ALONE TO THE ISLE OF SKYE

I KNOW of few things more delightful than to spend a winter's evening before the fire in the security of one's home planning the summer cruise, and if that is done after a good dinner, distances and headwinds lose much of their terror, and it is astonishing how far one can get—in imagination.

It was under such conditions that I planned to go to Scotland in 1938, and as I had recently been reading for the second time the adventures of Richard Hannay, I decided that the object of the cruise—and a goal always lends a spice to any expedition even though one may never reach it—should be that wild loch in Skye around which much of the tale *Mr. Standfast* was woven.

I realised that such a trip in a boat as small as *Wanderer II* would be something of an undertaking, and might well prove to be impossible in limited time. But that year I could spend four months aboard if necessary, for work on the book I was then writing could be done just as conveniently afloat as ashore.

Frank Carr[17] was also planning to visit the west coast of Scotland in his ex-pilot cutter *Cariad* that summer, but as he did not expect to reach Bowling from the east coast until towards the end of July, he was kind enough to lend almost the complete set of Admiralty charts to me ; I intended to start on the journey south again before then and could arrange for him to receive them on his arrival. To impecunious sailing people, such as myself, who wish to cruise extensively along a different coast each year, charts are indeed something of a problem. They are expensive to buy, and the owner of a small vessel needs to have on board as complete a set as possible as he may have to seek shelter in some small port or anchorage which may not have been on his original itinerary ; his very safety may then depend on having the large scale chart of that place and its approaches. But quite apart from the possibility of being needed in an emergency, the possession of the large scale charts adds much to the pleasure of a cruise as one may then sail closely to the coast and through little used inshore passages with safety.

Many of the charts which Frank Carr lent to me were very old, but on a rocky coast which does not change, such as I was intending to visit, that did not matter much and of course I had on board an up-to-date light list. I also had with me the Clyde Cruising Club *Sailing Directions for the West Coast of Scotland*. That is a very fine publication which deals most thoroughly with every loch and anchorage from Cape Wrath to the Isle of Man, and it contains many sketch charts of places not covered by large scale Admiralty charts. A revised edition was published in 1947.[18]

It was early in May when *Wanderer II* slipped quietly out of the Beaulieu River bound for Scotland, and I hoped to make Falmouth the first stop. Finding a light east wind off the Needles, I stowed the fore-and-aft canvas, set the twin spinnakers and got the yacht to steer herself while I sorted things out below—everything being on top and nothing to hand—and generally made preparations for the first night at sea, which I always dread as I usually feel sick and have difficulty in keeping awake after my soft winter living.

At midnight, when we were well S.W. of Portland Bill, the wind began to freshen and we were soon running fast in a lumpy sea. An hour later we passed through a fleet of trawlers ; I could not judge their course or speed, *Wanderer's* sidelights were masked by the sails and under that rig it was impossible to alter course much. However, as soon as we were clear I had to hand the spinnakers for the wind had increased a lot and we were going too fast, and then under staysail only we logged 5 knots for the next 3 hours, rolling abominably. As I had expected, I was cold, sick, and generally miserable, so I altered course for Dartmouth and in the early morning had to set all sail to topsail in order to get into that difficult place.

Although I know very well that when on a passage a fair wind should never be wasted, I have always found it difficult to act on that knowledge. With a snug anchorage under my lee the temptation to put into it for a rest and a meal is very great, even though a fair wind may be blowing to waste, and then by the

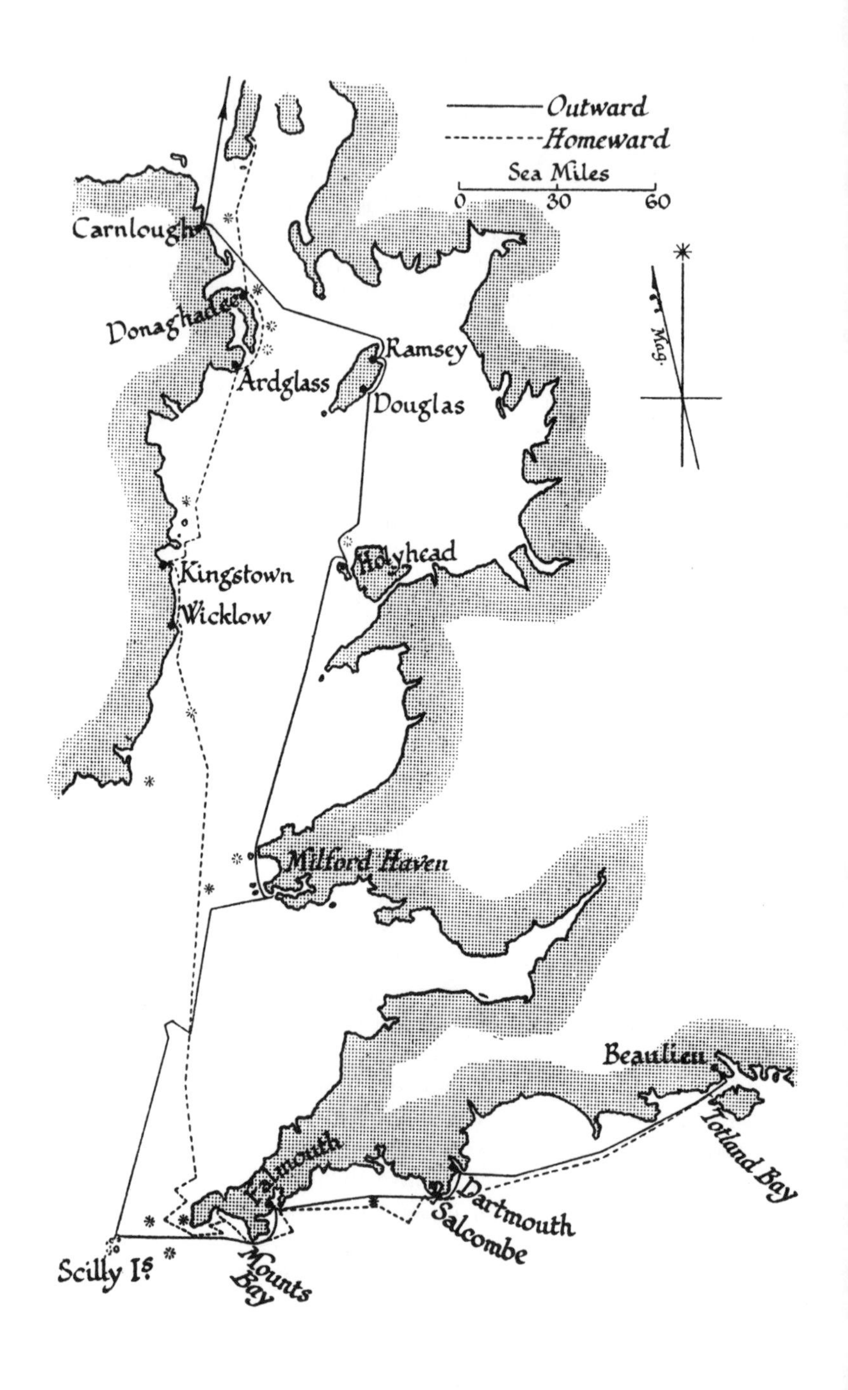

Outward
Homeward
Sea Miles
0
30
60
Mag.
Carnlough
Donaghadee
Ardglass
Ramsey
Douglas
Kingstown
Wicklow
Holyhead
Milford Haven
Beaulieu
Totland Bay
Falmouth
Dartmouth
Salcombe
Scilly Is.
Mounts Bay

time I have recuperated and worked out to sea again, as often as not I find a head-wind or a calm. And so it was on that occasion, for no sooner had I reached Bolt Head next day than the wind died, and because much time had been wasted beating out of the River Dart, the west going tide had finished. So I sculled into Salcombe and there wasted yet another night.

However, we did reach Falmouth the following evening, and from the moment we had cleared Salcombe Bar until we rounded St. Anthony, we had a perfect sail. The sea was smooth, the sun shone, and there was a pleasant S. breeze which held steady and true for the 50-mile passage, with just enough weight in it for the topsail and yankee to work to their best advantage.

Although I had allowed for the indraught into all the deep bays while going down Channel, each landfall showed us to be considerably to the north of our course, so while at Falmouth I got Mr. Cousens, the compass adjuster, to swing *Wanderer*. It was a quiet day, so the yacht remained on her anchor while I towed her stern round, steadying her head on each point in turn. Considerable deviation was found on westerly courses, but by fitting a tiny magnet to one of the cockpit seats, Mr. Cousens was able to reduce it to a ¼ point, and then made out a deviation card. I do not know what can have caused the deviation, for the compass had none the previous year, and no alterations had been made to any iron work or fittings since then.

Strong head-winds held *Wanderer* at Falmouth for several days, during which I saw a lot of Dwight Long. His ketch *Idle Hour* was re-fitting there in preparation for her crossing of the Atlantic, the last stage of her world circumnavigation. Dwight was lecturing each evening at the local cinema and selling postcards in an attempt to raise funds for a new mainsail and other gear.[19]

I also had the good fortune to meet Tom Kinnersley, and as he was due for four days' leave, he joined me, and in a fit of optimism I gave Oban as the next port at which I would collect letters, for, I argued, the prevailing W. and S.W. winds are fair winds for that place once one has rounded Land's End.

We left as soon as Tom was aboard bound for Holyhead, and with light and variable airs managed to reach the Lizard ; but there we remained for the rest of the day crashing about, becalmed in the swell, while we drifted to and fro in the tide race. In the evening a northerly breeze made and we started to sail again, but it freshened to such purpose that soon the topsail had to come in and the jib was changed for the smaller one ; after that we had a rough night. It was useless to continue to the north for it would take us several days to reach port against that wind and sea, so we decided to make for the Scilly Isles. If the wind changed before we got there, well and good, but if it did not Tom could at least get back to his regiment on time.

There was not much rest for the watch below that night, but my crew remained wonderfully cheerful although he was not used to such motion and said he was feeling as though he might be sick. So I gave him some glucose barley sugar which I kept for such emergencies. He swallowed a handful of the stuff and at once was exceedingly sick, for I had not then learnt that although glucose is a preventative it has to be taken some time, preferably several days, before sailing. Anyway he felt a lot better afterwards, and when we had shared a glass of rum and eaten a few biscuits, the world seemed not such a bad place after all, even though the sea was getting heavier.

I had decided to seek shelter in New Grimsby—the channel between the islands of Bryher and Tresco—for I knew from a previous visit that although the north wind blows in, there is always good shelter there, and as I had no intention of beating all the way from St. Mary's over Tresco Flats, we must enter from the north. There is nothing at all difficult about that entrance in reasonable weather, but when at 8 a.m., having passed Round Island, we saw a line of foam right across it, I began to wonder whether I was doing a seamanlike thing after all. But I assumed that white and heaving line was only the backwash from the rocks and cliffs on which the sea was spouting, and altering course ran boldly in towards it.

The wind fell light as we approached, and in something of a panic we reset the topsail and first jib, for it was essential to keep good steerage way. But all went well, and sliding off the back of the last white-cap we found ourselves safe inside in perfectly smooth water ; we anchored just below Cromwell's Castle, from which berth we could watch the sea tumbling about outside, had a meal, turned in for a few hours' sleep, and then spent the rest of the day tramping about Tresco.

Each time I go to Scilly I wonder more and more why I ever bother to go anywhere else, and if ever I own a yacht large enough to carry a good sailing dinghy on deck, I do not think I shall.

After one day of calm Tom had to leave me to fly back to Cornwall ; so, having put him ashore with regrets, I sailed alone, and single-handed I remained for the rest of the cruise.

The day was grey and damp with a light S.W. wind, and the barometer was steady at 30.00 when I left New Grimsby under all sail to topsail. At noon Round Island lighthouse bore E. 1 mile and the S.W. wind was moderate, so I handed all fore-and-aft sail, set the twin spinnakers, streamed the patent log and got *Wanderer* running steadily N.E. by N.½N. for the Smalls 106 miles away, where there would be a slight alteration of course for Holyhead. There was not sufficient wind to drive the yacht with her small area of canvas at more than 3½ knots and she would have done much better with mainsail, topsail and one spinnaker, but I wished to take life easily at the beginning of the long passage, and not to have to steer.

At dusk the wind veered to W. and fell very light, so that the fore-and-afters had to be set and I sat steering until 11 p.m. when visibility became very poor and by midnight we were becalmed in a thick fog. Those conditions lasted without any variety for 24 hours, during which time we sailed a total distance of 7 miles, some of them in the wrong direction while I slept.

It was a strange sensation to go on deck from the warm and cheerful cabin and find that swirling mass of grey vapour all around ; the effect was most bewildering, for a large swell had begun to roll in from the west, and there was not a straight or steady line anywhere on which to fix one's eyes in order to get some sense of balance. It was so lonely and depressing that I preferred to remain below where I tried to forget about it all, except when the mournful wail of some steamer's siren was sufficiently close to cause anxiety. My little radio set was a great comfort to me then, and the reception of many broadcasting stations was remarkably clear and loud. The barometer remained steady.

The second midnight out from Scilly some fitful puffs came from the west, soon hardening into a fine sailing breeze, and for the first time in 24 hours the sails ceased to chafe and slat as *Wanderer* settled down in her stride. Visibility was improving, too ; the sidelights were no longer reflected by the fog, and a little later some stars peeped out through the haze.

It was grand to be on the move again, but the wind was freshening, and the yacht needed careful steering under what was rapidly becoming a press of sail. At 3 a.m. I crawled forward and got the topsail off her. The wind was much stronger than I had thought, as I soon realised when I saw from the fore-deck the roaring bow-wave, the slack forestay and the hard curves of the sails ; so I took the big jib in while I was about it, but did not set the small one as we were going quite fast enough under main and staysail.

Under such snug canvas she was happy again, but in less than an hour's time even further reductions were necessary, so I hove-to and pulled down a reef in the mainsail, and no sooner was that done than I had to reef the staysail as well. I have already mentioned that *Wanderer's* mainsail is small and is divided into three portions by two deep reefs. The topsail is a working sail and is really the first reef ; consequently I do not often have to reef the mainsail, and at the time of that blow I had only twice had the second reef down.

At 5 a.m. we were suddenly overwhelmed by wind and sea and it was necessary to stow the mainsail without delay. I am not quite sure now how I managed that job, but I do remember making use of the topsail sheet as a vang with which to control the gaff, and inch by inch got it down and the boom into its stout crutch which is fortunately not of the folding variety ; the pram dinghy amidships prevented the boom from coming down on to the deck which is the best place for it in such weather. I cannot help wondering whether those people who talk so glibly of stowing the mainsail and setting the trysail, have ever tried it at sea in a small craft. The moment a sheet or halyard is started the canvas begins to flog, and I fancy it is not the weight of wind but that terrible slatting which carries the sails away. However, it was by then light enough to enable me to see what I was doing ; it was a wicked-looking dawn, crimson bars with greenish streaks between them spread over the eastern sky—a sailor's warning, indeed.

With the helm lashed down and only the reefed staysail set, we logged 5 knots on a broad reach, and for the first time since midnight I was able to go below, where, with infinite labour, I managed to get some hot food. And then I noticed the glass; it had fallen four-tenths in 5 hours, and was still tumbling down.

Obviously we were going too fast, for at times heavy crests were breaking aboard; so I handed the staysail and found that she sailed under bare poles at about 3 knots with the wind more or less abeam. That was with the helm lashed down; with it unlashed she ran to leeward at about 5 knots.[20] The wind was west, steady in direction but squally, and it had quickly turned the swell into a large but regular sea with foaming crests which looked far more formidable than they probably were, and every now and again one of them would burst aboard, apparently disturbed in some way by our small bow-wave. There was not a great weight in them, but it seemed an excellent opportunity to find out what riding to a sea-anchor was like.

In common with most cruising yachtsmen I had carried one of those contraptions for years, happy in the belief that should the need arise it would hold the yacht head to wind, or nearly so, and check her drift to about 1 knot. The sea anchor I had aboard was of the Voss pattern, with a mouth 4 feet square held open by crossbars of stout oak, and it was twice the size that is considered necessary for a 21-foot waterline boat. Commander Graham had told me that he never found a sea-anchor to be of much use, and I jumped to the conclusion that was because his was not big enough; the formula "diameter of mouth one-tenth of the waterline length" probably being correct for a vessel with a deep, square forefoot, but although their masts are well into them both *Emanuel* and *Wanderer* are somewhat cut away forward.

I got the thing into the cockpit and had difficulty in erecting it, for the wind twice blew it over the side. The hinged, iron-hoop type would, I think, be easier to deal with. To the swivel on the bridle I shackled a 30-fathom warp of 2½-inch Italian hemp led round outside the rigging, and to the end of that I shackled the anchor chain to avoid chafe. Then, streaming the anchor, I slowly paid out all the warp and a few fathoms of chain. The result was disappointing, for although the yacht's way through the water was checked considerably, the anchor did little towards bringing her head to wind ; she lay with the wind just forward of the beam. So some form of riding sail appeared to be necessary.

I had on board an unused storm staysail of about ten square feet, roped all round and still made up in stops as it had left the sailmaker's loft. Cutting off its hanks I lashed it securely beneath the boom, and then breaking it out with a preventer tackle, bowsed its clew down to the bilge pump, which is securely fastened in the cockpit. The effect was startling ; the boat came right up head to wind and the slatting of that tiny sail was dreadful. Every now and then she would pay off on one tack or the other for a few moments, only to come head to wind again very soon. The sail lasted for about an hour, and at the end of that time only the bolt rope remained ; so we lay as before with the wind nearly abeam, quite safely but in no comfort.

I went below defeated, but with a peculiar feeling of satisfaction that at least I had done all I could for the safety of my ship. But almost at once I had to make a journey to the bows, for the chain had jumped out of the fairlead and was biting into the teak rail. So great was the strain on it that I had to use a tackle with a strop on the bowsprit to get it back into the fairlead, and there I lashed it with a short length of small chain. Then once more I went below, changed into dry clothes, got something to eat and looked about me, considering the situation.

It was 9 a.m. ; the barometer had reached bottom at 29.35 (that glass was set high) and was just beginning to rise, while the wind was veering slowly towards N.W. and blowing harder than ever, howling through the rigging and giving the yacht a permanent list of about 45 degrees. The sky had cleared and the spectacle through the partly opened hatch was superb ; huge indigo seas were advancing from the west, their flashing crests of pure white breaking with a roar as they towered above us.

However, I was far too worried to appreciate the grandeur of the scene, for my reckoning put us some forty miles to windward of the inhospitable coast of Cornwall. Assuming that we were drifting in that direction at the rate of 2 knots, we would most certainly blow ashore if the gale continued for another 20 hours, and it seemed to me just then, exhausted as I was, that there was no reason why it should not do so. That was quite ridiculous, really, for after all the glass was rising and the wind was veering, but at the time I was so depressed that I seriously considered putting a letter in a bottle, for my chance of survival seemed extremely remote.

With much difficulty—for I had never before tried to use a sextant in heavy weather—I managed to get a longitude sight. It took a long time to work out, for the book of tables was thrown off the table again and again and writing was absurdly difficult, while my tired brain made very heavy weather of adding and subtracting figures. But when it was done the longitude agreed almost exactly with the D.R. ; that may have been coincidence but it was very reassuring all the same.

I was lying on the lee berth trying to get a little rest when at about noon a heavy crest broke with cruel force against the weather bilge. The boat was thrown bodily to leeward with a sickening lurch, and I was hurled so hard against the cabin panelling that I smashed the whole lot in, and damaged my hip and elbow. For a moment the daylight was obscured as the deck became submerged and a torrent of water poured down the companionway, extinguishing the cooking-stove. When I crawled on deck to see whether any damage had been done, I found that something had happened to the sea-anchor, for there was not much strain on its warp ; the yacht had paid off, was lying with the wind abaft the beam and was drifting to leeward much faster. There was nothing I could do, so I wedged myself in the cabin and listened to the radio.

I must have gone to sleep then, for the next I knew it was 4 p.m. and the gale had moderated to a strong wind. I got the sea-anchor aboard and found that it had collapsed, one of the oak bars having snapped clean across. Painfully I set the reefed mainsail and staysail, and allowing for our drift steered N.N.E. for the Smalls once more ; not that I had any intention of continuing on up the Irish Sea just then, for the sensible thing was to make Milford Haven for a rest, but we might have been set much farther to leeward than I thought, and I had no wish to find myself east of St. Ann's Head.

That was a wild sail. Hour after hour we drove along at 6 knots, and I might have enjoyed it had I not been bitterly cold and soaked to the skin. Twice I hove-to and changed into dry clothes, only to be rapidly drenched again, for no oilskins would keep out the deluges of spray, and I could do little to avoid them for the sea was heavy and confused, while steering was a necessity.

At midnight, the third one spent at sea, I picked up the Smalls light ahead, distant about 10 miles, and altered course to E. for St. Ann's Head at the entrance to Milford Haven. We took a long time to raise the lights on that head and on Skokham, for the tide was setting strongly athwart our course and the wind eased a little so that I ought to have shaken one of the reefs out of the mainsail : but my bruised arm felt weak and stiff and I was so exhausted with the buffeting I had received that I could not make the necessary effort. I had lashed the lighted riding light in the cockpit between my legs which I had covered with a sail bag, but the motion had shaken it out. I felt incapable of re-lighting it, so I remained at the helm in a sort of stupor, chilled to the bone and with teeth chattering.

At 5 a.m. we were up with St. Ann's Head off which there was a very wild and confused sea ; the patent log which was on the weather side was frequently submerged. Water streamed along both side decks at once, and some of it slopped into the cockpit. The motion was appalling. But we quickly smoothed our water as we reached into the Haven where it was my intention to bring up in Dale Road just within the entrance, but so much swell was finding its way right in there that I decided to sail on until I found a really peaceful berth in which to rest. So I bore away and ran swiftly up past Milford and Pembroke Dock, and at 7 a.m. anchored off Lawrenny. Slowly and clumsily I moved about the curiously steady deck stowing the sails and straightening the gear ; then I cooked and ate breakfast and turned in. At last my teeth stopped chattering, and as I dozed off I began to realise that *Wanderer* had survived her first really heavy gale in safety, and I was proud of her.

My hip and arm troubled me for some days, but when they

had recovered the weather was quite unsuitable for passage making with winds frequently of gale force, and I remained in Milford Haven for a fortnight. Twice I tried to leave but got driven back.

That is not a comfortable place for small craft. Even up the creeks 12 miles from the sea the tide runs hard raising a short, steep popple when the wind is opposed to it, and much of my time was spent shifting berth.

The great gale of 1st June caught *Wanderer* in the wrong place. While moving under reefed staysail only, the sheet fouled the stove chimney and whipped it bodily out of the deck, socket and all, and hove it overboard ; as the fire was alight at the time the cabin was soon in a dreadful mess with soot and ashes everywhere. The boom-crutch was washed off the lee deck, and in a sail of one mile the dinghy, which was towing astern, filled. However, with the kindly assistance of the estate carpenter and blacksmith at Lawrenny Castle, I was able to make a new chimney and boom-crutch, fit a new crossbar to the sea-anchor and patch up the smashed panelling in the cabin.

Ashore I chanced to meet one of the officers of H.M.S. *Broke*. She was on passage from Penzance to Milford, and must have passed *Wanderer* about twenty miles off during the height of the gale. Although she was steaming at very reduced speed her decks were awash and many of her company were sick. She recorded a wind of 55 m.p.h. with squalls approaching 70 m.p.h., and the sea was estimated to be between 15 and 20 feet in height.

The larger the sea-anchor that one can carry the better, but I doubt whether a really big one would keep a modern vessel with a cut-away forefoot end-on to the seas, unless she can set a riding sail or is prepared to lie by the stern. Probably *Wanderer* would have ridden quite well by the stern, but one has to remember that in a strong blow everything takes a long time and is very difficult to do, and once having streamed the anchor and found it did not work as it should, I was far too weak and tired to bring its warp aft even had I wished to do so, but as the cock-pit was not self-draining I never seriously considered riding by the stern. Perhaps all this is a very good argument for the yawl, but I have yet to see one whose mizen mast or sail would put up for long with the awful flogging that occurs when the yacht swings head to wind. A riding sail ought to be made of heavy flax canvas.

It does not appear to matter very much how the vessel lies so long as her way is checked, and I think that we were just as safe, if not so comfortable, beam to the sea as we were head to it. Well away from the shore I suppose that a sea-anchor might not be a necessity, but it would be more convenient than the warps, etc., which are sometimes towed from the stern to stop an easily driven vessel from sailing too fast under bare poles. But with a lee shore comparatively close aboard, it was necessary to check *Wanderer's* drift to leeward, and in that respect the sea-anchor did its work well, for working back on the chart from the landfall, I discovered that we had drifted at little more than one knot. So, as I am seldom a safe distance offshore when coastwise cruising, I shall continue to carry my drogue, but I sincerely hope I shall never have to use it again.

It was fine and sunny when at last I left Milford Haven with a moderate W.S.W. wind and all sail to topsail. The islands of Skokham and Skomar looked very jolly in the sunshine with the swell breaking on them, as we sailed close along the coast with a strong fair tide heading for Jack Sound, which divides Skomar from the mainland. Though the Sound is narrow, there should be no difficulty about negotiating it under power with the large-scale chart, and the Milford trawlers often use it. But as we approached the island the wind fell away for a few minutes and the tide swept us uncomfortably close to the rocks which were just showing then, for though I worked hard at the sweep I was unable to keep the leading marks in line. However, we were soon carried through, and picking up the wind again, ran quickly across St. Brides Bay and entered Ramsey Sound, through which the wind was drawing so that the yacht was completely under control in spite of the tidal swirls and overfalls.

At 4 p.m. we were off St. David's Head. There I streamed the log and set a course for the South Stack off Holyhead, N.E. by N. ½N. Though there was plenty of wind there was little sea and for 4½ hours we logged 6 knots ; but then the wind veered to N.W., although the barometer had dropped one tenth since noon, I had to hand the topsail and change jibs, and as a short steep sea got up our speed dropped. There were frequent heavy squalls with rain through which it was necessary to nurse the boat, and I had to remain at the helm throughout the night watching for them.

At midnight Bardsey Island light bore E., the wind was increasing and a steep sea was getting up. I altered course a half point more northerly to give the North and South Stacks a wider berth as I expected there would be a tide race off them through which I would not care to pass with so much wind.

By 5 a.m. we were making heavy weather of it with much water on the lee deck and a deluge of spray driving over all, so I pulled down one reef. There were patches of fog over the coast, and not until 8.30 a.m. did I make out the South Stack bearing E. about 3 miles away. It was a dead run from there up to the harbour of Holyhead in a steep and dangerous-looking sea which was breaking heavily against the breakwater, and I was very glad to get to a safe anchorage in the W. corner of the harbour, having averaged 5½ knots from Milford.

The direct course from Holyhead to the Mull of Cantyre passes west of the Isle of Man, but the light N.W. breeze which took us clear of the harbour, veered to the N. off the Skerries, heading us, and then died right away. We lay becalmed for 6 hours during which the tide set us away to the N.E., so that when the wind came again at midnight from S.W. and the glass started to drop, I steered for the Isle of Man, for the bad weather I had encountered since leaving the Isles of Scilly had lowered my morale, and I had no wish to be caught at sea in yet another strong blow.

At breakfast time Douglas Harbour lay only about a mile away, when with great suddenness the wind blew directly from it with gale force. With the utmost difficulty, because of the steep angle of heel and the deep water on the lee deck, I reduced canvas to the double reefed mainsail and reefed staysail, and started to beat in. Even under that snug rig the yacht was hard pressed, and with the gaff jaws only 4 feet from the gooseneck the mainsail had so little drive in it that we had to wear at the end of each tack as it was impossible to stay. That lost us much ground and we actually took 3 hours to beat into the harbour.

At noon we worked in between the pier-heads and anchored near the other yachts. Almost at once the Elins of *Lalla Rookh* came to help me stow the sails and then took me off to their ship for a hot meal. Only those who understand the absurd privations of the single-hander in such weather—hungry, short of sleep, and completely worn out by the work and the motion—can appreciate to the full my feeling at such kindness. The Elins had been watching my progress with some anxiety, and so had the lifeboat lookout ; he did not think that *Wanderer's* canvas would stand the strain, and had summoned the crew to stand by ready to come to my assistance if necessary.

I spent a few days at Douglas, then left with a fresh W. wind and sailed up the coast to Ayre Point, the northern tip of the island, but found such a heavy sea running that I put back into Ramsey Bay, where in company with five coasters, four trawlers and a man-of-war, I rode out a strong S.W. blow. As soon as the wind moderated I set out again although the day was gloomy with rain and visibility was little more than a mile, for the frequent delays were becoming irksome. From Ayre Point I set a course which should take us to the Hunter Rock off Larne, for as I intended to go to the west coast of Scotland and not into the Clyde, Northern Ireland, besides being a weather shore, was more or less on the way.

The cumulative effect of the tides on that crossing is to set one to the south, and I had allowed for it, but insufficiently, as I discovered when I made a landfall 10 miles south of the desired one. All the afternoon I had heard the fog signals of the Skulmartin and South Rock lightvessels, but as they both make explosions and are only 10 miles apart, I was inclined to confuse one with the other. When the mist cleared I altered course and reached up the coast past the Copeland Islands, across the mouth of Belfast Lough, and passed close to the Hunter Rock light buoy soon after 11 p.m. The topsail and jib then had to come in, and as I did not care to beat into Lough Larne in the dark with a rapidly freshening wind, I carried on along the coast with the intention of anchoring for a rest in Carnlough Bay about ten miles to the northward.

Soon I had to take in a reef, and then, close under the cliffs, I had to pull down the second one and reef the staysail as well.

The night was pitch dark, driving rain had long since blotted out the Maidens, the Hunter Rock and the lights of Larne, while only a darker darkness showed where the shore lay ; the squalls off the Antrim Mountains were fierce, and I got the full force of the gale on rounding Path Head. It was a slow wet beat into the bay, where I brought up off the town in three fathoms as dawn was breaking.

All that day and the next night the wind blew hard, but we were comfortable enough in that roadstead with the wind off-shore. The following morning, however, a teasing little swell was setting in from the east, but there was no wind at all. Presently the pilot came out in a skiff and suggested that I should go into the dock where I would be more comfortable, and when I explained that I had no engine, he at once offered to tow me in.

Carnlough should, I think, be better known, for though unattractive it is an excellent jumping-off place for the west coast, and is the last completely sheltered harbour until West Loch Tarbert is reached, some 50 miles farther north. It consists of a tiny walled basin with an entrance only 40 feet wide, and one has to go in carefully for there is no room inside in which to manœuvre. There is a depth of 6 feet in the entrance and 8 feet inside, and when the yacht has been made fast to the quay, a breast rope may be taken to the opposite wall to keep her off. There is not much rise of tide, and except for the " puffers "[21] who come over from the Clyde to load limestone, and make rather a dust about it, the dock is a comfortable little haven ; high walls keep the wind off, only a slight scend comes in with east winds, and shops are very handy.

There was not much wind the morning that I left Carnlough until we were abreast of Rathlin Island, and then it came from the west and soon increased to gale force. The glass fell rapidly, while rain deluged down. I could do nothing except reduce canvas to the reefed staysail and carry on. There was no room to heave-to or ride it out with the Cantyre shore a bare 5 miles to leeward, and it would have been foolhardy to attempt to round the dreaded Mull in that weather, and seek shelter under its lee. I thought for a while of reaching back to Red Bay or Carnlough, but doubted whether we would be able to beat up to an anchorage against so strong a wind. So I continued to the north.

One gale is very much like another, except that those encountered near the shore are always more frightening. But one seems to come through eventually ; and when I sighted the island of Gigha through the murk under the lee bow I found that the worst was over, for we weathered it easily and, rounding its north end, entered West Loch Tarbert. Circumnavigating the rocks which lie in the fairway, we eventually found shelter in the lee of Eilean Laggan, 8 miles from the sea and almost at the loch's head, and there the anchor was let go in Scottish water at last.

Listening in that evening, I learnt that the wind attained a velocity at times of 77 m.p.h., and no less than 2.31 inches of rain fell in West Scotland during the day.

I lit the coal fire and kept it going for several days, as everything on board was damp and sticky with salt. I attended to the ravages of the gale—a stitch here and a splice there—studied the charts and the sailing directions and did some more writing, and all the while the rain teemed down, the wind howled and the clouds flew fast from the west.

But on the fourth day the clouds parted, the barometer began to rise slowly, and with a pleasant S.W. breeze I beat down the loch and ran aground on the southern shore. West Tarbert is not an easy place to navigate because of its unmarked dangers, and it was while attempting to avoid one of those that I stood too close in to the shore. We remained aground for an hour or more, for although the tide was flooding it has a maximum rise there of only 4 feet, but when the Islay steamer passed I made use of her wash to haul *Wanderer's* bow round with the kedge and warp, and setting all sail to heel her over, got off without any further difficulty.

I then sailed quietly up the Sound of Jura, looking in at Loch Killisport on the way to Loch Swen, and in the evening ghosted up that glorious waterway, and at dusk slipped into the little lagoon of Tayvallich, which is the most perfect harbour I know of. The entrance to Loch Swen is protected by the McCormaig Islands, the tide only rises a few feet and there is practically no tidal stream. Then, towards the head of the loch, is a bight

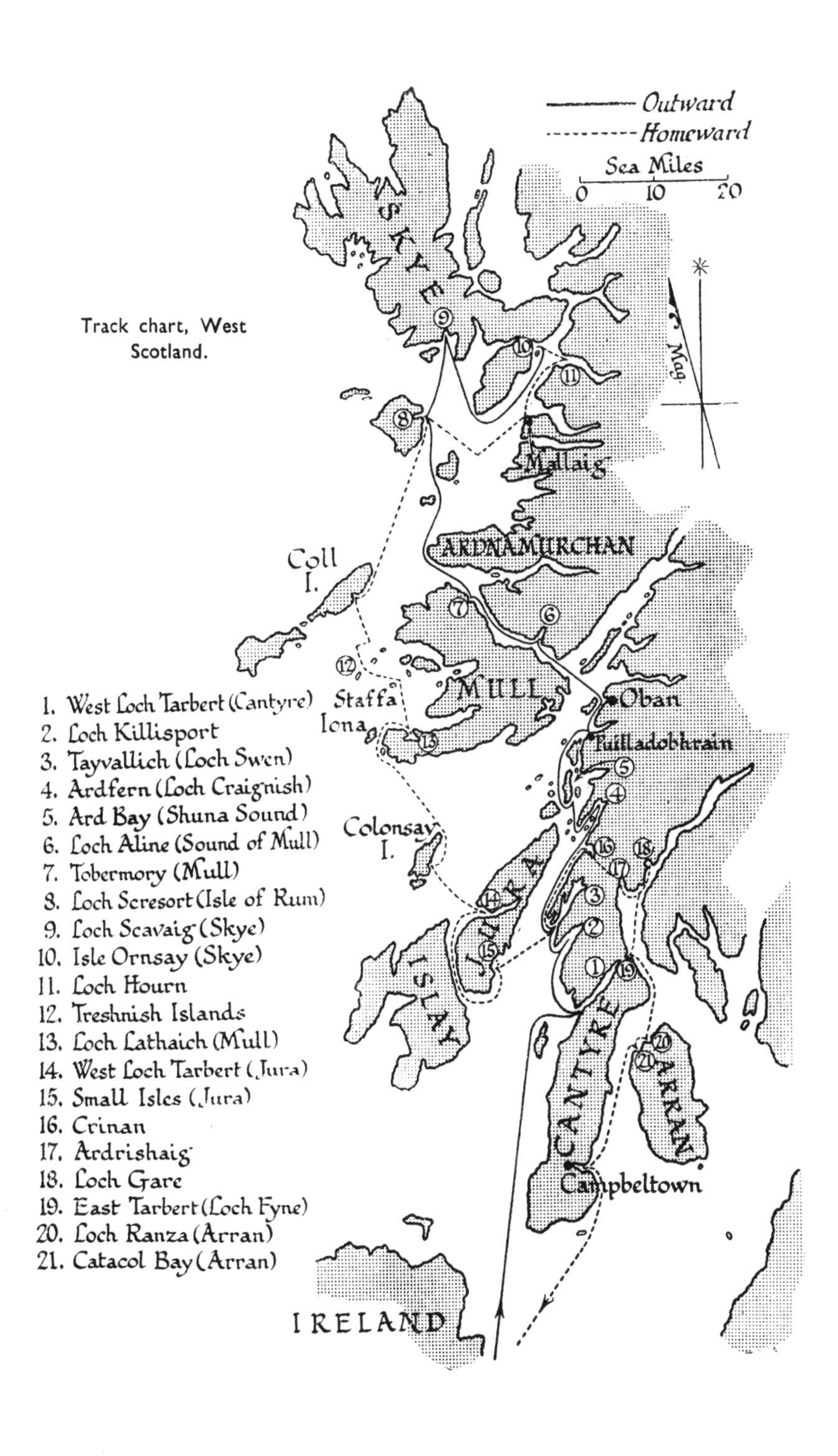

Track chart, West Scotland.

to port, and at the inner end of that is Tayvallich harbour ; the entrance is exceedingly narrow while its points are staggered, so the lagoon is landlocked. There is a neat little jetty at which to land, a shop and a water tap within a few feet of it, and beautiful surroundings.

One frequently has to beat out of the Scotch sea lochs, for they mostly run N.E., and the prevailing wind is S.W. So it was the day I left, but once clear of the McCormaig Isles we sailed rapidly up the coast past the entrance to the Crinan canal, to Ardfern at the head of Loch Craignish, making our way there through the narrow passage east of the islands.

The next day was almost calm. Passing through the tide rips in the Dorus Mor, I had to use the sweep vigorously to avoid being carried into that part of the flood stream which sets directly toward and through the Gulf of Coirebhreacain, and at sundown brought up for the night in a tiny bay on the west side of Shuna Sound.

Early in the morning we were away again on the first of the flood. There was not an air, so I had to scull all the way through Scaba Sound, and ignominiously passed Pladda lighthouse stern first in the 7-knot tidal swirls. Then we picked up a light air from the west, and leaving the Isles of the Sea and Sheep Island to port, headed for the perfect little haven called Puilladobhrain (the otter's pool). We reached the entrance in a rain storm which soaked the chart and the sailing directions as well as *Wanderer's* summer finery, and I had some difficulty in identifying the various rocks and islands. But eventually we brought up in the wild little pool which had not a ripple on it and not a sign of human habitation anywhere around.

From Puilladobhrain to Oban is a sail of only 6 miles, and there I went next day to collect my mail and buy some stores. I anchored off the Brandy Stone, where there was a depth of over 10 fathoms although I went in close towards the shore, but I only remained long enough to do what was necessary in the town as I do not care for popular yachting centres which are spoilt by the hot angry noise of outboard engines from which their owners have removed the silencers, and as the weather continued to appear more settled than of late, I wanted to get on to some more peaceful place.[22]

I sailed away in the afternoon and from the north entrance could just fetch close-hauled across the Firth of Lorne to the Sound of Mull, reading my mail pleasantly in the sunshine as we went. But thunderclouds were gathering over the mountains of Mull, and as the storm worked towards us the wind boxed the compass and then settled at N.W. so that we had to beat up the Sound. The evening was very beautiful as at dusk we ghosted into lovely Loch Aline and brought up in the S.E. corner. The afterglow from the sunset was still lighting up the sky at midnight.

Two other small yachts without engines came in just after I did, and in the morning we left in company for Tobermory, and drifted in a complete calm for some hours before a fresh N.W. wind sprang up.

On weighing the anchor at Loch Aline I found that the fid in the stock had broken. That had happened once before, so I decided to have the stock fixed permanently in position by a blacksmith at Tobermory, for I had never found any need to unstock it, and at the same time I would have the bend with the knob at the end of the stock cut off as it sometimes fouled the bobstay when being weighed or let go. I therefore picked up a vacant mooring off the town with great difficulty as the wind under the land was fluky and uncertain and some swell was running into the harbour. But the owner of the mooring asked me to move almost immediately, so I did what I ought to have done before, and shackling the kedge to the anchor chain rode to that while the bower was being altered ashore. The alterations were a great improvement. The bower weighs 42 lb., the kedge 35 lb. and both were to Claud Worth dimensions. They were rather heavier than the anchors usually carried by so small a yacht, but they have never dragged except when foul, and I have more confidence in them than in any mooring. There are 30 fathoms of $\frac{5}{16}$-inch chain and 30 fathoms of $2\frac{1}{2}$-inch lightly tarred Italian hemp. *Wanderer* also carries a 56-lb. weight with a specially shaped bow shackle ; it can be slung on the chain and lowered down to prevent snubbing. She has a chain pawl but no winch.

While lying at Tobermory we never stopped rolling day or night, for the wind was between N. and N.W. The oldest inhabitant of Mull, he was 90 years of age and a seafaring man, told me that was the most treacherous summer he could ever remember, and I heard similar statements made at many of the places I called at during 1938.

When I left Tobermory bound for the island of Rum, visibility was very poor with a drizzle of rain, the glass was dropping and the forecast had been strong S.W. winds. Those were not very promising conditions for rounding Ardnamurchan, but the wind was light from the east, and it seemed a pity to miss the opportunity of a fair wind round that headland which is so respected by Scottish cruising men that when a yacht has rounded it she wears on her bowsprit or stem-head a bunch of heather. The point is the most westerly of the Scottish mainland and is exposed to the open Atlantic ; a very considerable sea rises off it even in moderate winds, but there are no offlying dangers, the tides do not run hard and there are good anchorages not many miles away. I do not think, therefore, that it offers quite such a serious obstacle as Portland Bill or Land's End do, but I have not seen it in heavy weather.

We were about a mile S.W. of that grey and desolate-looking point when the wind died away and breezed up again a few minutes later from W. It freshened quickly so that sail had to be shortened and we were sailing fast in a lumpy sea as we approached the passage between the islands of Eigg and Muck, both of which were invisible. The chart bore a note to the effect that there was abnormal variation in that locality, but gave no hint as to the amount, and I was a little anxious until the S.E. corner of Muck appeared faintly through the mist on the weather bow. Soon I was able to make out the coast of Eigg, and when we had passed A Ghodag, a reef 6 feet high, I altered course for Rum, and an hour later had that high mountainous island close on the port beam. Visibility then improved, but the peaks, several of which are well over 2,000 feet high, were enveloped in mist from out of which and down the mountainsides into the sea rushed many torrents, zig-zagging now and again, and then leaping straight over the edge of some precipice ; a most impressive sight.

The only safe anchorage that island has to offer is in Loch Scresort halfway along the eastern side. I gave the southern entrance a wide berth to avoid the reef which runs out there, and then beat in to an anchorage off the slip on the southern shore, the yacht being hard pressed by savage squalls. But as is the case in most of the lochs, we lay very comfortably windrode, for there was no tidal stream there.

I spent the next day ashore tramping about the moors, and I climbed one of the nearer peaks. It was a day of mists and fleeting sunshine. and in the clear intervals I could look down from my eyrie to where *Wanderer*, a toy boat in the distance, lay at anchor, and over and beyond her to the majestic peaks of the Cuillin mountains in Skye, while dark shadows chased one another across the intervening sea. Before I had climbed down to the lower slopes again a thick mist had enveloped the mountain, and my only means of direction was the downward slope of the ground. But about 500 feet or so above the sea I came out of the wet mist with relief, descended to the dinghy, and fetching the watercans ashore was just about to fill them at a nearby burn when two men appeared. They were the first people I had seen since anchoring the previous evening, for the large house at the head of the loch was shuttered and closed while I had not been close to the few small cottages. I said " Good evening " and asked whether there was a well nearby as the burn looked to be very peaty. They shook their heads and one replied in a surly manner : " No one is allowed to land without permission." I was then ordered off, but I filled my cans with the brown water from the burn before getting into my dinghy with as much nonchalance as I could muster in the circumstances.

Rum is private property, but it is the only island on which I have ever received a hostile reception, for islanders are as a rule the most friendly of folk.

I was therefore not surprised to find the following passage in John McLintock's delightful book *West Coast Cruising :* " We pass Rum by, the largest and least visited of the Small Isles. Rum prefers it so ; Rum the rugged misanthrope, the isolationist that repels advances and discourages visitors. You cannot buy any stores on Rum ; they will not sell you anything . . . . Unless you are a deer you are not welcome, for the island exists solely as a deer forest. . . ."

The next morning with a light N.W. breeze I sailed for Loch Scavaig which is thrust, as it were, right into the very bowels of the Cuillin mountains whose 3,000-foot peaks throng the southern shore of Skye. *The West Coast of Scotland Pilot* tells of the fierce squalls that drive a vessel round and round her anchor and mentions that in strong winds between W. and N.E. the loch is unapproachable by sailing craft. There is no Admiralty chart of the loch on a sufficiently large scale to be of any use, but the Clyde Cruising Club book contains a sketch chart which gives all the information that is necessary. Feeling very small and nothing worth, I handed the topsail as I expected squalls, and crept cautiously into that place which is so grim and wild and desolate that it defies description. Having passed through the narrow channel between Eilean Glass and the drying rock which lies off its western end, I anchored behind the island, launched the dinghy, moored at once with the kedge—the anchors being laid east and west—and then had a chance to look about me.

On two sides the shores of the loch rose almost sheer for a 1,000 feet, and by craning my neck I could just see the black peaks of the mountains towering above them. In one corner a waterfall came tumbling down to sea, and into the other swept the overflow from Loch Coruisk across a low ledge of slippery rock. The place must surely be one of the most lonely and isolated in the British Isles, for the nearest habitation is some eight miles away across the mountains, a day's march in such country.

I landed on the flat rocks near Coruisk's overflow and climbed several hundred feet up the mountainside. From that point of vantage the little pool, with *Wanderer* lying in deep shadow in the centre of it, and the whole lock with its approaches lay spread out like a map below me, and I felt quite sure from his description that it was of this place John Buchan was thinking when he wrote *Mr. Standfast*. Having thus reached the objective of my cruise, and seen it in its awful solitude, I suppose I ought to have sailed away again while that was possible, but I had an inexplicable urge to lie for just one night in that wild place, hemmed in by the silent brooding mountains.

My imagination was too busy to let me sleep much, and again

and again I got out of my bunk to stand in the companionway and look about me, though there was of course nothing to be seen, neither was there anything to be heard except the rushing of the waterfall and the hissing of heavy rain which fell throughout the night. But at dawn a breeze made from S., and by breakfast-time had freshened a lot, blowing straight into the loch. A steep little sea was soon running in the entrance, against which I doubted *Wanderer's* ability to beat with safety, for if she chanced to miss stays in the narrows she would at once blow ashore either on to the island or the half-tide rock.

To seaward the sky had a slightly yellow tinge, while overhead nothing could be seen except the heavy grey clouds in which the peaks were hidden. At noon the wind veered a little, and as though that was the signal for the launching of the squalls of which I had heard and read, the first of them caught the boat with great suddenness on the port bow. Her head paid off until it was brought up with a jerk by the anchor chain, and no sooner had she swung round to face the wind than there was calm for a few moments ; then the second squall came to hit her from another direction. As the day progressed the squalls became more frequent and furious, and fell upon us from all points of the compass, as often as not blowing vertically off the mountains, pinning the little vessel down with her rail awash, although I had by then stripped her of most of her running rigging.

I had lowered the 56-pound weight down the chain, and it did something towards easing the snubbing, but again and again I felt sure that the chain must part or the anchors come home, while the squalls tore round and round in that devil's cauldron, whipping the spray from the sea and whirling it away overhead to be lost in the low mist which made a roof for the dark pit in which we lay. The heavy rains had turned the waterfall overnight into a rushing mountain torrent, whose roaring dominated the whole place in the quiet spells between the squalls ; but while the squalls lasted one could hear nothing for the roar of the wind, and when I happened to be on deck during one, movement was impossible ; I could only crouch down and hang on, feeling beaten, stunned.

The second night in that place was dreadful. The seas beat

against the island under whose lee we lay, and the spray, driving over, rattled on the deck like hail. Not a glimmer of light showed through the cloud pall to illuminate the wild scene, as the boat was hove over first on one side, then on the other, while the anchor chain jerked and rasped on the bobstay.

I was indeed thankful to have such sound and heavy ground tackle, for the squalls and whirlwinds continued throughout the second day, and not until the evening did they show any signs of moderating. About 10 p.m., however, there was a long calm ; for some time I sat below " listening " to it for I could not believe that it was more than a temporary lull, and any moment I expected another devilish squall. But there was nothing except a few light puffs from N.W., and presently I realised that the chance to leave had come. Quickly I rove what gear was necessary for the lower sails, with difficulty weighed the anchors, for they were deeply buried in the mud, and sailed away. There was just sufficient light coming in from seaward to enable me to dodge the rocks ; but Garsbheinn—the Hill of Blasts—did not let *Wanderer* go without one final wicked squall which did its best to dismast her. But we were soon out in the open, sailing over a large but easy swell under the full moon, thankfully leaving grim Scavaig astern to brood sullenly beneath its heavy pall of storm clouds.

Reeving off the rest of the gear as we went, I set the topsail and yankee, and then had a quiet uneventful sail round Point of Sleat and up the Sound of that name, which divides Skye from the mainland. As a rosy dawn was breaking I anchored inside Isle Ornsay close to some other yachts whose smoky riding lights were just beginning to fade, and felt I really had returned to civilisation.

. . . . .

Reluctantly I decided to go no farther north, for there was the long passage back to the Solent to consider, and I wanted to see something of the west side of Mull and its islands, as well as the Clyde, on the way.

The following day was damp and cold as I beat down the Sound of Sleat. I had a look at dark Loch Hourn, and then beat on to Mallaig, considering that would be quite enough of windward work for one day. But the place was crowded and looked uncomfortable, so I carried on for the island of Eigg, one of the "Cocktail Group," as someone has irreverently named the Small Isles. But the fair tide had done before I reached the anchorage there, and the wind was freshening from the S.S.W., so I did a very unenterprising thing and reached over to Rum, bringing up in my old berth. At least I had lost no ground but the morning brought a very strong S.W. wind and heavy rain, so I remained at anchor and wished I lay off some more friendly isle. I did not land.

Rain was still falling the following morning but the wind had taken off a little ; so I left under very snug canvas, only to get completely becalmed in a heavy and confused sea under the lee of the island. But in the afternoon there was a sudden miraculous change ; a brisk west wind came along to roll the clouds away, the sun shone on the sparkling sea, and all the mountains of the isles and the mainland came out in their glory of purple and blue, while even the dark Cuillin bared their heads at our parting.

With a bone in her mouth and every sail full and drawing, *Wanderer* tramped along on her south-west course for Coll, and in the evening came-to in Loch nan Eather on the S.E. side of that low and windswept island. I intended to spend part of the next day there, but was awakened early by the motion, and on looking out found that the wind was blowing straight onshore, and I thought it best to get away at once before the sea got any worse for there was not much room in which to manœuvre.

All day we turned to windward, but although progress was slow it was quite an enjoyable sail over the sparkling blue sea in bright sunshine. The Treshnish Islands looked very jolly as we sailed between Lunga and the curious Dutchman's Cap and beat on towards Staffa where I intended to land and have a look at Fingals Cave. I sailed right round that island, but could find no sheltered berth within dinghy reach of the landing place, so I went on to Loch Lathaish which is on the northern side of the Ross of Mull, and there chose a very secure berth behind the little island in the S.E. corner.

It was just as well that I had not stayed at Coll, for the next day there was a strong S.E. wind and I remained at anchor. I was able to get everything I required in the way of stores from a remarkable little shop in the tumbledown village, which seemed to stock all the most up-to-date things. There was great excitement ashore, for that happened to be visiting day for the weekly steamer.

In the evening the wind fell right away ; I landed at dusk, climbed a hill overlooking the anchorage, and there sat smoking a pipe amongst the heather while I contemplated that wonderful land, and—with a feeling of gratitude—the little white boat who had brought me so far in safety to see it all. Away on the horizon Staffa and the Treshnish Isles floated serene in the mist like monstrous ships.

I had hoped to call at Iona, which one usually does by leaving the yacht in the Bull Hole on the Mull shore and crossing by ferry, for there are no good anchorages off the island itself. But I was not prepared to devote a whole day to the expedition, so I decided to anchor temporarily in the Sound and just go ashore for an hour to have a look at the cathedral. But when I arrived in the Sound of Iona I found a strong tide and some swell rolling in. I might have stopped even then had I not spied a pleasure steamer at anchor belching forth her cargo of sightseers, and I preferred to retain an unspoilt memory of that green and lovely isle, so I sailed on, passing inside the Torranan Rocks, on which the swell was breaking heavily. For a while I could not make out which was which, but eventually the rocks and channels sorted themselves out, as such things always do, and passing Ruadh Sgeir, the most easterly of the group, and the only one to have a beacon on it, I set the masthead spinnaker for the first time that cruise, and had a wonderful sail to Colonsay. Reaching down that island's eastern shore we looked into Scalasaig, which is the recognised anchorage, but finding most of the available space taken up by a steam trawler, we ghosted round the next point—the wind by then had died for the night—and came-to in the little bay called Loch Sturrsneg.

Only the gentle lap of the swell on the rocks broke the silence of the evening, as the sun set over the island in a riot of glorious colour, while the distant Paps of Jura turned from blue to purple, and from purple to black as the light waned. A strange sad feeling came upon me as I sat on deck and watched the miracle. I was not lonely, for a sailing ship is company for any man, but I wanted a companion with whom to share all that loveliness. Life is so short, impressions so fleeting, and if only one could store up such scenes of beauty for some future glimpse. . . .

I was unlucky with islands. Eigg, Coll, Staffa, Iona, and then Colonsay ; I did not set foot on any of them. Once again in the morning the wind was in the S.E. and though there was not much weight in it, I will never willingly leave my ship unattended off a lee shore ; so I sailed, and had breakfast under way. It was grey and damp, with mist on the mountains, and last night's lovely picture seemed a dream of long ago.

I was bound through the Sound of Islay with the intention of stopping at the Small Isles which, of course, have no connection with the other Small Isles south of Skye, but form an uninhabited group close to the S.E. shore of Jura. It was much too early to attempt to pass through the Sound, for in the narrowest part of it the tide runs at 5 or 6 knots. So I whiled away the time until the ebb was due to begin by sailing into West Tarbert, the one in Jura. To anyone who does not know the west coast of Scotland other people's logs must sometimes appear rather confusing, for there are so many places bearing the same name ; there are, for example, no less than five Tarberts, for the word means a narrow isthmus.

That particular Loch Tarbert is a wild and lonely one ; the chart did not extend as far as the loch head, but one day I have promised myself I will return and explore it properly ; however, one needs good weather for such an expedition, and by the time I arrived the wind had freshened a lot and visibility was getting poorer. So I only got a glimpse of the place through the mist, although I penetrated its rocky waters as far as I dared.

The Sound of Islay is 12 miles long, the wind was drawing straight through, and we had to beat every inch of the way. But by then the tide was in our favour, so, leaving the great white distilleries to starboard, we were soon through and tumbling about in the Sound of Jura, where the wind was strong from the S.E.

Sailing rapidly up the Jura shore I slipped in behind the Small Isles to my desired berth, but finding quite a lumpy sea running even in there, I came out again. Lowlandman Bay, a little farther to the north, was out of the question with that wind blowing straight in ; I did not wish to revisit West Tarbert (the Cantyre one, which was my first stopping-place in Scotland), so I headed for the entrance to Loch Swen, knowing from my previous visit that at Tayvallich I would find perfect shelter.

The sail up and across the Sound of Jura was most exhilarating ; a steep, white-crested sea was running, for wind and tide were opposed, and the sun had come out at last. As soon as we reached smooth water in the lee of Knap Point I set the topsail, not that the yacht needed it, but I wanted to find out how fast she would sail when really driven. In the loch the wind was stronger than it had been outside, and was just abaft the beam, and I very soon wished that I had not set that sail ; *Wanderer* stormed along with a great roaring bow-wave curling away from her stem, she seemed to squat by the stern, dragging a steep wave along behind her and she carried considerable lee helm, which was something she had never done before and I felt that I no longer had complete control of her. So I edged over towards the weather shore, pulled the topsail down and handed the jib. I believe she went just as fast under the mainsail and staysail only, but she no longer dragged a stern wave with her, neither did she carry any lee helm.

My log records that we covered the 7 sea miles from Eilean Liac to the point outside Tayvallich in 55 minutes, but I have wondered since whether I might not have made an error in the time, for she has never sailed at such a speed since.

The maximum speed of the tide in Loch Swen is 1½ knots, but the tides were neaps on that occasion and it was slack water. It is seldom that one has an opportunity for checking one's speed with shore marks where there is no tide, and I cannot help thinking that tide has quite a lot to do with the high averages we sometimes read about. I would not for one moment suggest that the writers are exaggerating, but on a coastal passage it sometimes happens that one has a fair strong tide off the headlands and a foul but slack one in the bays between, and yet one may say with perfect truth that there have been 6 hours of tide each way.

I remained at Tayvallich for several days, doing a little painting, rigging and writing, while the glass tumbled down and gale warnings were broadcast several times a day ; but gales are of little consequence in that snug retreat.

When the weather settled down again I could not decide whether to make the most of it and start on the homeward trip, or to go into the Clyde. Having come so far it seemed churlish not to have a peep at that famous yachting ground, so I left it to the weather ; I would go whichever way the wind would let me. But by the time I had reached the entrance of the loch there was a flat calm ; so as the tide was running north, we of course went north with it and only just managed to reach Crinan after several hours of sculling before it started making the other way. Lowering sail outside I sculled into the sea-lock, to the amusement of some onlookers who were convinced that my engine had broken down, and we were soon moored snugly in the little basin for the night, in company with several other yachts who gave one the impression that they lived there permanently.

I was greatly relieved that all was so easy, for I had been trying, with little success, to work out a plan of campaign for entering that sea-lock where there is no hauling-off buoy ; and to this day I cannot imagine how a sailing yacht without an engine gets in during a breeze of wind, especially if that breeze happens to be blowing onshore. Even under bare poles she would carry too much way, and the lock is not long enough to permit her to bring up slowly by surging the stern warp. Perhaps that is another use for the sea-anchor.

Crinan is certainly the gateway to the Isles, and a very convenient gateway too, for it saves one the long and possibly uncomfortable passage round the Mull ; but those who know the Cantyre peninsula must often have wondered, as I did, why anyone bothered to make a canal 9 miles long when one joining East and West Tarbert need only have been a mile in length. As a matter of fact, that was the original idea, and the isthmus was surveyed in 1771 ; but apparently the estimate for making a cutting was too high, and a simple cutting would not have served, for the tides at East Tarbert rise 11 feet, while at West Tarbert they only rise 4 feet, and sometimes they do not rise at all; also the times of high water differ by about three hours. So locks would be needed, and where there are locks a water supply is needed; that must have been the real difficulty.

At 10 a.m. my horse and horseman arrived, and having made the tow-rope fast some distance up the mast to clear the bushes on the bank of the canal, we started off on what turned out to be one of the most pleasant journeys *Wanderer II* had ever undertaken. She was not built with an eye to canal work, it is true, but she behaved very well and slid gently along at a steady 3 miles per hour with hardly a ripple to tell of her passing. Not a sound broke the sleepy peace of a perfect summer day but the drone of insects and the soft clop, clop, clop of the horse's hooves on the grassy tow-path.

We met very little traffic, and what there was had to keep out of our way, for it was all under power. Fortunately, we did not meet any other vessel under tow, for in that case we would have had to keep clear, as west-bound traffic has the right of way, the towpath being on the north bank.

I had been told that it is almost impossible to pass through the 15 locks single-handed without sustaining some damage; but if one is lucky enough to get as good a horseman as I did there need be no difficulty at all, for he makes fast the lines and checks one's way as each lock is entered. I believe the secret of successful lock work is to have the bow and stern warps made fast as far apart as possible; then, as the water level rises—or falls, it is only necessary to tend one of them.

Only once did we get into any sort of trouble, and that was entirely my own fault. Having made fast in an up-lock I had gone below for a moment to get some ammonia with which to discourage the clegs—a species of stinging fly which was very troublesome—and when I got on deck again the bow warp had slackened and the sluice water had forced the bows away from the lock side, causing the edge of the transom to grind against the stonework. Heave as I would, I could not get her straight again; but the lock-keeper, seeing my difficulty, promptly shut the sluices.

And so we slipped on through that delightfully narrow waterway with its overhanging trees and flowering bushes, leaving the murderous clegs astern, for they mostly inhabit the western portion of the canal. Several blasts from the foghorn were needed to get the swing bridges open in time, for as it was a Monday the women who attended to them were mostly engaged with the week's washing. Eventually we arrived at the highest point—*Wanderer* had never been 64 feet above sea level before—and started on the downward grade, which was much easier but rather wet owing to the leaks in the lock walls.

At the last lock but two we made a longer pause than usual while I called at the canal office to pay my dues : one shilling per foot overall measurement, with a minimum of twenty-five shillings. That seems a cheap price to pay for cheating the Mull, and one may remain ten days without further payment. My tug cost £1, and his owner appeared to be delighted with the small gratuity I gave him and saw me safely into the basin at Ardrishaig, where I remained for the night.

We took 5 hours from Crinan to Ardrishaig, a distance of 9 miles, but a yacht with an engine can get through much more quickly than that ; I once did it in 4¼ hours in a 61-foot M.F.V. during the war. The only damage *Wanderer* sustained was a small scratch on her transom and one burst fender, but as that was a wretched canvas affair stuffed with cork it was a good riddance ; the modern rubber ones are so very much more satisfactory.[23]

Early next day I locked out. Fortunately it was still calm, for there is no hauling off buoy that end either. Since the new sea-lock has been constructed one may enter or leave at any state of the tide, as at Crinan, and we were soon at anchor off the pier, afloat once more in clean salt water ; not that the canal is dirty, but one soon collects a certain amount of grit by jumping ashore to help the lock-keepers or to have a look at the boat in unfamiliar surroundings.

By noon there was a breeze from the east so I sailed away and brought up for the night in Loch Gare, going on right up to the head of Loch Fyne and down to East Tarbert the following day. Starting with a reef in the mainsail and the small jib, the yacht was somewhat pressed, but we had barely sailed two miles when we were becalmed ; so out came the reef and up went the topsail and yankee, but before reaching Inverary we were reduced to lower sail again. And so it went on, kites and reefs alternatively in sunshine and in rain until we were off East Tarbert.

That is a good, though rather congested harbour, but I had not realised how crowded it might be, or I would have run in under staysail only. It is always a problem for the sailing man to know how much canvas to carry into a small anchorage, and I incline to the belief that it is better to carry too much rather than too little. Nothing is more ridiculous than to drift helplessly on top of some other vessel without proper steerage way. But that time I overdid it, and was compelled to sail absurdly round and round in small circles while I got canvas off, for the place was packed with yachts, and I was determined not to select a berth from which I would have difficulty in getting safely under way again. Perhaps I am too timid, but I suffer so much from harbour panic that I always choose a secluded anchorage if I can ; quite frequently, however, some other vessel with a friendly feeling (but also with an engine), brings up so close to me that I cannot get away without risk of fouling her, for it is not always possible to guarantee on which tack the anchor will break out.

That time I did get the berth I wanted, just to windward of all the other craft, and there I remained for several close and thundery days with no wind. It was a cheerful little place with much coming and going of steamers at the pier. Several Loch Fyne fishing boats stood on legs or lay beside the quay, clean and freshly varnished, while the activity among the many yachts seemed most unusual after the wild and deserted anchorages to which I had been accustomed among the islands and along the west coast.

Having spent a night in Loch Ranza at the N.W. end of Arran, from which I was driven by a fresh onshore wind at 4 o'clock in the morning, I had a fast and quite delightful sail down Kilbrennan Sound to Campbeltown. There I anchored off the stone pier by the town, and spent the afternoon filling the water tank and buying a few fresh provisions, for I had decided that if the N.W. wind continued next day I would start on the long return journey to the Solent ; with the prevailing S.W. winds that blew so hard that summer, a fair wind across to the Irish coast ought not to be missed.

Considering the many weeks I had been on the Scottish coast, I had seen very little of it. I had passed by many lovely anchorages and I had failed to explore any of the islands, but I had seen enough to know that one day I would return—perhaps in a larger vessel and perhaps in better weather—and find out something more about the most magnificent cruising ground in the British Isles.

CHAPTER XII

FROM SCOTLAND TO THE SOLENT

WISHING to make an early start I was astir before dawn on Saturday, 13th August, but there was no wind at all until 11.30 a.m., when a light breeze made from N.N.W. The dinghy was already on deck, and all sail to topsail was set, so I weighed anchor at once, ran out of Campbeltown Harbour and down the Cantyre coast. Ship Rock lighthouse on Sanda Island was abeam at 1.45 p.m., when I streamed the log and settled down to steer S.W. by S. for the Maidens, for Ireland would be a weather shore if the wind backed to S.W., as the weather forecast had stated that it would during the day.

To begin with the tide was on the port beam, but as we dropped the Mull of Cantyre astern we had it more ahead, and with the freshening wind blowing against it, a small, steep and confused sea was soon running. But it was glorious sailing in the brilliant sunshine, the little crests sparkled, and the mountains of Scotland, blue in the distance, came out of their misty retirement to bid me farewell.

Throughout the afternoon *Wanderer* ran happily on her way for the wind, instead of backing as the meteorologists had said it would, veered to N. and freshened. Nothing therefore would be gained by closing with the Irish Coast north of Belfast Lough, so at 5 p.m., having fixed our position by cross bearings of the Mull of Cantyre and Ailsa Craig, I altered course to S. by W. for the Copeland Islands, and two hours later had the Maidens abeam about 4 miles away. The tide by then was in our favour, and the wind had freshened to such purpose that we were logging 6 knots. I was unable to leave the helm for more than a few seconds at a time, and as I did not consider that it was safe to run under twin spinnakers in the busy and comparatively narrow waters of the North Channel, I decided to put into the little walled harbour of Donaghadee on the Country Down coast for a rest. Chapel Bay on the S. side of Great Copeland

Island, would have been a more convenient stopping place, for there we could have lain windrode and well protected without the bother of entering harbour, but night was upon us by the time we had reached Donaghadee Sound, which divides Great Copeland Island from the mainland, and it was so dark that I could only just distinguish the dim outline of the island as we swept past with a strong fair wind and a 3-knot tide under us, so I did not care to attempt to reach the anchorage. The absence of the red flashing light buoy on the Deputy Reefs was a little disconcerting, but fortunately both the other light buoys were in position, and we were soon through the tide-rips and heading for the occulting light on Donaghadee south breakwater. I handed the topsail and staysail, and was just wondering whether it might not be prudent to get the mainsail down as well before running into the harbour, which I could see from the chart was very small, when a black shape suddenly loomed up under the lee bow ; as I put the helm down there was a bump alongside and someone leapt on board and hitched the painter of his boat to one of the after samson posts.

" I am the pilot," he said as he scrambled into the cockpit and laid hold of the helm, " will you be having th' mainsail down, captain, sorr ? "

I had never before had occasion to take a pilot, for I consider that half the pleasure of cruising is to find one's own way with lead and chart into difficult places, but as he was on board I decided to accept his services, and going forward I had got the mainsail part way down when he gybed, and heading a little to starboard of the occulting light, shot between the massive breakwaters, and rounding up head to wind, shouted at me to let the anchor go. There were some lights in the harbour and inky shadows under the high walls, so I was a little bewildered, and it seemed to me an uneasy sort of berth my pilot had selected ; but I did his bidding, and while I stowed the jib he ran out a stern line to the southern breakwater and we then hauled *Wanderer* into a narrow berth between the other yachts which were already lying in the S.E. corner of the harbour.

To have entered the place and to have brought up in safety there without any assistance would have been difficult, for the harbour is only 180 yards wide and on that occasion was unusually crowded. I gave the pilot a drink, paid him off and remained there most uncomfortably for the night, our crosstrees rubbing against those of our neighbours, for the northerly wind sent some swell in to suck and gurgle on the walls.

Sunday, 14th August. The morning was fine with a light N. wind. I landed for milk after breakfast, and on my return at 8.30 a.m. I cast off the stern line, made all sail and then weighed the anchor. It was foul of two chains, but as there was practically no wind in the lee of the breakwater and the water was shallow, I had no difficulty in clearing it, and two men in a passing rowing boat kindly gave me a tow through the entrance.

With the masthead spinnaker set I had a very pleasant sail down the coast, passing inside the Skulmartin and South Rock lightvessels and across the mouth of Strangford Lough where, although the ebb was well away, there was no sign of any tide rips where indicated on the chart. There the wind fell so light that I decided to put into Ardglass for the night instead of continuing to Dublin Bay as I had originally intended ; we did not enter that little harbour, which is only 28 miles from Donaghadee, until 5.15 p.m., and as we ghosted into it the wind dropped right away. I brought up just inside the breakwater on which almost the entire male population of the place was seated fishing.

I remained two days at Ardglass. On the first of them there was no wind at all, and on the second a great deal too much from the S. with a rapidly falling glass and an uncomfortable swell setting into the harbour. The little place was full of bustle and industry, for the herring fishing was in full swing, and on the quay were many girls cleaning and packing the fish. The smell was almost overpowering for the offal was dumped in the harbour and there was no great gathering of gulls to clean up the mess as there would have been in any Cornish port. Most of the fishing vessels came from Peel in the Isle of Man, and all of them had pointed sterns.

Wednesday, 17th August. It blew very hard throughout the morning and gale warnings were broadcast, but as the wind was a little north of west, we would be able to sail a point or so free for Dun Laoghaire, 60 miles farther down the coast.

The wind had tailed *Wanderer* too close to the breakwater to allow me to get her under way in safety, so I ran out a line to the warping buoy which was moored nearby, then weighed anchor, and under single reefed mainsail, reefed staysail and small jib, slipped and ran out of the harbour. As soon as we were clear I set course S.W. by S. which, allowing a quarter of a point for leeway, would take us outside Rockabill to the Bailey at the N.E. corner of Dublin Bay. As the coast receded, although it was never much more than 15 miles to windward, we found a short, steep sea ; as it was forward of the beam it hindered our progress and deluged as with driving spray. Snug though her rig was, *Wanderer* was hard pressed in the squalls which were at times of great force, and though the Mountains of Mourne looked very lovely I did not appreciate their proximity.

At 9.30 p.m. Rockabill light bore W. A S.W. gale warning had been broadcast with the 9 o'clock news, but the wind was easing, so I shook out the reef in the mainsail and staysail, and soon after set the topsail. But half an hour later the wind backed to S.W., heading us off to S., and it quickly freshened so that the topsail had to come down and shortly afterwards it was necessary to take in a reef again.

Thursday, 18th August. At 2.30 a.m., when Lambay Island bore by account N.N.W. 5 miles, I tacked, and in driving rain and strong squalls stood inshore with the intention of putting into Howth for shelter ; but I had no chart of that harbour, and when I had read it up in *The Irish Coast Pilot,* I came to the conclusion that it was not a safe place for a stranger to blunder into on a dark night ; so I held on that tack only until Howth light became masked by Ireland's Eye, and then put about again.

At 5 a.m. the Bailey bore W. and with more wind and sea to battle against as Dublin Bay opened out, I had to stow the jib as the yacht was overpowered. I did not pull down the second reef in the mainsail because with so little leading edge the boat will only just go to windward and barely makes good one knot, but even so it was 8 a.m. before we brought up among the other yachts lying off the club in the blessed shelter of Dun Laoghaire harbour. The Customs officers were quite surprised to find that so small a vessel had arrived in such weather, quickly gave me pratique and left me to sleep.

Strong S.W. winds kept me in port for two days. I received much hospitality from members of the Royal Irish Yacht Club, and I was interested to see the Dublin Bay 21-foot class racing in the harbour without a single reef among them; they appeared to be desperately pressed and were luffing most of the time.

Sunday, 21st August. I hoped to be back in the Solent by 3rd September to attend the meet of the Royal Cruising Club in the Beaulieu River, and although the quickest method of getting there would be to sail boldly down the Irish Sea without putting in anywhere, the weather was so uncertain and the barometer so unsteady that I decided to sail down the Irish coast inside the banks, so that in the event of further bad weather I could seek shelter.

There was no wind until the afternoon, when I left under all sail to topsail and yankee, passed between the Muglins and Dalkey Island and slipped pleasantly down the coast. There were a few fresh puffs from off the shore in which I had to luff to ease the strain on the yankee, and one shower of rain which produced a most spectacular double rainbow; but in the evening the wind fell light and it hardly seemed worthwhile to continue, especially as I would be unable to get any rest in such narrow waters. I therefore made towards Wicklow and brought up there in the empty outer harbour at supper time.

The following morning was grey and damp with a moderate S.E. wind and another gale warning. Two men in a pulling boat came to tell me that the outer harbour was not safe in strong winds, and offered to tow *Wanderer* into the river. I could see no danger in my present berth, for the two breakwaters protect the harbour from all winds except N.E., and it seemed very unlikely that the wind would blow from that direction. However, I gave the locals credit for knowing more about their home port than I did. So I passed them a line, weighed the anchor, and then found to my dismay that their combined efforts were unable to tow the yacht to windward; in fact they were losing ground rapidly, and by the time I appreciated that the situation was getting out of hand, we had drifted too close to the north breakwater to anchor again and pay out a sufficient scope of chain. So I set the mainsail immediately, and beat into the narrow river, keeping the boat ahead to pull our bow round at the end of each short tack. We made fast to the north quay with the bower anchor out in the stream to keep us away from it as its foot almost dries at low water, and there we lay for three nights while the glass rushed up and down and the wind blew hard from S. In the drizzle which persisted throughout my stay, Wicklow looked a dreary and desolate place, its quays unused and grass-grown, its warehouses empty and its river, which is really the overflow from Broad Lough, little better than an open sewer. I very much wished that I had remained in the clean outer harbour, but the business of moving there in so strong a wind would have been almost impossible without assistance, which I was chary of accepting for a second time.

Thursday, 25th August. During the night the wind moderated, the sky cleared and in the morning there was only a light breeze from N.N.W. The Rev. Mr. Vandeleur helped me to get clear of the harbour under lower sail, and he left me off the entrance. There I set the topsail and No. 1 jib, rounded Wicklow Head and steered S. by W.¾W. for the Blackwater lightvessel 28 miles away, passing inside the Arklow Bank. There was a good whole sail breeze during the morning, but after lunch, which I ate very comfortably in the cockpit, it eased a little and we did not reach the lightvessel until 3 p.m. I sailed very close to her and threw her crew a tin of cigarettes, but my aim was poor and it fell into the sea to be swept away by the tide before they could reach it with their net. As we surged past the vessel's stern, a piece of wood with a small canvas package tied to it with spunyarn landed in the bunt of the mainsail, slithered down and dropped on deck. I retrieved it from the scuppers, and undoing the canvas found that the packet contained five stamped letters—the lightship's mail. There was insufficient wind to enable me to beat back against the tide to make a second attempt with a gift of cigarettes, so we waved good-bye to one another, and streaming the patent log I set a course S. by W. for the Longships off Land's End, distant 147 miles. But very soon the wind backed so that S. by

E. was the best that we could lay, a course that would take us to the Smalls, so if the wind did not veer by the time we got there we could put into Milford Haven to wait for a slant. At 6 p.m., however, we were becalmed and I was able to prepare and eat an excellent meal in peace ; then by the time I had washed up and lit the sidelights there was an air from N., so I set the masthead spinnaker to make the most of it and remained at the helm throughout the night which was quiet and starlit with excellent visibility ; course S. by W. again.

Friday, 26th August. At midnight the log read 15 miles and the Tuskar light, just visible from a few ratlines up the rigging, bore about W. by S. A school of porpoises kept company with us for several miles, gambolling and blowing, their bodies aglow with pale green phosphorescent light as they circled round the yacht and down beneath her keel. I missed the friendly creatures when they went frolicking off in another direction.

At 4 a.m. I picked up the loom of the Smalls and on reading the log was surprised to see that it had advanced only 4 miles since midnight, for though our progress had been leisurely it surely could not have been as slow as all that. So I hauled the line in, expecting to find that weed had fouled it, but discovered instead that the rotator and the small weight just ahead of it had gone. As the line had been cut through cleanly, I could only suppose that one of the porpoises had taken it in mistake for a fish. I had a spare rotator and weight which I bent on to the line, but I did not stream the log again until 5 a.m. when I was able to fix our position by means of the Smalls light. That light was just dipping below the horizon when I stood in the cockpit, my eye was 5 feet above sea level and the chart stated that the light was 126 feet high ; so I turned up the distance-off table for dipping lights in the nautical almanac, and entering it with the above figures found that the light was 15½ miles away. Its bearing S.S.E. completed the fix. It is, of course, only possible to use this method of getting a position when the sea is reasonably smooth, and cross bearings of two objects—when available—are much to be preferred.

By dawn I was feeling tired, so I stowed the fore-and-aft canvas, set the twin spinnakers, blew out the sidelights and turned in to sleep soundly until 11 a.m., when a number of short blasts on a whistle brought me on deck in a hurry. There close alongside lay a steam trawler offering me the weather forecast and fish for breakfast. We exchanged a few remarks on the weather and our respective destinations as both vessels rolled along lazily in the swell, and then as the trawler sheered off, her skipper leant out of the wheelhouse window and shouted : " If you ever want anything don't hesitate to ask a trawler." He gave one final toot on his whistle and headed away to the east.

All day the very light but fair breeze held, and although the wind was often shaken out of the sails by the swell, for they are of rather heavy canvas, we continued slowly on our way out of sight of land, while I slept and ate and read and attended to a few small carpentry and rigging jobs. Of course we would have sailed much faster if I had replaced the twins with the mainsail, topsail and masthead spinnaker, but then I would have had to remain at the helm, and I wished to conserve my energy. A noon latitude sight agreed with the D.R., placing us in latitude 51 degrees 33 minutes N. and later on in the day a longitude by chronometer sight when the sun was on the prime vertical put us in west longitude 5 degrees 55 minutes, which was only one mile east of where I thought we should be.

Saturday, 27th August. At midnight our run for the past 24 hours was only 63 miles, and soon afterwards the light breeze backed to N.W. and the spinnakers would no longer keep *Wanderer* on her course ; so I took them in and setting mainsail, topsail, staysail and yankee sat steering for two hours, but the wind then fell so very light that I stowed the yankee on the bowsprit end, backed the staysail and turned in until breakfast-time, when I took another longitude sight. The sun was a little hazy and the sight was quite unreliable, placing us in the longitude of Lundy Island. There was also a solar halo as well as other indications of a break in the fine weather, a backing wind and a slowly falling glass, while the B.B.C. spoke of a deep depression approaching. All day the yacht sailed herself, but bit by bit as the wind backed I had to get the sheets in until at noon she was close-hauled. She was just able to carry the yankee with the lee rail awash, sometimes laying the course, but more often breaking off slightly to leeward of it. The sky by then had clouded over, the sparkle had gone out of the day and the sea had a sullen look.

At 3 p.m. I sighted land ahead and hoped that we might be able to weather it, but it was much too far off to be identified, so I had another sleep for with the impending approach of bad weather I did not know when I might get the chance again.

At 10 p.m. cross bearings of Godrevy and Pendeen lights placed us 6 miles N.E. of the latter, which position agreed almost exactly with the dead reckoning. Such a perfect landfall is, of course, due more to luck than to good judgment, for it is impossible to know the exact course made good while sleeping, and even when awake one cannot watch the compass all the time. If only the wind had been a point more westerly during the afternoon we would have weathered the Longships easily, but as it was we could only point a trifle to windward of St. Ives Bay, and for a while I considered putting in there to wait for daylight or a fair wind ; but as I felt fresh and well rested after two and a half comfortable days at sea, I decided to go on round Land's End.

I therefore put *Wanderer* about, and as the wind was freshening I handed the yankee and set the No. 1 jib. An hour later, when most sensible folk ashore would be thinking of going to bed, a downpour of rain came to blot out everything, and almost at once the wind hardened so that I had to hand the topsail and change jibs. Again I put about and fetched in close to the land until I could just see Pendeen light dimly through the rain high up above me. I was so shocked at its nearness that I at once stood offshore and did not again attempt to close with the land in such thick weather. Throughout the night I beat to the south against the tide in tacks lasting threequarters of an hour each, and saw nothing except the blurred lights of steamers as they crossed our bow or stern or came at us head-on. Soaked through in spite of the new oilskin smock I had bought at Campbeltown, I crouched in the cockpit, easing the yacht through the stronger squalls in which she was over-canvassed, and trying with an electric torch to indicate my presence to the passing ships whose lookouts were apparently unable to see my navigation lights.

Sunday, 28th August. Risky though it was to leave the helm in such poor visibility, I went below at the end of every tack to mark the position on the chart, for it was essential to keep an accurate reckoning. Down in the cabin I could hear the mournful tolling of the Seven Stones submarine bell and occasionally the double boom of the Longships, and I wished heartily that I was anywhere but there. I suppose the prudent thing would have been to haul out of the steamer track and lie-to until daybreak, but I was loath to give up those hard-earned miles to windward, and I hoped to find less shipping after the Longships had been passed, for it was not my intention to cut close round the Runnelstone.

At about 3.30 a.m., after one of those periodic visits to the cabin, I returned to the cockpit to see the dreaded triangle of lights—red, green and white—bearing down upon us. I shone my torch on the sails and then directly at the ship, but still she headed for us. Quickly I pulled a flare from the tin which was ready to hand just inside the companionway, tore off its cap and ignited it with the little plug from the other end. It burst into flame at once. A deep voice from the steamer bellowed " Hard a-port." There was a muffled clanging from the engine-room telegraph gong. The red light disappeared and the ship swept under our stern, her black glistening hull and white superstructure revealed for a few moments in the eerie blue light and then she disappeared in the murk on the quarter. Before the flare died down I noticed that the log wheel was no longer spinning, and on hauling in the line found that the rotator had gone. That steamer must have cut the line though it was only 75 feet long.

At 7 a.m., according to my reckoning, the Runnelstone buoy bore E. 3 miles away ; the wind had moderated, but although the rain had stopped at last visibility was still poor. I did not head for the Runnelstone as I had not sufficient confidence in my D.R. without the aid of the log, so I continued to sail close-hauled heading S.E., determined to give the land a safe berth until I could be more certain of our whereabouts.

But an hour later the sky began to clear, the mist blew away and I could see the buoy about 2 miles away to the north with the land behind it. Thankfully I altered course for the Lizard, but in a very short time the wind died away to leave us crashing dreadfully in a turbulent sea without steerage way. However, the calm did not last for more than a few minutes, after which the wind sprang up with startling suddenness from the opposite quarter, N.N.E., and was soon blowing hard. I pulled down the first reef, reefed the staysail and continued for an hour on the course, reaching fast, but when I had to take in the second reef and hand the jib, I knew that once we had rounded the Lizard it would take many hours to beat against so strong a wind into Falmouth Bay. I was wet and cold and feeling very tired after such an anxious night, so, deciding to seek shelter in Mounts Bay, I hardened in the sheets and beat up for the weather shore. But there was so much weight in the wind and so steep a sea, for the wind was opposed to the old sea from S.W., that we did not reach an anchorage close to St. Michael's Mount until 5 o'clock that evening. We had made good a distance of 206 miles from Wicklow at the very low average speed of 2.6 knots, and had taken no less than 19 hours to beat the 28 miles from off Pendeen.

When the wind eventually moderated and backed to N.W. I made a quick passage round to Falmouth to clear Customs and post the letters from the Blackwater lightvessel, and then continued up Channel without delay, for there was still just a chance that I might reach the Beaulieu River in time for the meet. But at the Eddystone the wind came easterly, and when we had beaten as far as Salcombe it fell calm, so I sculled in to an anchorage and there remained completely becalmed for the best part of two days.

The run from Salcombe to the Needles was pleasant but as the wind remained steady neither in strength nor in direction, much sail shifting was necessary. At times we could carry the masthead spinnaker, and at others were reduced to lower sail and small jib with spray flying and lee deck awash, and at dawn off Anvil Point I actually found a small fish flopping about in the scuppers. The ebb was running hard by the time we reached the Needles Channel, and as it was impossible to get through Hurst narrows against it, I brought up for a few hours in Totland Bay. Then as soon as the strength of the ebb was done I got under way once more, and running up the Solent in curiously smooth water, entered Beaulieu River. Quietly we beat up Patience Reach and eventually came to an anchorage off Gins Farm among the many fine cruising yachts gathered there, for we had after all and in spite of our delays, arrived in time for the tail end of the meet.

Wanderer looked a little weather-worn in such grand company, her sails and rigging stiff with salt, her brightwork scoured by rain and spray, but she wore proudly on her bowsprit end a bunch of Scotch heather picked in the Isle of Skye, to show where she had been to since she left her river anchorage four months before to sail 2,000 miles.

CHAPTER XIII

ON THE BRITTANY COAST

I FELT that I had experienced more than enough bad weather during my Scottish cruise, and remembering the perfect sailing conditions we had in *Dyarchy* along the Brittany coast, and having had reports of similar weather from others who had been there, I decided in 1939 to sail south in search of sunshine.

The cruise began from the Solent, but as I had the assistance of very efficient sailing friends—Adlard Coles as far as Portland, and Stephen Brown from Portland to the Yealm—the trip down Channel was easy and comfortable and Helford was reached without incident towards the end of May.

There I took aboard stores and water. A large anti-cyclone covered the British Isles and much of the Atlantic, and apart from a local light air each morning which twice tempted me as far as the river mouth, I remained becalmed at Helford for several days, which was bad for my morale.

But on looking out at 4.30 a.m. on the 29th May, I found a moderate E. wind blowing. From aloft the sea appeared to be ruffled out to the horizon, so I hoped it would prove to be more than a local breeze, and having made all sail to topsail and large jib, I weighed the anchor at 5 a.m. and beat out of the river. There was a steep little lop outside, but we were able to fetch down to the Manacles a point or so free and had the buoy abeam at 7.45 a.m. There I streamed the log and took my departure for Ushant.

My intention was to pass outside that island and make a passage direct to Belle Ile, which was as far to the S.E. as I expected to go, and from there work my way home in easy stages, calling at any place which might take my fancy. But most of my previous attempts to make long passages single-handed had not succeeded, and there was no reason why this one should. I quite expected to get tired long before my destination had been reached, in which case I could put into one of a number of convenient ports.

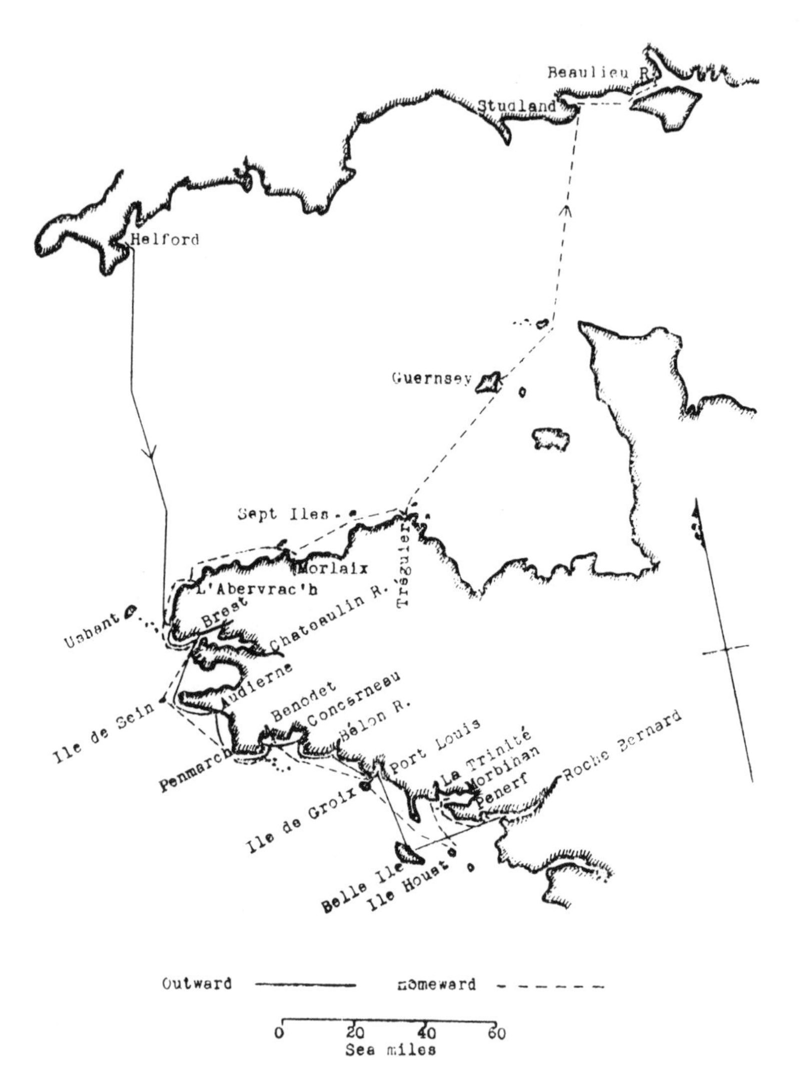

Wanderer's track on the Brittany coast

The day was a glorious one ; the sky was clear, the sun blazed down on the dark blue white-crested sea, and with the wind a little abaft the beam *Wanderer* hurried along, her course S. by W. ½W. She was just able to carry the topsail, and although the slight sea was steep enough to throw her about a little and made it difficult for me to hold a steady compass course, she averaged a fraction under 6 knots for 8 hours. But as she would not steer herself on that point of sailing, and as the wind was not sufficiently far aft to allow the twin spinnakers to be used, I had to remain at the helm.

By noon the wind had increased and the sea was beginning to get up, so I hove-to for a few minutes while I handed the topsail and changed jibs, then bearing away again continued on the course. But throughout the afternoon the wind continued to freshen and hauled round a little S. of E. and the glass was dropping ; fearing that a south-easter might be brewing, I altered course at 2 p.m. to S. for Ile Vierge so as to be up to windward should the wind veer further, and in a position to seek shelter in L'Abervrac'h if necessary.

An hour later I had to reef, and at 4 p.m. a very awkward sea was running. Much heavy spray was coming aboard, I was soaked and had had enough of steering, so I took in the jib, and backing the staysail hove *Wanderer* to on the port tack to wait for conditions to improve. We must have taken rather more water into the cockpit than I had thought, for *Wanderer* does not leak yet 200 strokes of the diaphragm pump were needed to clear the bilge.

Having changed into dry clothes and prepared and eaten a meal with absurd difficulty, I felt quite cheerful but thought I was being a little faint-hearted to lie-to in brilliant sunshine ; had the sky been overcast I would almost certainly have entered the wind in the log-book as of gale force, but although there was a good deal of weight in it, it was the sea rather than the wind that was the deciding factor. The motion, now that our speed through the water had been checked, though sudden was not very violent, and the boat seemed well able to look after herself, so I lay on the lee berth and listened to the radio which is always a comfort to me on such occasions. The 9 o'clock weather forecast indicated that the wind would continue strong from E. to S.E., but as the sea had eased noticeably, I let draw the staysail and continued for Ile Vierge light which I sighted on the weather bow at 1.45 a.m. I altered course for it, but under her reduced sail *Wanderer* made such poor progress close-hauled, and yet could not carry any more canvas, that I decided to make for the Chenal du Four instead of L'Abervrac'h.

A huge full moon was riding in the sky drawing a broad silver path on the sea, and the scene was quite enchanting. But I was growing very sleepy, and as I sat drowsily in the cockpit with my arm over the tiller and my feet braced against the lee coaming, I kept dozing off and I had to take a turn of the mainsheet round my waist to prevent myself from tumbling down to leeward. I was beset, too, by a queer hallucination. I thought there was someone aboard with me—I even spoke to him at times—and whenever a lurch to leeward caused me to knock my knee or elbow against the woodwork, I thought it was the other fellow who was being hurt, and I said to myself: "He'll be a mass of bumps and bruises in the morning." No doubt my fatigue was due to the early start, for I have found that if I can have my sleep right out in port before starting on a passage, I can remain awake through the night without much difficulty, though there is, of course, always a drowsy feeling just before dawn.

But presently I noticed that we were sailing more upright and that there was far less noise, and I realised that the wind had moderated. I shook myself properly awake, and going forward let out the reef and set the small jib, and *Wanderer* picked up her heels again, throwing a shower of spray over her weather rail. The horizon ahead of us and on both bows was by then dotted with pairs of masthead lights, lifting and dipping on the sea, and though the boat seemed well able to look after herself and was nicely balanced, I did not care to leave the cockpit with so much traffic about. Those were the first vessels I had seen since leaving the steamer track off the Lizard, for as most ships make their landfalls at or take their departures from either the Bishop or Ushant, the entrance to the English Channel is a very lonely place.

Dawn that morning was a wonderful affair. As the sun lifted his clear red orb out of the eastern sea, so the moon touched the horizon in the west. The sky was flushed with pink light which was reflected by the tops of the seas, but the troughs were dark and chill as though the night still retained a hold in them. On the port bow lay the low rocky coast of Finisterre, and on the starboard Ushant, dark and forbidding in spite of the sunshine.

Smoothing our water as we went we brought Le Four lighthouse abeam at 6.45 a.m., and there I handed the log reading 94 miles. The Chenal du Four, which divides the mainland from Ushant and the other off-lying islands, is not at all difficult to navigate provided one has reasonably clear weather and a fair tide, for it is excellently marked and it only gets narrow and interesting towards its southern end. I steered a compass course for La Valbelle, the first of the buoys, which was invisible 5 miles away ; we were soon up with it and I began to think about seeking an anchorage in which to rest. With the offshore wind the Anse des Blancs Sablons, a clean bay on the mainland only 5 miles farther on, appeared from the chart to offer what I wanted, so I stood in towards it and *Wanderer* sailed herself while I went forward to prepare for anchoring. The bower anchor, which I carry on deck with its stock up-and-down the port rigging, had been securely lashed before putting to sea, and I was working on that lashing with my spike, for the wet had set it up very tight, when I heard a cry, and looking over my shoulder saw very close ahead a small black boat at anchor right on our course. I sprang aft, and pushing the helm hard down luffed just in time to avoid a collision with her, though the end of our boom just touched the boat's stem as we swept past. I shouted my apologies, and instead of the scowls and curses which I deserved for my carelessness, I received cheerful waves and a roared "*Bon jour*" from the fishermen in her.

At 8.45 a.m. I brought up in 3 fathoms L.W. in the bay with the Little Ilet bearing W. by N., having taken 25 hours from the Manacles, for 5¼ of which we were hove-to. The distance was 103 miles. There I seized all my wet clothes up in the rigging to dry in the hot sun and blustering wind, and turning in slept heavily in spite of the swell which found its persistent way into the bay. The wind blew hard from the E. all day with a clear sky, and I was glad to be in so sheltered a berth ; but in the evening when it began to back I took a reef in the mainsail and staysail and prepared for sea, as the bay would no longer offer shelter when the wind got round as far as N. by E. But it steadied at N.N.E. and I was therefore able to remain safely for the night.

Belle Ile still lay more than 100 miles away, but now that I had made the coast, there seemed to me, after a careful study of the charts, to be little point in going straight on. With tides to consider and pilotage to attend to there would not be much opportunity for rest, so as Brittany was after all my chosen cruising ground, I decided first of all to make Brest and arrange for letters to be sent on, and then to go south in easy stages. To be able to make such a complete change of plans without having to consult anybody is one of the very few advantages of sailing alone.

After breakfast next morning the wind veered to E. and moderated, so I got under way immediately in an endeavour to catch the last of the S. going tide, for it runs at from 5 to 7 knots in the narrows by the Grande Vinotiere. There was little time to spare, so I cut inside the Vinotiere tower and just managed to get round Pointe de St. Mathieu, passing inside Les Vieux Moines as the flood tide started to make, and began the 12-mile beat to Brest. That port has the most lovely approach of any on the coast, and the Goulet, its mile-wide entrance channel, looked particularly attractive on that summer morning. The sea was alive with sailing craft, and *Wanderer*, going well, held her own with a wine carrying ketch and slowly outsailed a couple of Camaret crabbers. In the Goulet the wind suddenly freshened ; I had to hand the topsail and jib in a hurry and then had some anxious moments with a line of large buoys and other obstructions which were laid across the channel, until I found the one narrow way through. There was no mention of the obstruction in the latest Notice to Mariners which I had obtained before starting, and no doubt it had something to do with the war scare.

I brought up in the Port du Commerce, and was at once boarded by two douaniers in immaculate uniforms and bare feet (a sensible rig as their boat was waterlogged) and then I went ashore, wired for my mail and obtained a *passeport des navires étrangers* for a few francs. That was the only formality, and during my stay in French waters I was not bothered again.

For two days I remained at Brest while a N.E. gale blew coal dust all over the yacht. I would have sailed to some cleaner spot, but we were so closely surrounded by other craft that I doubted my ability to get under way in so strong a wind without fouling one of them. However, as soon as the wind moderated I slipped away and anchored in the Anse de L'Auberlach, a charming place in the Rade only 5 miles from Brest. There, unreeving all the gear, I scrubbed it from end to end and wiped down the shrouds and stays, for everything aloft was grimed with coal dust and would have marked the light weather sails which were not tanned. I also scrubbed the deck and sides and had a great clean up below, but it was several days before the last traces of our stay at Brest were completely removed. For some time my antics had been watched with interest by the villagers, and presently a party of them in Breton costume rowed off to sell me strawberries, and incidentally to find out what I had been up to.

The Rade de Brest is a jolly place for day sailing with many pleasant anchorages, and when I realised that threequarters of a fathom could be added to the soundings marked on the chart, I had a carefree time, and sailed at low water over several shoals where only a quarter of a fathom was shown. The Admiralty and Royal Cruising Club charts (all of which I had on board) were taken from the French survey which is reduced to the lowest possible low water ; when planning the cruise I could see little point in having the French charts as well, for they were poorly printed, had no compass roses and were of course marked in metres, but I would have been glad of them later when I reached Quiberon Bay.

I returned to Brest to collect my mail and then sail on, but was compelled to remain there for the night becalmed. That evening the harbour presented a most extraordinary sight : its surface was coated with a scum of oil and filth in which were suspended all manner of foul things, while here and there a packing case or broken barrel reared its head above the oil.

As soon as an air made in the morning I crept away, used the sweep to clear the obstructions in the Goulet and brought up off

Camaret, where I anchored in just over 1 fathom L.W. with the lighthouse bearing N. The crabbing fleet was away at sea and the harbour, all of which dries, looked very depressing with a few rotting hulks standing on legs in it.

The following day I beat out of the bay with a light N.W. breeze, bound to the south and east, but got becalmed at the north end of the Toulinguet Channel. The tide was weak and setting fairly through it, so I had ample opportunity for studying the curious rock formations, the Tas de Pois in particular looking most spectacular.

At noon a breeze came away from W. and it was pleasant to be on the move again. The course for the Raz de Sein, 13 miles away, was S.W. by S., and *Wanderer* slipped along just free with a slight swell on the beam. But the wind brought with it a mist which soon thickened into fog. I got cross bearings of Tas de Pois and Cap de la Chevre before they vanished, and then concentrated on the steering. The Raz de Sein is a channel 1½ miles wide between the Chaussée de Sein, which extends some 10 miles seaward, and the mainland. Although it presents no difficulties to the stranger, I did not intend to try to pass through it in so thick a fog, for the tides run hard there. But I held on in the hope that visibility would improve before I arrived in the neighbourhood, and that would not be for some time as the tide was adverse and not due to turn in my favour until 7 p.m. If the fog did not clear I could put about and head out to sea north of the Chaussée clear of all dangers and wait until it did.

During the afternoon two motor vessels passed close. I saw nothing of them but could hear quite clearly the voices of their crews above the mutter of the engines. I also picked up occasionally the faint moan of a whistle buoy which could only have been La Vandrée 6 or 7 miles away. The sails were soon heavy with moisture, and large drops of water gathered along the bottom of the boom to swell for a moment before being flung off as that spar brought up with a slight jerk at the end of the leeward roll. As we sailed along we took with us our own small circle of fog-bound visibility, widening at times as the sun tried to break through, then closing in again as we ran into a thicker patch of the smother.

At 5 p.m. my dead reckoning placed us 3 miles N.E. of Tevénnec, the most northerly danger of the Raz, and that was as close as I dared to go. I was preparing to put about and stand out to sea when the sky grew lighter to windward; so I held on for a few minutes, and there was then a general clearing of the fog to the southward, enabling me to get a fix by cross-bearings which agreed very well with the D.R. and would enable me to pass through the Raz even if the fog were to thicken again. It remained clear, however, but we made slow progress against the tide and did not round La Vieille lighthouse until slack water at 7 p.m. *The Channel Pilot Part II* mentions an eddy to the N. of La Vieille with a width of one cable, but I was unable to find it, though even had I done so it would have been of little help for I could never have passed the lighthouse until the tide slacked, as the wind was very light. For a short time we lay becalmed in the Raz; the blue sky which the dispersing fog had revealed began to cloud over, the air turned suddenly cold and a fresh wind made from N.E. With sheets eased and helm lashed *Wanderer*, now in the Bay of Biscay, sailed herself to the S.E. past a desolate coast on which lay the rusting remains of a wreck, while I had supper; at dusk we fetched into Audierne roadstead and brought up east of the line of leading lights in company with a fleet of crabbers, and rolled gently on an easy swell all night.

In the morning I sailed into Audierne harbour and with the lead found the small pool just below the bridge, the only spot in which one can remain afloat and which we occupied in *Dyarchy* four years before. But the labour of getting properly secured there single-handed seemed hardly worthwhile, for there is very little room, the bower anchor must be dropped in the correct spot (when the electric pylon is in line with the Gendarmerie) and sufficient chain veered to bring one's stern within about 50 feet of the bridge to which stern lines must be taken and made fast to the railings. So I ran slowly out again, and after much sail shifting had a glorious reach in bright sunshine and smooth water to the Menhir tower off Penmarch, and there lay becalmed for several hours crashing wretchedly in the tidal overfalls and plagued by a swarm of evil black flies. At one time we got set rather close to the rocks and I had to use the sweep to get clear. Some motor fishing boats were dodging about among the inshore rocks on which were several towers, and no doubt they belonged to Port du Guilvinec or Guénolé, but neither of those places appeared to be at all suitable for a stranger.

Not until the evening did a breeze make and take us round the corner into the Anse de Benodet, and just as it was growing dark I slipped into Loctudy and brought up where the anchor is shown on Admiralty chart 3645. But the strong tide made that berth an uneasy one, so I got under way again and moving farther to the N., brought up by the lead in one of the pools where there is sufficient water. The little whitewashed village of Ile Tudy looked very foreign in the bright starlight.

The approaches to Benodet and Concarneau contain a great many rocky dangers, but so excellently are they marked that I experienced no difficulty at all in making my way across the bay to Concarneau, and there beat through the narrow passage into the inner harbour. But I had to make two attempts to get in, for on the first I met a Dutch coaster coming out, and as there did not seem to be enough room for both of us, I ran out and waited for her to get clear. As soon as I had rounded the high walls of La Ville Close, the inner basin opened out. It was a most colourful picture containing as it did a great fleet of tunny-men preparing for sea, some on legs with their bowsprits steeved up against the battlements, others lying afloat in closely packed tiers. I brought up in the S.W. corner where I thought I would be well out of the way, but the harbour master insisted that I must go alongside ; as a sewer was discharging from the wall against which he ordered me to lie, I made sail, and running out through the narrows again, brought up off the Mole de la Croix, an exposed berth if the wind should come onshore, but it appeared to be settled in the N.E.

I landed in the evening and explored La Ville Close, a most interesting fortified island town with massive gateways and battlements, and dark, narrow cobbled streets.

Although I had read many accounts of cruises to Brittany, I was unable to discover anyone who had visited the Bélon River which, with the Aven River, discharges its waters into a small bay 12 miles S.E. of Concarneau. As little known places have a great fascination, and as I would have to pass it on my way along the coast, I decided to explore it. *The Bay of Biscay Pilot* dealt with that neighbourhood in two short paragraphs only, while the chart, having a scale of one inch to the mile, was rather small, but it showed that the river had a bar which dried 3 feet exposed to the S.W. When I left Concarneau the wind, though squally, was still at N.E., and though the day was cold and grey, I could hardly have had more favourable weather conditions for my venture.

Skirting the coast, I passed inside low and grassy Ile Verte, and on arrival in the bay found a party of small black luggers in a tightly packed mass fishing in the middle of it. Then the sun came out, and at once I saw what a charming spot I had come to, its brightly coloured cliffs, woods and fields making a homely patchwork not unlike the Devon landscape.

The tide was at about half-flood as I started to beat in over the bar, sounding as I went and keeping closer to the southern shore to begin with as the chart indicated more water there. The depths, however, were fairly uniform, and even when I stood right across to the northern side I still got soundings of from 1½ to 2 fathoms. The bar appeared to be of sand and extended from the little bay on the south shore and just outside the river's mouth almost as far as the stone quay which is also on the southern side. There the water deepened and the channel was very close to that shore. From there on the deepest water was slightly to starboard of the middle of the river, the starboard bank being generally rocky and steep-to while sand and mud flats extended from the northern one. The water was so clear that the lead was no longer needed ; by looking over the side I could see *Wanderer's* keel and its shadow on the river bed ; I had only to watch until the two got close together and then put about—a simple and pleasant, but unorthodox method of pilotage.

A mile from the bar the river turned to the S.E., narrowed, and then widening again branched into two. I brought up in the narrows where there would be about 3 fathoms at L.W. There was not much stream, but tides were neaps. On both sides of my anchorage trees came crowding down to the water's edge ; on one shore lay three blue tunnymen almost ready for sea, and off the other several luggers rode at moorings close to a clean stone slip. That night the silence was profound, and broken only occasionally by the distant mournful baying of some dog.

I awoke at dawn to the sound of rain drumming on deck and the sighing of wind in the treetops. So far as I could make out from so sheltered a place there was a good deal of wind from about S.W. ; the glass had fallen heavily in the night and was still dropping, and delightful though the place was I had no wish to be weatherbound there, so I decided to clear out before the bar became impassable. But there would not be sufficient water over it until noon, and while I waited I prepared for a dusting ; I lashed everything, had a good meal and put a reef in the mainsail ; and then I shook it out again for I thought that in so short and hollow a sea as we were likely to encounter, it would be better to have too much canvas than too little.

At midday I weighed the anchor and started to beat slowly down the rain-swept river against the flood, getting completely becalmed every now and again. Halfway to the bar I met a reefed lugger scudding up the river ; as she passed her helmsman waved me back and shouted something which I could not understand. I acknowledged his wave, but carried on to see what the bar looked like, and found that although the seas on it were steep and curling they did not look dangerous and there was very little broken water, all of it well over towards the north shore. So I continued, and although once or twice a vicious little sea slapped *Wanderer* hard on the weather bow just as she was coming up to the wind, she did not miss stays, but it was with considerable relief that I felt the seas grow easier and knew that we were across the bar, and leaving that area of churned up sand astern I headed down the coast for Port Louis with the wind abeam and sheets eased.

That was a wet and most uncomfortable passage. The short sea was confused and quite out of proportion to the weight of the wind, which in the open was only about force 5, and I was glad when we got under the lee of Ile de Groix after two hours of it. But by the time we had reached West Pass, the main channel of approach to Lorient and Port Louis, the wind had increased again, and blowing against the first of the ebb, raised an alarming sea in which *Wanderer* sheered wildly as she rapidly overhauled a small red motor cruiser which was also running in. The motor boat had a party of seven or eight aboard, and as they were all sitting right aft in the open cockpit, there was so little freeboard left that I feared she might be pooped, so I hauled the mainsheet right in to reduce speed and remain near. But she got through the narrows safely, and following her in I brought up in the roadstead off Port Louis just within the harbour entrance and remained for three wet and windy days.

That berth is well sheltered from S.W. but there was sufficient tide to cause the yacht to sheer restlessly about, often with her stern to the wind, but as I could discover no better place on the chart, I had to put up with the discomfort and the rain which drove remorselessly down the companionway. The harbour was grey and depressing, and in such weather even the gay colours of the tunnymen looked farcical and faded like those of a third-rate circus, while the rust streaks from their chainplates caught the eye too readily. Ashore a sailmaker was at work on a topsail which he had spread out between the puddles in the main street, much to the inconvenience of the traffic, but even he had to give up when the sail became so hard and stiff that he could no longer force his needle through it.

In time the rain clouds rolled away, and *Wanderer*, under all sail to topsail, made a fast passage to Belle Ile. The N.W. wind was fresh and there was a heavy sea running, but the sun shone and the sail was a most exhilarating one. The topsail had to come in before we brought the Birvideaux abeam, where the breakers were dashing high against the glistening column of the lighthouse. Then rapidly we closed with Belle Ile, which looked like a proper deep sea island with its fringe of white foam and brilliant sea, and rounding Taillefer Point we found smoother water, but the good wind served us right up to the entrance of Le Palais harbour. There, shooting between the high stone walls, each crowned with a miniature lighthouse, I let go the anchor in the centre of that sun-drenched and surprisingly empty basin, having averaged 6 knots from anchorage to anchorage, a distance of 25 miles. Launching the dinghy at once, I ran out a warp to one of the heavy chains which hang down at frequent intervals along the northern wall, and hauled our stern to within a few feet of it as is the custom there.

A lighthouse tender, a disreputable crabber and a small party of sardine boats drying their pale blue nets, were the only craft in the avant port. But a day or two later a large fleet of crabbers from Audierne sought shelter in the harbour from a strong S.W. wind, and brought up in closely packed rows each side of *Wanderer* with not more than two feet of water between their sides and hers, but they were tightly moored and never touched her. When that evening the wind died away and the sky cleared the scene was very beautiful : the lighted doors and windows of the quayside cafés threw golden reflections on the water of the harbour between the stout hulls of the crabbers which lay in even rows, their rigging etched black against the sky, and over them loomed the massive shape of the citadel. A strong smell of French tobacco and a subdued hum of conversation drifted over the fleet.

I spent nearly a month cruising in the neighbourhood of Belle Ile, Quiberon Bay and the Morbihan, mostly with fresh to strong S.W. winds, and visited a great many amusing little places, at some of which I remained several days while my typewriter chattered late into the night. But a detailed account of my short day sails would be very tedious, so I will only mention one of the highlights of that most enjoyable time : my visit to the Vilaine River.

As I approached the bar late one afternoon, the wind freshened ; blowing against the last of the ebb it raised a very hollow sea, and I could well understand what it must be like in heavy weather when, according to the sailing directions, the seas break right across. The entrance is about a mile wide, and two sets of leading lights keep one in the best water ; the ebb had about an hour yet to run, and the least depth I found on the bar was 2 fathoms.

The anchorage just within the entrance looked uninviting with the wind and tide opposed, so I continued running up the river and was soon off the edge of the chart which only showed 6 miles of it, but I found it to be well marked with buoys and beacons. On we sped in the grey of the evening, our hissing wake streaming out astern to break on the glistening muddy banks ; farmsteads with their barns and ricks, cliffs and woods and little fields slipped quickly by, each corner rounded presenting a new and lovely vista. Many quiet anchorages presented themselves, tempting me to stop, but each time I had to go on to see what lay just round the next bend. Eventually, however, as the breeze seemed to be dying for the night, I brought up abreast a bed of whispering reeds near a fine curved bridge and an outcrop of rock behind which, almost hidden, crouched the little town of Roche Bernard.

. . . . .

That, I decided, would have to be the end of the outward trip if time was to be found to visit the Morbihan and some other places which I had passed by when coming down the coast. So I spent one day only in the Vilaine River, where we had got sufficiently far east to be on the same meridian as Weymouth, and then went to Penerf. With the aid of the sketch chart in *Yacht Cruising*, which is a most valuable companion for any cruiser on the Brittany coast, I found the entrance simple enough though one or two new beacons had been added.[24] But the anchorage off Cadenic village was most uncomfortable on the ebb with the fresh W.S.W. wind, and I thought so little of the place which looked so grey and dreary under a leaden sky, that I did not land, but sailed in the morning as soon as it was light enough to see, in company with the dawn-starting sardine boats. If only there had been a hint of warmth and colour in it the scene would have been most attractive as we crossed tacks with the outward bound fleet, their black hulls well heeled beneath their double lugs ; most of them were reefed, and although they all carried bowsprits none of them had jibs set. In the comparatively sheltered water of the harbour *Wanderer* had the legs of them and headed the entire fleet out of the harbour by way of the Plateau des Passes. But in the rougher water out at sea, while she pitched, the luggers strode steadily on, and though sailing fuller overhauled her rapidly in the short turn to windward to the Penvins buoy, as was only to be expected for they were of greater length. There our courses diverged, and while they continued to windward for their fishing ground, I skirted the off-lying rocks and made my way to the Morbihan.

I spent an entertaining week exploring that inland sea which, although it is only 10 miles in length, contains about 50 islands. Many of them are only flat rocks or patches of shingle, and the chart would have been of much greater assistance if the heights of the islands had been marked on it ; but as soon as I realised that the conspicuous pink house was on Ile Ar Gazek, the riddle of the islands solved itself. All the same I wished that I had obtained the large scale French chart of that place, but I managed without it and contrived to sail through most of the little channels without getting stuck. But tides in the Morbihan run very hard, particularly near the entrance, and many an anchorage that looked feasible proved to be impossible on that account. I visited the Auray River, the banks of which were lined for miles with oyster farms, limewashed tiles of a curious shape being used for their cultivation, and then sailed on to La Trinité, which is the recognised yachting centre of those parts, to pick up a friend who had come out to join me for a day or two.[25]

We spent a night under the lee of Ile Houat, then passing through the Teignouse passage had a quiet sail to Port Tudy on the N.E. side of the Ile de Groix. With great cunning we beat into that tiny walled harbour, but finding no possible berth in the avant port, which was tightly packed with tunny-men, we entered a basin which opened out to port, and crossing the bows of three very smart tunnymen, anchored just beyond them and took a stern line to the quay. Our neighbours proved to be regatta winners, which perhaps entitled them to lie apart from the common herd ; at low water, mid tides, they sewed a couple of feet, while little *Wanderer*, looking a pigmy thing beside them, lay afloat in just one fathom.

After tea we walked out to the end of the breakwater and watched more of the tunny fleet come sailing in, all of them carrying topsails and large jibs of many colours. It seemed that there could not possibly be room for any more, yet still they came, each forcing a berth for himself among his friends already there. It appeared that we had selected the one berth in which it would be possible to remain undamaged. We had a splendid dinner at the Hotel Marine at the top of the hill, and afterwards sculled round the harbour in the gloaming, reading names and

Tunnymen at Port Tudy, Ile de Groix

examining the colourful vessels at close quarters, until the after-glow of the sunset faded and it grew too dark to see.

We woke up in the morning to a very different scene. Hurrying grey clouds drove low across the sky from W.S.W., while savage rain squalls tore down upon the little harbour, and the wind sang shrilly among the masts and topped up fishing rods of the tunny fleet. The barometer had fallen half an inch in 20 hours, and not wishing to be there when the place became completely choked with craft, as it was said to do in bad weather, we left after breakfast with the idea of sailing to Benodet, 30 miles up the coast ; but as soon as we drew out from the lee of the island the yacht was almost overpowered by wind and sea, so we bore away for Port Louis where my crew unfortunately had to leave me, and there I remained for three dreadful days of westerly gales and rain.

The news I received on the radio each evening showed that the international situation was steadily worsening, and I thought that the sooner I could get round the N.W. corner of France and within easy reach of the English coast, the better. So when the wind backed to S.S.W., a beam wind for my purpose, I made use of it although it was still very strong, and had an anxious passage in a heavy tumbling sea with a lee shore close aboard to Benodet, where I found good shelter on the west side of the river abreast of the pink château. The fishermen on the quay thought that I had been very foolish and told me that the local steamer had been unable to make her daily trip to the Iles de Glenan, as there was too much sea for her even in the lee of the rocks and islands.

The passage round Penmarch and across the Baie d'Audierne was slow and tedious with a persistently heading wind, so that instead of reaching the Raz de Sein in the afternoon, I did not arrive there until 2 a.m. The south-running stream had just finished, so it seemed a pity not to make use of slack water to call at the Ile de Sein, which was one of the things I had planned to do while on the coast. I therefore determined to make the attempt dark though the night was.

There are three channels of approach to the roadstead off the N.E. side of the island, and two of them, the N. and N.E. channels, are indicated by white sectors in the red, white and green occulting light on the island. I chose the N.E. channel because it was the nearer of the two, but as I approached it the wind backed right round to S.W., compelling me to harden in the sheets and beat in. But as we progressed the white sector grew narrower and our tacks grew shorter, so that we seemed to be out of the white and into one of the coloured sectors before the yacht had properly gathered way. With a large scale chart it might have been possible to continue ; but I did not care to risk standing outside the safety sector with only the Admiralty chart, more especially as the wind was freshening and drizzle had set in, dimming the light which would be my only guide until I could find the unlit Nerroth tower where an alteration of course would be necessary. So I reluctantly bore away and ran out of the channel. The breakers on Tévénnec rocks showed grey and close for a moment as we swept past on the flood which by that time was running hard, and then in open water we stormed across the mouth of Douarnenez Bay with straining sheets and a phosphorescent wake.

Dawn found us in the Toulinguet Channel sailing almost blind with visibility reduced to about a quarter of a mile by sheets of driving rain. Camaret did not attract, for it offers an uneasy berth at any time, and the weather seemed to have taken a real turn for the worse, so although I was by that time wet and tired, I thought it worthwhile to continue through the Goulet de Brest, and by breakfast-time we were snugly at anchor close to the almost invisible shore in the Anse de Fret.

While the bad weather lasted I revisited some of my old anchorages in the Rade and explored the Chateaulin River for several miles beyond the suspension bridge and outside the boundary of the chart. There was some activity there among the laid up ships of the reserve fleet and in the naval harbour at Brest. With such reminders I did not linger when the weather improved, but at once beat out of the Goulet against a light W. wind, when *Wanderer* made such poor progress against the sea that was still running in, that I feared we might miss the tide through the Chenal du Four. It was therefore necessary to set the yankee, and before going to the bowsprit end to hank it on to the topmast stay, I backed the staysail so that the yacht might lie with the seas abeam. But in spite of that she worked round head to sea, and before I had completed hanking on she pitched sharply and washed me off the bowsprit, for rather stupidly I was kneeling on that spar in an attempt to keep dry instead of sitting astride it. I managed to retain a hold of the bobstay, and nearly had my arm pulled out as she rose quickly to the next sea, and then as she plunged once more she gave me a blow on the shoulder. So I let go, and dropping aft to the rigging scrambled aboard there where the motion was less wild. Then I got the sail set and we were soon down to Les Vieux Moines. There we picked up a fine S.W. wind which pushed us through the Chenal du Four at great speed ; we ran through several banks of fog, but none of them lasted long enough to cause any pilotage difficulties, and after we had cleared them there was too much wind for the yankee, so I replaced it with the No. 1 jib. We rounded the Four lighthouse in bright sunshine, encountered the usual vile seas off the Porsal, and then went tearing into L'Abervrac'h where there was some more fog produced by kelp burning on the shore. The leading marks were obscured, but I found the channel buoy all right and steered by compass for the Petit Pot de Beurre tower.

It was magnificent sailing as *Wanderer* smoked along at her maximum speed with the swell breaking white on the rocks each side, and the Pot de Beurre was soon abeam. There I altered course to S.E. by S., the second pair of leading marks also being invisible, and with lee rail buried we stormed up the channel and finally checked our mad career just below the stone slip off L'Abervrac'h, and at last I had a chance to look about me and see what sort of place I had blown in to.

It was a queer, grim spot. To seaward lay a maze of rocks and islands on which the seas were churning white, and the lofty tower of Ile Vierge light played hide-and-seek in the mist. Near at hand, and almost obscured in kelp smoke, was the little village. Although the wind was blowing off the land, and although we appeared to be cut off from the sea by the rocks, our berth was an uneasy one, so I moved a little farther up beyond the slip, and although that was a slight improvement I shall go round the next bend and have some real peace if ever I visit L'Abervrac'h again.

My arm and shoulder were bruised and stiff after the yankee

episode, so I remained a day at anchor, and had the pleasure of seeing *Fairlight* come sailing in and of dining with her company ashore.

The wind was still at W. but light the morning that I left. I passed out through the Malouine Channel, which, although only a cable wide between the rocks, is quite straightforward with the Sugarloaf and Pot de Beurre towers kept in line over the stern, and it saves one several miles if bound to the N. or E. Outside I set the masthead spinnaker for the first time on that cruise—the twin spinnakers were not used at all that summer—and had a pleasant run along the coast. In the evening I passed inside the Ile de Bas with a freshening wind—a passage which I would never willingly attempt again single-handed, for the pilotage there is a wholetime occupation—and having with great difficulty sorted out the rocks and towers in the approach to Morlaix, I brought up in the river near to the white mooring buoys off the Tour de la Lande. That is an isolated berth a long way from the shore, but I only intended to stop for one night. The Penze River, a little to the westward, offers a much more comfortable anchorage for a little vessel.

The morning was overcast and the W. wind strong, when at 11 a.m. under lower sail and small jib *Wanderer* hurried out of the harbour through the main channel, past the Château du Taureau to the Stolvezen buoy, and passing inside La Méloine shoal, on which the seas were spouting, headed for the channel inside Les Sept Iles. She was too early on the tide and rather over-canvassed, and as she ran she rolled heavily, often dipping several feet of her boom in the sea. Once or twice small crests toppled aboard over the stern, to stream along the side decks and pour out over the rails and through the scuppers amidships. Triagoz lighthouse was abeam at 2 p.m., and with the tide then in our favour the seas grew easier as we ran on inside Les Sept Iles, but we were running dead before the wind and rolling just as heavily as before.

The course for Crublent buoy off Tréguier was E. and with so much wind steering was by no means easy. Visibility was not more than a mile, and as the time to make the buoy approached I grew very anxious. But at 5 p.m. it materialised dead ahead in the most uncanny manner, and gybing I headed in towards the entrance of the river. The leading marks 4 miles away were, of course, invisible, and a heavy rain storm had obscured the red and black towers on the outer dangers, so for a few minutes I had to steer by compass and endeavoured to allow for the tide which was setting strongly athwart our course. But very soon the towers appeared through the rain ; we surged between them, rounded Petit Penir, and then lay close-hauled for La Corne lighthouse at the river entrance with lee deck buried and spray driving over all. A few short tacks brought us into smooth water, and with less wind under the lee of the land we fetched up the river.

Then at last the sun came out, and as I took off my oilskin, lit my pipe and guided *Wanderer* up that lovely river in the rain-washed evening light, I tasted once again the greatest joy which small boat cruising can offer : the satisfying contentment of a rough and anxious passage successfully achieved. Quietly we wound our way between the woods and fields, and finally brought up in the little bay below the town of Tréguier. Only the deep tolling of the cathedral bell broke the silence as I put the last tier round the mainsail and went below to prepare the evening meal.

I was ashore early in the morning to buy my last French loaf and vegetables in the busy little market where stalls had been set up around the cathedral. Then I took the dinghy aboard and glided away down the river with many a backward glance at the slender spire and the huddled old grey houses, until a bend of the river hid them from view. As the banks fell back on either hand and the tumbling sea opened out ahead, we felt the true force of the wind which was still fresh from a westerly direction. By noon La Corne was well astern, and off the outer-most buoy I streamed the log and set course for St. Martin's Point on Guernsey, 40 miles to the N.E. With the sea on the quarter and the sun shining brightly it was a jolly sail, but I had to watch my steering, for under her press of canvas *Wanderer* kept trying to edge to windward of her course. So long as I kept her heading N.E. she took little helm, but the moment I let her come up the smallest amount she would swoop right round with the wind abeam and cover herself with spray.

Hour after hour the spinning log registered 5½ sea miles, and it appeared that the boat was almost in as great a hurry to get home as I was. Our course should have passed the Roches Douvres at a distance of 3 miles, but when I sighted the lighthouse there it was a long way off, due no doubt to the fact that in spite of my care we had been sailing to windward of our course. So I steered a point more easterly and an hour later sighted the wedge of Guernsey faintly ahead. The sky then clouded over and the wind hardened, but at 8 p.m. we rounded St. Martin's and in smooth water reached up the coast to Peter Port where I anchored close to the other yachts in the S.W. corner of the harbour at 8.30.

Next day the Customs called to look among the potatoes for Colorado beetles, but finding none left me to do as I liked, so I went ashore and there had the good fortune to run across Max Barber. He wanted a passage to England, and I was delighted to have a crew for the last leg of my voyage after so much lone sailing, so we left the harbour at 9 p.m. But as we approached the Race of Alderney the wind headed us and freshened to such a degree that I did not care to attempt to beat through it with wind and tide opposed, Accordingly we put about and stood out towards the Casquets, but found such a steep and dangerous sea running, that we turned and ran ignominiously back to Peter Port where we arrived at 2 a.m., having had a particularly unpleasant time in the overfalls off Platte Fougére.

But our next attempt was more fortunate. The wind had backed to W.N.W. and had moderated when we left the harbour at 9 a.m. under all sail to topsail and yankee. We passed through the Race of Alderney, where there were only a few small overfalls and tidal swirls, and at 12.50 p.m. took our departure from Alderney lighthouse which bore S.W., 5 miles. With the intention of calling at Studland Bay or Poole we steered N. by E.¾E. for Anvil Point, so as to be a little to windward of the course in case the wind should veer.

It was perfect sailing over a large but regular sea ; the sky had cleared, and with the wind abeam *Wanderer* was just able to carry full sail. With her lee rail down and sheets well eased she drove ahead at speed for England. As each deep blue sea with its sparkling crest advanced upon her, she mounted smoothly up its leeward side, paused for a moment on the summit and then slid gently down into the trough beyond. Aloft the sun cast a delicate tracery of rigging shadows on the dark brown canvas and the cream curves of the yankee, while cumulus clouds of dazzling white sailed majestically across the sky. We took it in turns to steer, and steering was fun. There were moments, particularly when on the crests, when the little yacht showed a strong desire to turn and face the wind and sea, moments when firmness, understanding and an ability to anticipate her movements were required to hold her steady on the course. But Max was a first-rate helmsman, and I had no misgivings about leaving him in charge on deck while I prepared some food.

After tea the wind increased a little, so I took in the yankee and set No. 1 jib, and from then on our speed increased from 6 to 6¼ knots, and we kept that speed up right across to Anvil Point, where we picked up the east-going tide to help us round the corner past Peveril Ledge and Swanage. The white cliffs of Standfast Point were gleaming palely in the moonlight as we rounded Old Harry and slipped in to the calm water of Studland Bay. There, close under the bulwark of the land, the shouting wind that had served us so well that day was hushed to a gentle whisper as we let the anchor go at 10 p.m.

As I wrote up the log after dinner that night I glanced back over the times and distances of the more recent passages of the cruise, and I discovered that since leaving Brest *Wanderer* had never averaged less than 5½ knots, while that last cross-Channel sail had turned out to be the best of all—6.3 knots from anchorage to anchorage. Of course the strong fair tide in the Race of Alderney had raised the figure a little, but from our departure off Alderney to our landfall off Anvil Point we had averaged 6 knots. It was the fastest passage that the little vessel has ever made at sea.

The next morning we sailed swiftly to the Solent, cleared Customs at Lymington and then moored *Wanderer* in Beaulieu River after a cruise of 1,500 miles. A fortnight later war was declared.

CHAPTER XIV

THE NEW DYARCHY

DURING the war I had got married, and the thing Susan and I wanted to do more than anything else was to fit out *Wanderer II* and have a gentle unambitious cruise in her along the southern coasts of Devon and Cornwall—a sort of honeymoon cruise. But our wartime occupations did not finish until the summer of 1945 was well advanced, and as much work would be needed to get the yacht ready for sea, we reluctantly had to postpone her launching until the following year.

But Roger Pinckney had organised things better and had managed to fit out his new *Dyarchy*, so when he and his mother asked us to join them for the same sort of gentle cruise as we had been planning, and to the same cruising ground, we accepted gratefully, for we had both sailed with the Pinckneys in our single pre-war days and wanted to repeat that pleasure.

Dyarchy (the name of the old pilot cutter was retained when she was sold) was designed by Laurent Giles & Partners, was built in Sweden just before the war and is the finest vessel of her size that I have ever seen. Her colour scheme—black topsides with a wide rubbing strake of varnished oak—her bold and sweeping sheer, her powerful overhanging bow with its rounded sections and upthrust bowsprit, her transom stern with its marked tumble-home, and the perfect proportions of her gaff rig, all combine to give her a rakish, almost piratical appearance. Dark-coloured vessels always seem to be more slender and delicate than they really are, and from a distance *Dyarchy* looks a fairy, lissom creature ; not until one has gone alongside, climbed over her bulwarks and stood on her wide clear deck, does her strength, sturdiness and size become fully apparent.

Although she has been compared with her predecessor on more than one occasion, the new yacht has practically nothing in common with the pilot cutter except a transom stern and gaff rig ; the old boat's forward waterlines were hollow and the

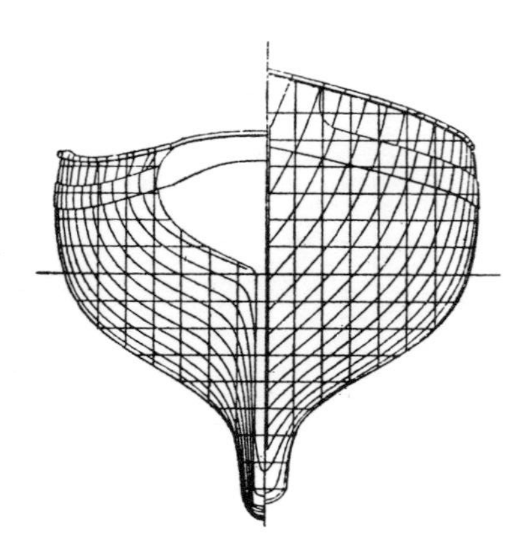

Lines and sail Plan of *Dyarchy*.

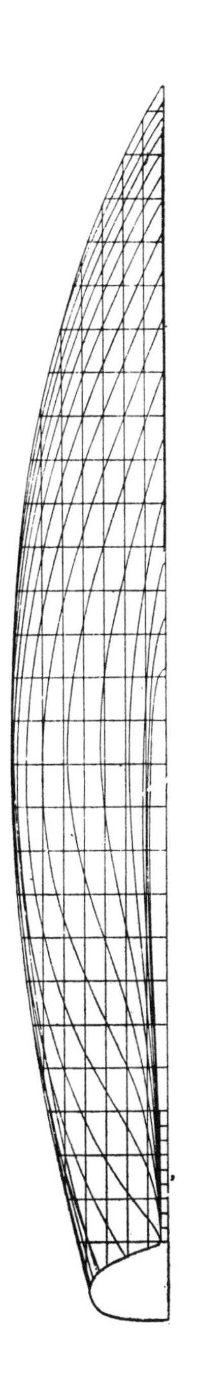

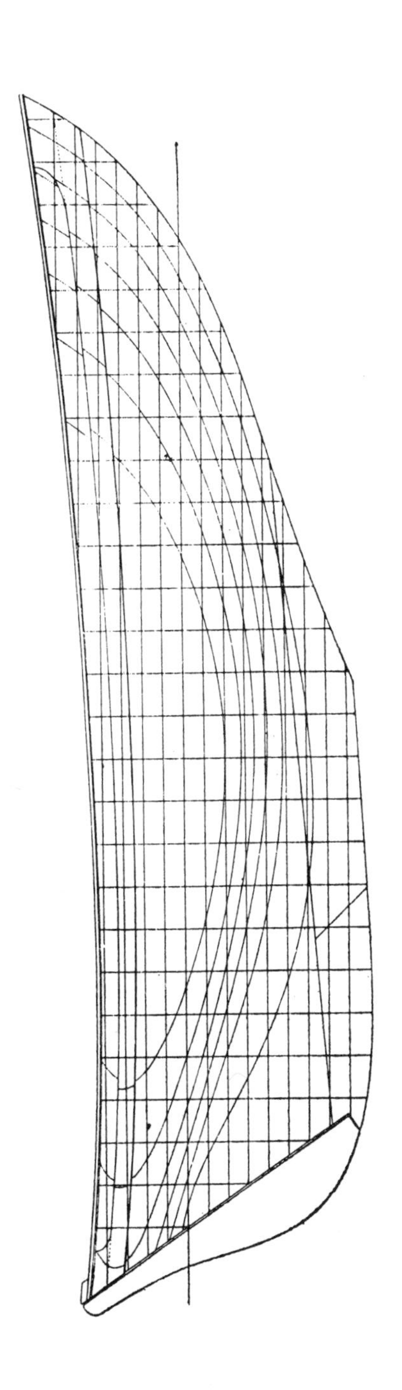

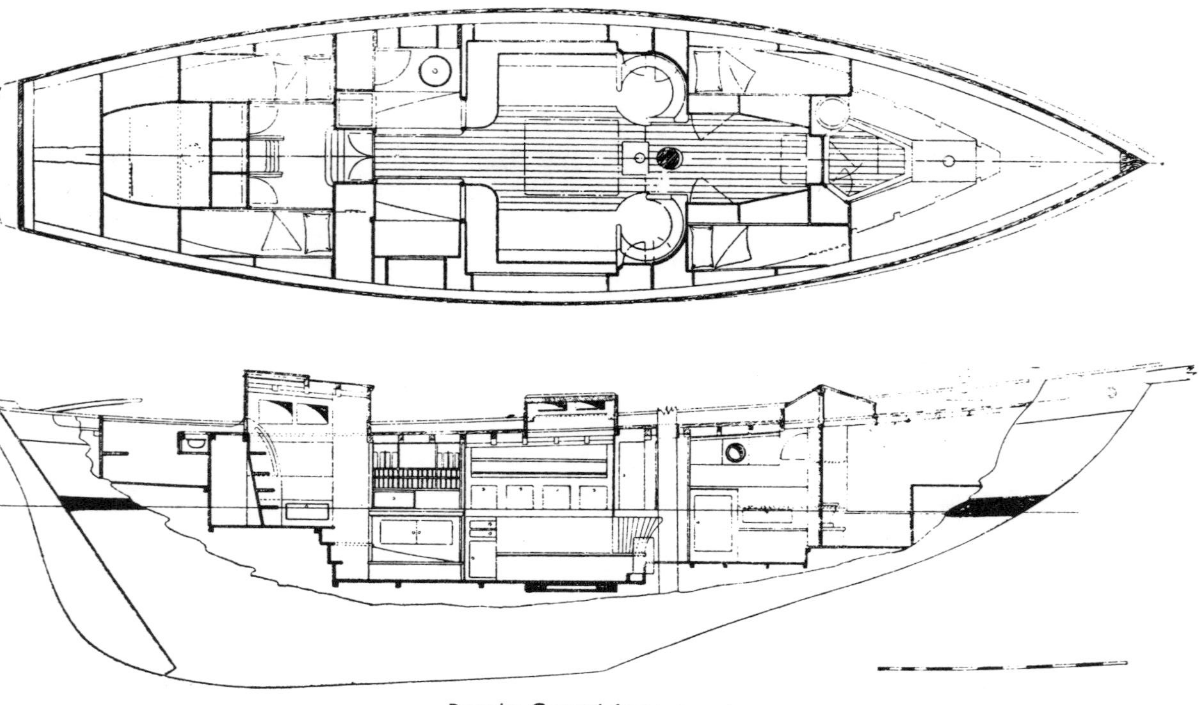

Dyarchy, General Arrangement.

midship section U-shaped ; the new boat has more rounded graceful lines with no suggestion of a hollow or even of a flat forward, and her sections are a masterpiece of curved harmony. She measures 46 feet 6 inches overall, 38 feet on the waterline, has 12 feet 3 inches beam and draws 7 feet 6 inches of water. Her iron keel weighs 9 tons, but as she was found to be too light aft, half a ton of lead was taken aboard shortly after her launch, and more was added later as she was still inclined to kick her heels. That extra ballast, about one ton in all, has since been inserted in the deadwood. There is now no inside ballast, so that in spite of her heavy displacement of 21 tons, 10 tons is on the keel. I am sure that no cruising yacht ought to float on her marks when launched, for bit by bit a good deal of extra gear in addition to stores and water is added to put her down, and it is far more satisfactory to ship ballast as may be necessary than to have to remove something from the keel or paint in the waterline higher year by year as some people have to do. Except for the Oregon deck and western red cedar fittings below, construction is entirely of oak.

The gaff cutter rig of 1,350 square feet suits the ship well, and because it has been properly thought out and modernised, it is efficient. All the standing rigging is of 19 strand Fairlight wire which cannot be spliced and is fitted instead with bronze sockets, the wire being splayed out in the taper of the sockets where the strands are kept apart by a special metal filling so that the join retains 100 per cent of the strength of the wire. The halyards are also of wire, those for the jib and staysail leading to small winches, while peak and throat halyards have tackles on their standing parts, thus saving weight windage and stretch aloft. The working jib is set on a stay which can be run inboard for hanking the sail on and is set up automatically by the halyard. The topsail arrangements are quite unique ; two-thirds of the luff of that sail runs in a groove formed on the mast above the upper peak band ; a small traveller, through the centre of which the halyard is rove, runs freely in the groove to centre the halyard and lead the head of the sail into the groove as the topsail goes aloft. Preventers and runners are set up simultaneously by massive levers each side of the cockpit, but because of the great strain imposed on them the blocks and other fittings in connection with that gear have had to be strengthened considerably. Appledore reefing gear is used on the mainsail, but so powerful is the ship that only on a few occasions has it been necessary to reef, and her topsail, like that in all other Laurent Giles designed gaff rigged yachts, is a working sail and is regarded as the first reef.

Dyarchy soon showed herself to be an efficient sailer, fast and weatherly. On her maiden voyage she sailed 1,300 miles in 23 days, 300 of them dead to windward without a stop, and Humphrey Barton sailed her 1,500 miles in 27 days when he brought her home from the Baltic.

Her accommodation is unusual for a 27-tonner in that it was originally designed to sleep only four people, for her owner had once sailed to Spain in his old ship with a party of seven, and he decided that was three too many. But in fact the settees in the saloon can be used as bunks in case of necessity as they extend beneath the sideboards at their aft ends, and they have been used too often to be kept a secret any longer. The general arrangement is as follows: The deep self draining cockpit has the helmsman's seat across its aft end and a wide bridge deck, in which is housed the compass, at its forward end. From this a flight of easy steps leads down into the deckhouse which has a bunk each side and lots of lockers; beneath its floor is installed a 10-17 h.p. Albin petrol auxiliary engine driving a folding propeller under the quarter, giving a top speed of 5½ knots and a continuous cruising speed of 4½ knots; it also charges the battery for the navigation and cabin lights. Three steps down and the galley with sink, larder and Calor gas cooking stove is to port, the chartroom and oilskin locker balancing it to starboard. These compartments are not bulkheaded off from the central alleyway or from the saloon, but each has a flat-topped wooden rail at the right height to form a seat for cook and/or navigator. The saloon has sideboards at its aft end, two settees, an enormous armchair built in each side of the mast, a Courtier stove and plenty of lockers and bookshelves; the table collapses into the floor. Tanks to hold 100 gallons of water are fitted beneath the settees and under the cabin sole. Forward of the saloon, and separated from it by part bulkheads and a curtain, is the double cabin with its own skylight and a door into the forepeak, which contains a w.c., chain locker and racks for sails. A 10-foot 6-inch pram dinghy, with enormous carrying power and stability, stows capsized over the skylight, its bilge keels being shaped in the form of handrails for convenience when going forward at sea. Prismatic deadlights let in sufficient, if somewhat subdued, light when the skylight is covered.

The topsides and bottom planking is close seamed without caulking, as is the Scandinavian practice, and it was only to be expected that they would leak when *Dyarchy* was launched from her wartime berth ashore ; but those responsible never thought to treat them with soft soap or pump the yacht out, with the inevitable result that she sank. Fortunately that happened in shallow water ; it did little damage beyond putting the engine out of action, and for the 1945 summer cruise we were without auxiliary power. A brief account of that cruise may therefore be of some interest in showing that, although an engine is a very great convenience and a help in keeping to a set timetable, it need not be regarded as essential in a handy vessel even when she is working in and out of narrow places.

We joined *Dyarchy* at Lymington on the 21st July. Her mooring was a long way down towards the mouth of the river, for with the necessity of keeping the fairway clear for the Railway steamers, there is no berth available farther up in which she could lie afloat. She was too far away for convenience, so Roger Pinckney and I sailed her up the river with a moderate west wind and ran her on the mud opposite the Royal Lymington Yacht Club. There we spent the afternoon loading gear and stores, and embarked the rest of the party, Mrs. Pinckney, Susan and Morrice McMullen.[26] We floated off the mud towards high water and in the evening sailed down the river and picked up the mooring again for the night.

Next day was fine and sunny with a fresh W. by N. wind. We got away at 9.30 a.m. under lower sail and fetched out of the Solent and down the Needles Channel on the starboard tack. Clear of the land we found a slight sea running, just steep enough to have knocked some of the way off the average yacht, but *Dyarchy*, heeling only a little, forged her way to windward with never a pause, her powerful bow turning over a great foaming bow-wave and trampling it under foot before it had a chance to climb up over the weather bulwarks, and only occasionally did a tiny wisp of spray flick up over the rail. Except for a small patch forward of the rigging, her steady deck was dry, and one could lie on it well out of the wind in the lee of the bulwarks.

That was a new experience for Susan and me. In the small boats to which we were accustomed, windward work was usually a wet struggle, and always a slow and uncomfortable business. But now we began to see that there was something in " a good thrash to windward " in a really able and sizeable ship, a satisfying feeling of achievement and delight in the powerful, thrusting progress as the miles streamed effortlessly away astern, and the wind hummed a steady note in the rigging.

At 1.30 we tacked, and fetching into Weymouth Bay at tea-time, we beat into the harbour. There is not over much room there, and the wind was uncertain, but *Dyarchy* did not appear to mind the difficult conditions, although there was one anxious moment when we lay without steerage way in such a position that we might have fouled the quay, for in common with all deep heeled vessels with little grip of the water forward, her head will pay off when a puff catches her without steerage way. But she wriggled cleverly up the harbour without incident, and we made fast alongside the quay by the town where we remained for two nights and a day and rove off some new halyards and did a little varnishing. We also started to scrape the surplus glue from the decks which had recently been payed.

It was easy enough to leave Weymouth with a moderate west wind. We simply cast off from the quay, pushed the ship's head off with the boathook and setting the yankee spun her round on her heel and set the rest of the canvas as we ran out of the harbour. At 11.15 a.m. we beat past the pitch of the Bill in short tacks close inshore, but there was little smooth water there, and the race which was only in playful mood that day boiled and roared all round us, but no water came on deck. Then on the port tack we stood up the west side of Portland peninsula, but as we proceeded the wind conveniently backed and allowed us to sail on that tack right round the curve of West Bay. The sun shone, the sea was smooth, the coast looked very jolly away to starboard, and we all thoroughly enjoyed the easy conditions ; this, we said, was exactly what we had been

The new *Dyarchy*

waiting for and looking forward to throughout the long war years.

During the afternoon the wind slowly dropped and at 6 p.m. we lay becalmed close to Exmouth Bar buoy which occasionally clanged its bell in an idle, sleepy sort of way. While Susan peeled the potatoes Morrice set about catching some fish for the evening meal and Roger went below to sort out the folios of charts ; presently he came on deck with the interesting news that through some oversight there was not a single chart on board of the waters west of Portland. We supposed that did not matter very much for we all thought that we knew those waters well enough, but it was not long before we started to disagree as to which of the points to the S.W. of us was Berry Head, a matter of some importance as we were bound for Brixham where Morrice would have to leave us. At 8 p.m., however, there came a nice northerly breeze and we made off in approximately the right direction. Presently the light on Berry Head began to flash and settled the arguments, and at 10.30, in brilliant moonlight against which the sails glowed a luminous pale pink, we entered Brixham Harbour and picked up a trawler's mooring, for we did not care to anchor on a bottom known to be foul with heavy chains.

The day we left was overcast and cold with poor visibility and a moderate N.N.E. wind. Under all sail to topsail we fetched out of the harbour, and having rounded Berry Head, ran down the coast towards the Start, but as we were still without a chart and were inclined to edge away from the land, nobody was very surprised when the point did not materialise, and not until we had gybed and headed in a more westerly direction did it appear quite suddenly and very close through the drizzle. We then had a swift sail along the coast to the Prawle where we encountered a very strong squall, in which the ship simply stormed along for a minute or two ; I had never before travelled at such speed under sail. Crossing Salcombe Bar to the eastward of the leading marks where there was ample water, we fetched right in to North Sand Bay, and then beat up the estuary against the ebb. Neither the buoy marking the Wolf Rock nor the beacons on the Poundstone and Old Harry were in position, but no difficulty was experienced on that account and at lunch time we brought up in the Bag.

Salcombe, as I have mentioned elsewhere in this book, is not the easiest of places for a sailing vessel to enter or leave because of the squalls and calm patches which are almost invariably encountered at the entrance, and it was therefore very interesting to see how easily and surely *Dyarchy* managed, and not once did she show any hesitation in going about.

At Salcombe Mrs. Pinckney had to leave us for a spell, and we missed her very much when, having done some shopping and collected the missing charts for which Roger had wired at Brixham, we sailed away. A faint air from N. wafted us down to the bar, and there we lay becalmed for a time until a light breeze made from W. enabling us to beat slowly along the coast and across Bigbury Bay to the entrance of the Yealm. There used to be two good pairs of leading marks to take one over the bar in the best water, but we could see no sign of them, and then, just as the wind came ahead, we touched bottom and stuck. On careful investigation we could just make out the green painted posts to which the leading marks used to be attached, and found that we had touched exactly where their lines intersected, where one has to turn a little to the northward off the first pair on to the second pair. But the tide was making, so we soon floated off and with uncertain airs beat into the river where a passing motor boat kindly towed us to a mooring beyond the landing place on the south shore. (The leading marks have since been replaced.)

The evening was perfect with bright sunshine, so the three of us landed and walked along the footpath to Wembury Church, the winding river with its steep wooded banks looking very lovely. There is something so peaceful and friendly about those West country rivers on which the war has left no visible mark, that I for one would be quite happy to visit them every year and never go farther afield.

The following day we finished scraping the deck, and very smart it looked after it had been scrubbed with bathbrick. But bare decks need a lot of attention if they are to be kept in good condition, and much though I like their appearance and the feel of them beneath my bare feet, I think that if ever I own a ship with a bare deck I shall paint it.

As it was necessary for Roger to return to his home for a day or two, it was decided that Dartmouth with its good railway service would be the most convenient place from which to do so, so we left the Yealm bound for the Dart in the morning. Having set all sail to topsail and yankee, we slipped from our buoy, and with the lightest of airs, mostly from a westerly direction, beat out of the river against the flood. That was an extraordinary achievement for so large a ship, as the fairway is narrow and much blanketed by the high surrounding land, but *Dyarchy* ghosted along so well in the calm patches that not once did a puff catch her without steerage way. It is not until one has sailed of necessity without an engine that it is possible to realise what can be done under sail alone, though as we were to see that evening an engine can sometimes save one a good deal of tedious and abortive work.

As soon as we had cleared the entrance we set the genoa in place of the yankee and stood away with a nice S. breeze for Bolt Tail, but by noon were almost becalmed and not until after dinner did we pick up a N.E. wind off Salcombe. At 9 p.m. we tacked off the Start, and laying up the coast inside the Skerries Bank were off the mouth of the Dart by 11 p.m.; the wind freshened there, so we handed the genoa and setting the working headsails started to beat in. The entrance has good leading lights with coloured sectors, but the white sector, in which it is necessary to keep, grew very narrow as we progressed, and our tacks got shorter and shorter. Abreast of the castle the wind became fluky, as it always does just there, and the ebb was against us, but we managed to work up as far as the Kingswear railway pier which we were quite unable to weather as the wind had almost died. So we drifted back over our hard won ground, and having made two fruitless attempts to reach one of the large mooring buoys off Warfleet Cove, we anchored inside them at 2.30 a.m., all of us feeling a little tired and rather cross at having failed to reach our objective by so narrow a margin. Leaving the mainsail and topsail set, we turned in until 6.30 a.m. when we got the anchor and with a moderate N. wind beat into the river and moored with bower and kedge just above Philips yard off the mouth of Mill Creek.

The fine weather continued, and for three days Susan and I acted as ship-keepers, eating and sleeping, bathing and drifting about the river in the dinghy. It was our first real holiday for several years and we idled our time away most happily.

On 3rd August, with Mrs. Pinckney and Roger aboard once more, we left under all sail and beat out of the river with some difficulty against a light S. air, for once again we had the tide against us and in an attempt to cheat it we stood in a little too close to the Royal Dart Yacht Club, and touching bottom were held there for half an hour. We cleared the entrance at 12.30, but finding so little wind outside we did not get round the Start until late that night. An occasional air stole out to us from the shore, but the land breeze, which in such fine weather we felt sure of getting, never materialised. At 7.30 in the morning, when we were off Bolt Tail, the destroyer *G 72*, commanded by Maurice McMullen's brother, circled round and spoke to us. In her new light grey paint she looked very fine in the morning sunshine. At 10 a.m. we got a light E. air to which we set the spinnaker, but throughout the day it slowly veered so that the spinnaker had to be replaced with the genoa, and by 8 p.m. we were heading almost into Fowey. But then the wind came away good and fresh from N.W., the first breeze with any heart in it that we had had for more than a week ; after passing the Dodman we had to take the genoa in and set the working headsails and then stormed along towards Falmouth.

I experienced then for the first time *Dyarchy's* one unpleasant habit, the lee helm which she carried on certain points of sailing when the wind was fresh. It was an uncomfortable feeling for those who are accustomed to the weather helm which most yachts carry and made it very difficult for a new helmsman to get the feel of her. She was as near to being perfectly balanced as it is possible for any vessel to be, which possibly accounted for the lee helm, and the manner in which she would steer herself and hold a steady course without the helm being lashed when running, was quite uncanny, yet she would not sail herself to windward at all. Since then, however, the lee helm has been cured by raking the mast as far aft as possible and by setting the jib 9 inches in from the bowsprit end, alterations which have also affected windward sailing, for the ship can now be persuaded to sail herself close-hauled, though she is very sensitive and will not do so if her crew move about.

It was very dark as we rounded St. Anthony and beat into Falmouth Harbour which we found to be crowded, so Susan went forward to keep a lookout, Roger steered and I attended the headsheets, by no means a difficult job although there were no winches. I was indeed glad that the responsibility was not mine as *Dyarchy*, rapidly overhauling a small motor-boat, hurried along, threading her swift way between the anchored ships and sometimes shooting head to wind when she encountered a sudden obstruction. But Roger handled her superbly, and at 11 p.m. the anchor was let go off the yacht club after a very interesting sail of 66 miles which had taken us nearly 38 hours.

We awoke to a brilliant sparkling morning with a fresh N.W. wind, and having got water and papers ashore, we sailed about in the harbour and then reached across to the Helford River. The destroyer who had spoken with us the previous day was running trials in Falmouth Bay, and the 75-foot M.F.V., whose job it was to keep the course clear, came tearing after us with shouted instructions to get out of the way ; but she was quite unable to catch us as we were doing more than 9 knots. Meanwhile the destroyer was signalling to us with her searchlight ; the message, to which we could not reply except by waving our arms, read : " Good afternoon, *Dyarchy*."

We beat into Helford River which, except for a party of Mulberries moored on the bar, looked just as charming and unchanged as when last I visited it in 1939 ; we brought up off the entrance to Abraham's Bosom and remained for two days enjoying the hospitality for which that place is so well known.

G. 75 was still tearing round and round in the bay when we left, and the M.F.V. was still fussing, but we kept well out of the way of both of them. The N.W. wind soon freshened, but as it was offshore there was no sea, *Dyarchy* drove along at great speed and the roaring of her bow-wave was most remarkable. The favourite vantage point was right up in the eyes of her, where one could sit ahead of the bow-wave and watch it thundering away on the lee side. We wished to spend a night at Looe, a place none of us had ever visited by yacht, so as soon as St. Georges Island had been passed we went about and fetched in towards the harbour ; but we were too early on our tide, and as it would have been a very difficult manœuvre to beat in with so much wind blowing out through the narrow entrance, we abandoned the idea and stood on for Rame Head, bringing up in Cawsand Bay at teatime. That was a very pleasant anchorage and we spent the evening exploring the village, a new discovery for all of us, and found it most attractive.

We left the next morning with the wind still at N.W. but light, and as we sailed across Plymouth Bay firing on the big gun range started. It was most alarming, for the shots, which landed in the sea with tremendous splashes to starboard of us, appeared to pass right overhead. There was nothing we could do except sail slowly on and we were indeed thankful when we had placed the Mewstone between us and the shore battery. No doubt most yachts passing that way have the same nerve shattering experience, and they possibly can expect to receive little consideration, but the range also interferes with all shipping wishing to enter or leave Plymouth from the eastward and compels them to make a long detour out to sea.

In Bigbury Bay the wind died away, and for the rest of the day we only got a few light airs to take us to Bolt Head. There, as the ebb was just beginning, we crept into Salcombe Bay and had to drop the kedge for an hour to avoid being set on to the Eelstone. But an hour later a breeze made from N. and enabled us to beat into the harbour, but it died away before we had reached our desired anchorage, so we towed with the dinghy to one of the R.A.F. mooring buoys which at that time were still lying below the town, and made fast to it for the night.

From Salcombe we made a passage homeward to the Solent. Drifting slowly seawards we took threequarters of an hour to get clear of the harbour and then picked up a pleasant W.S.W. breeze and were off the Start by 12.15, where we set the spinnaker, streamed the log and steered E. to clear Portland Bill.

It was a brilliant day once more with a steady wind and smooth sea ; we had our meals picnic fashion in the cockpit where the wide bridge deck made an excellent table, and took only short spells at the helm, though the ship hardly needed a steersman so steadily did she run. At 7 o'clock that evening land was sighted on the port bow and at 8.30 Portland Bill was abeam. There the wind moderated and we ran into a confused lop which we hoped would go down as we dropped the Bill astern, but it persisted and there was a slight swell from S.W. so that the boom crashed and the sails slatted wretchedly. At 10.15, still in a vile uneasy sea, we picked up the light on Anvil Point, and handing the spinnaker, which we had carried on one side or the other ever since leaving Start Point, we headed in for it with the intention of bringing up in Swanage or Studland Bay for the rest of the night. But the strong inshore tide swept us away to the N.E., the sea grew calmer and the wind veered to N.W., so we continued for the Needles and as the flood had finished by the time we got there we anchored in Totland Bay. That is a very convenient place as it can be made by night just as easily as by day, even though the green light which Totland pier used to show has not yet been replaced. One can creep up on the edge of the Needles green sector where slacker water will be found on the ebb, and then stand straight into the bay, bringing up by the lead, for the bottom is clear of dangers. There is only a slight tidal stream in the bay.

Two days of our holiday were still left, so after breakfast we beat up the Solent with a light E. breeze, but getting becalmed off Newtown Creek we launched the dinghy and towed *Dyarchy* in to an anchorage there, returning to Lymington the following evening after a day sail in the Solent.

Although we could well have done with a little more wind, that had been one of the pleasantest of cruises, which was rather more than any of us had expected, for anything for which one has planned and to which one has looked forward for years rarely comes completely up to expectations. But the Pinckneys had not lost their magic touch, and the new *Dyarchy* had proved to be as happy a ship as the old one. I believe that she was the first yacht to sail from the Solent to the West Country after the war.

. . . . .

Having sailed in the old *Dyarchy* on several of her Easter cruises to Guernsey, when with almost unfailing regularity we used to leave Lymington at midnight on the Thursday-Friday night and eat our lunch in Peter Port, I was very keen to see whether the new ship would follow in the tradition of her predecessor. So in 1947, as Susan and I had not quite finished fitting out *Wanderer II* in time for Easter, we asked the Pinckneys with a little hesitation—for we knew that they already had a good and sufficient crew—whether they would take us with them, and, bless them, they said they would be delighted.

We joined the yacht on the Wednesday, a day earlier than usual. She was lying on the mud opposite the yacht club, handy to the landing place, and that evening when the rising tide had floated her upright and the stores had been put aboard, we weighed the kedge from the dinghy, got the bower, and under engine slipped down the river in the calm of the evening. There was no wind in the Solent except that of our own making, so we anchored off Jack-in-the-Basket, and having attended to a few last-minute jobs such as reeving the headsheets we turned in.

In spite of the self-invited guests the yacht did not seem at all overcrowded. There was Roger ; his mother, a wise and calm old lady who celebrated her eighty-first birthday that year ; Joan Wood, who was as much at home aloft as she was on deck ; Hugo Duplessis, a keen hand and an excellent helmsman ; Susan, and myself.

At 10 o'clock next morning we made all sail to topsail and genoa and slipped down the Solent on the first of the ebb with a light S. wind. It was good to be sailing again after the bitter snowbound winter, but scarcely had we reached Hurst narrows, where the spring tide runs at 5½ knots, when a wisp of fog licked down over the island shore and obscured the Needles. It was followed at once by others ; they coalesced, advanced with speed, and before we had got Cliff End abeam everything was blotted out—no land, no buoys, nothing. Silently we slid along heading for the sound of the Needles foghorn which repeated its rasping note every 15 seconds, and very soon the Warden buoy loomed out of the fog ahead, clanged its bell as we passed close by, and quickly vanished again. After that we saw nothing at all. An invisible steamer passed to starboard groping her way up the channel, the Needles foghorn changed its bearing from ahead to abeam, and then at 11 o'clock, when it had dropped away on the quarter and we reckoned that we had given an ample berth to the wrecked Greek ship which lay on the Bridge close to it, we streamed the log, and the wind having backed a little, we were able to lay our course for Alderney, S.W. by S., a point free on the port tack.

By noon we had sailed out of the fog which, as we saw nothing of the Isle of Wight, must have been clinging only to the land. As the wind freshened *Dyarchy* settled down in her stride, but the day had turned grey with a cold rain, and all of us except the helmsman very soon went below, some to cluster round the stove in the saloon, while the more squeamish sheltered in the halfway sanctuary of the deckhouse from which they could conveniently visit the lee rail in a hurry when the urge came.

I, having eaten rather too many sausage rolls for lunch, was dozing by the fire in one of the armchairs, when a sudden loud crack startled me into wakefulness. Having farther to go I was, of course, the last to reach the deck, where I learnt that the bobstay had carried away. Considering that the genoa was set at the time, it seemed remarkable that the bowsprit had not carried away as well, but although that spar bent upward a little, it took no further notice of its lack of support. Without delay the genoa was handed and bundled down below, the chain bobstay, which was whipping about from the cransiron, was secured and the staysail was set. The loss of a bobstay is the sort of thing that may happen to anyone, *Latifa* carried hers away during the Bermuda race of 1938, but it is interesting to reflect that it is nearly always a shackle, rigging screw, or some other fitting that parts under strain, and very rarely the actual wire, rod or chain. And so it was on that occasion ; the shackle securing the bobstay's lower end to the stem fitting had broken, and that was a new shackle fitted only a few days before.

By then the wind had increased considerably, and *Dyarchy* seemed to be getting along just as fast without her genoa ; but she was carrying some weather helm, and would no doubt be easier to steer with a small jib set. Although her overhanging bow made it almost impossible to reach the frequently submerged stem fitting, Roger, with the aid of his mother's walking stick and great cunning, did eventually manage to get the hook of a tackle into it ; but just as the jury bobstay was ready to be set up, the hook shook free, and as by then both he and I were soaked through with surprisingly cold sea water, the attempt was abandoned.

There was no further excitement until 4.30 p.m. when the lee staysail sheet carried away. But that had been expected for it was a very old one, and in anticipation the weather sheet had been belayed. Without any bother a new sheet was rove and then, as most of us were already on deck and rather wet, and as the wind, now backed to S.E., had freshened even more, it seemed a good opportunity for getting the topsail down.

The novel method of setting that sail has already been described on page 183. It is an excellent arrangement and has proved to be thoroughly satisfactory in many miles of sailing, but to my old-fashioned way of thinking it has one drawback : without any sort of leader there is nothing to keep the sail close to the mast as it comes down, once its luff rope had left the mast groove. However, as that sail had been up and down countless times without the slightest trouble, a leader would appear to be unnecessary.

Roger took the helm ready to bear away a little when the time came to keep the topsail pressed against the mainsail as it was lowered, Joan and Hugo tailed on to the tack to pull the thing down while I took the turns of the halyard and sheet off their pins and started to ease away handsomely. Then something went wrong. The sail, having started to come down, jammed. Joan came to my aid and gave a swig on the halyard which freed it, and then that sail went mad. As soon as its luff had slid out of the groove, instead of nestling snugly against the mainsail as it should have done, the thing took charge and blew away aft like a kite, swaying from side to side and jerking furiously at its three tethered corners. With devilish ingenuity it flicked its halyard round to leeward of the gaff and beat the leach of the mainsail as though determined on its destruction. I could do nothing to help get it down as I dared not let the sheet or halyard run, and in order to get the halyard round to weather of the gaff again, Roger had to bring the ship up into the wind. Just as he did so the topsail threshed its sheet undone—it was made fast with a cliphook—and emptied of wind the combined efforts of Joan and Hugo got it down on deck, but not before it had flogged one of its cloths to ribbons, split a seam and badly mauled its clew. The loose sheet, meanwhile, had tied itself in a clove hitch round the topsail halyard.

I thought at the time, and I still think that the responsibility for that disaster was entirely mine ; either I slacked away too fast, not fast enough or at the wrong moment ; but I still do not know which, for Roger, instead of cursing his inefficient crew as he had every right to do, wiped the spray from his beard and said the fault was his.

Without her topsail *Dyarchy* felt easier, but she did not slacken her pace, and at 5.45 p.m., having covered 49 miles in 7 hours, land was sighted on the weather bow. That proved to be Alderney, and as it seemed doubtful whether we would be able to fetch Alderney Race, it was decided to go through the Ortac Channel instead, provided that daylight should last long enough.

That passage, which lies to the west of Alderney and Burhou, is wide and quite simple so long as the Ortac—a remarkable rock 79 feet high with almost vertical sides—can be seen. Although we were sailing at nearly 9 knots dusk was upon us by the time we had brought Verte-tête abeam, having lost the starboard bow nameplate—a piece of beautifully carved oak—in the heavy seas on the Pomier Shoal ; but we experienced no difficulty though it took us nearly an hour to get through the channel against the spring flood. The sea running there was particularly steep and uncomfortable, and every now and again a deluge of spray drove across the deck and cockpit.

Conditions generally were far from pleasant. We were all wet and a dollop of spray had come through the unlatched skylight to soak the lee settee, while through the grating in the alleyway one could hear the bilge water sluicing to and fro as the ship lurched. But none of us cared much about those things for we all knew that we would be in shelter very soon.

For a time we sailed blind in driving rain, but presently the light on Platte Fougère appeared comfortably under the lee bow, and we began to feel the shelter of the rocks which lie to the N.N.E. of Herm, as we entered the Little Russel and brought the excellent leading lights into line. Having passed the Roustel light we sailed quite suddenly into a patch of furiously jumbled sea. The motion was violent in the extreme ; the ship plunged, cascades of water seethed along the lee deck, and several times she actually lost steerage way, an almost unheard of thing for her. But all the time the tide, now in our favour, was carrying us towards the harbour of St. Peter Port, and at midnight we rounded the northern breakwater close-to, for the harbour master has a lookout hut there and generally asks the visitor where he has come from. But that night there was such a mist on his window from the warmth within, that although our white mainsail passed within only a few yards of him he did not see it, and a minute or two later we rounded up head to wind in the yacht anchorage and let go, having taken 14 hours and 10 minutes for the passage.

Dyarchy, therefore, had not improved on the old pilot cutter's time on that occasion, but it was obvious that she could easily have done so had she started three hours later and thus avoided the strong adverse tide when closing with the islands. The trouble with these modern ships is that they sail so fast as to upset one's old established customs.

Having disposed of a piping hot steak and kidney pie which Joan and Susan had ready by the time the gear had been stowed and all made snug on deck, we felt warm and well content, and turned into our bunks to sleep soundly in spite of the swell which found its way into the harbour.

Throughout most of Good Friday the rain poured down, the wind blew hard, the swell continued to roll in and no one felt very energetic ; but before breakfast on Saturday we motored into the Old Harbour in a gleam of sunshine and made fast alongside the quay where we filled the water tanks from a most convenient hosepipe. While we waited for the ship to dry out we renewed our acquaintance with the little town, which looked very much the same as in pre-war days, and did our shopping, receiving kindness and courtesy everywhere.

When we returned to *Dyarchy* she had already sunk far below the level of the quay and had taken the ground. We scrambled aboard by way of the ratlines which Mrs. Pinckney took well in her stride along with the rest of us, and having collected brushes and sea-boots, we dropped down over the ship's bows and were just in time to give her bottom a quick scrub before all the water ran away. Then we had lunch and afterwards painted one side of the bottom with undercoating and anti-fouling. With six paint brushes at work—Charles Kinnersley, a young Guernseyman, had joined us for that operation, and was just the right height to do all the more awkward bits under the turn of the bilge without bending—it took only an hour to get each coat of paint on, and *Dyarchy*, with her 7½-foot draught, presents a large expanse of bottom when one comes to paint her. A step ladder had been brought along from Lymington for convenience when painting in the waterline and was a very great help.

How delightful it always is to lie alongside in someone else's ship! There are no worries over the dinghy, each one of the crew can come or go as he or she pleases. And when at Guernsey what fun it is to walk along to the entrance of the Old Harbour, now hard, dry sand, and look up at the towering stone quays with which the ship was level when she entered the place only a few short hours ago. Then up into the town for cigarettes (duty free) and back on board in time for tea.

But in with the evening flood came a slight scend, just enough to jar and grind the yacht against the quay in spite of fenders, and although we laid out the kedge abeam to keep her off, the warp had to be slackened a little while before she was due to ground again, and not until her keel had settled firmly on the bottom at 11 p.m. did we get any peace.

On Sunday we turned her round so as to paint the other side of the bottom, but the rain, driven by a fierce S. wind, poured down all day and the bottom never dried. So we had to remain alongside for yet another day in order to complete the work, and then we motored away to the Outer Harbour.

Five other yachts belonging to members of the Royal Cruising Club were due to spend Easter at Guernsey, but the only one to arrive before we left was John Morris's *Mercy Jane*. She had been cruising on the Brittany coast and called in at Peter Port on her way home from Iles Chausey. In spite of the bad weather she had not spent more than 24 hours in any port, and although she was built as recently as 1939, she had no engine.

On Wednesday morning we started homeward bound with a moderate N.N.W. wind, but as we approached the Race of Alderney it fell light, heading us, and *Dyarchy* was sadly handicapped without her topsail which we had been unable to get repaired at Guernsey. We made one tack in the Race and brought Braye Harbour in Alderney abeam, but there the fair tide was beginning to slacken and our progress was so slow that

A view of *Dyarchy* from the bowsprit end, showing the wide clear deck and the high bulwarks

the engine was started to take us away from that neighbourhood and prevent us from being swept back into the Race.

The wind then died completely, and when Alderney had been dropped 10 miles astern, the engine was stopped, and for the rest of that afternoon, right through the night and all the following morning we were almost becalmed. Now and again gossamer airs came along and to them we set the spinnaker or genoa according to their direction, but none of them lasted very long, so as our time was getting short and food was running low, we made further use of the engine from time to time. During the night we took 2½-hour watches, one each, and the only need for a watch was to keep a lookout for steamers, one or two of which passed close by.

At 1.30 p.m. we made out the Needles ahead, and an hour later, just as a pleasant easterly breeze sprang up, the engine ran out of fuel. We at once set the genoa and had a delightful sail over a calm blue sea, and at teatime slipped close round the bows of the wrecked Greek steamer into the Needles Channel where the tide was ebbing, but by keeping well over in the slacker water by the island shore we made good progress. Even in the narrows the tide could not stop us, and we were soon slipping up Lymington River where we carried the genoa as far as the yacht club. There at dusk we anchored.

The passage home had taken 36 hours, and was one of the slowest that *Dyarchy* has ever made.[27]

CHAPTER XV

AN AUTUMN CRUISE

IN THE AUTUMN when days grow short and nights turn cold most people lay their yachts up for the winter, and that was what I had usually done with my boat before the war. But for many weeks in the summer of 1946, *Wanderer II* had swung idly at her anchors while Susan and I worked on our new yachting annual, and not until it had gone to press late in October were we free to take a short holiday.

We hoped to pay a brief visit to Devonshire, but we made no serious plans for a cruise as we quite expected that the weather would confine us to the Solent, but it was a quiet warm day when we took the dinghy aboard, weighed our muddy anchors, and with a light E. air beat slowly down the Beaulieu River on the first of the ebb. In the Solent the tide carried us amidst oily swirls towards Hurst narrows, and there for a little while we had to work at the sweep to avoid being swept upon the Shingles. A heavy swell running in from the S.W. was piling upon the shoaler heads in dark rollers with almost vertical advancing faces ; for a time each great wave appeared to remain poised as a precarious wall of almost overbalanced water; then a speck of white would appear on its head, spreading rapidly to left and right before the whole swell collapsed and rushed forward in a tumbling cascade with a roar which could be heard a long way off. It was not a pleasant spot near which to remain becalmed, but the ebb hurried us along, and faint occasional airs filled the yankee first on one tack then on the other to give a little steerage way. By 3 p.m we had passed out from between the Bridge and S.W. Shingles buoys, and were rolling about uncomfortably in the open sea, thankful to be safely there but wondering where we would get to, if we ever got anywhere.

An anchorage seemed desirable in such light weather, so we headed for Poole, but night was upon us long before the bar buoy had been reached, and as there was so little wind we decided to bring up in Studland Bay and continue to the westward in daylight. The sky was overcast, there was no moon, and we crept into the black cavity of the bay in total darkness, sounding as we went, and having reached the 3-fathom line we were just about to round up and anchor, when the dilatory breeze increased quite suddenly to a fresh N.E. wind, making Studland Bay a lee shore. So we hastily replaced the yankee with the working jib and beat back to the bar buoy. Not wishing to spend the night at sea, we shaped a course up Poole Swashway for a flashing red light which I assumed to be on the port hand buoy at the bend in the channel. All the other lights had vanished in a chill evening mist which had come with the freshening wind.

Susan went forward to keep a lookout for the unlighted buoys with which the sides of the channel are marked, and she soon reported one on our weather bow. That I felt sure must be a starboard hand one, but wishing to make quite certain, I put *Wanderer* about and headed for it, only to discover to my dismay that it was a port hand barrel buoy. Obviously something was wrong, so I continued right across the channel and fortunately found one of the starboard conical buoys. Again we went about, heading N.N.W., my intention being to keep to that side of the channel. We passed close to two more buoys, but then when no more appeared and the mysterious red flashing light, for which I dared not steer, was on the beam, I felt completely lost with no more lights in sight. A cast of the lead gave three fathoms, so we anchored, and launching the dinghy rowed away in her to investigate. We found that the red light was on a dolphin built on the training wall at the west side of the channel, though the chart, an old pre-war one, did not indicate such a light, and the *Nautical Almanac* avoided the issue quite simply by stating that as many lights had been discontinued, reduced in power, or modified in some way, the section dealing with them had not been included in the 1946, edition.

We find that the best way of getting about in our 7-foot pram dinghy is to sit on the centre thwart and take an oar each, but even so we had quite a hard struggle against the wind and the sluicing tide to return to *Wanderer*, whose riding light looked very distant and forlorn. We rested alongside her for a little while and then pulled away to the eastward where we eventually found No. 7 conical buoy. That definitely fixed our position well in the channel, and as the mist persisted we thought it best to remain there until daylight. Although the yacht rolled heavily there was no vice in the seas which were broken to a large extent by the Hook Sand to windward, but it was an anxious night nevertheless, and we would have done better to have remained at sea ; the wind freshened a lot at times and we kept a constant lookout for traffic, but nothing came near. At the first hint of dawn the mist thinned, we got our anchor and sailed into the harbour, bringing up in South Deep.

Ashamed though I am of it, I have related this pilotage error in some detail because it shows once again how very important it is to have up-to-date charts, or at least to correct the old ones from Notices to Mariners. That is a lesson which I thought I had learnt many years ago, but as I believed I knew the entrance to Poole so well from many visits in clear weather, I had not bothered about that particular chart. I have since learnt that the dolphin bearing the red flashing light was in position on the training wall before the war, and yet I could not recollect ever having seen it.

All day the wind hummed in the rigging, and in the afternoon we could no longer keep our tired eyes open, so we lay down for an hour's rest. But it was dark when we awoke, the cabin clock pointed to 7 o'clock and, bemused as we were by sleep, it was some time before we could decide which day it was or even whether it was morning or evening. Lethargically we got up, cooked and ate a meal, and at once turned in again to sleep soundly until daybreak. Apparently the office life we had been leading for the past few months was not the best preparation for cruising, and of course we were six years older since last we had knocked about in little boats.

We had an early breakfast and at 8.30 a.m. ran swiftly out of the harbour with all sail to topsail set to a moderate N.E. wind. The S.W. stream was just starting as we reached the bar, and the opportunity, as Susan said, was too good to be missed, so we decided to make for Brixham. Quickly we slipped past Old Harry, Anvil Point and St. Albans Head, and then with much more wind the topsail had to come in together with the No. 1 jib, and not until Portland Bill bore N. 5 miles at 1 p.m. did the wind ease sufficiently to allow the small jib to be set.

Under a low grey pall of nimbus we hurried along throughout the afternoon on a course to take us to Tor Bay, and every hour with perfect regularity the patent log recorded another 5½ sea miles. I was very glad that my single-handed days were over, for *Wanderer* would not steer herself on that point of sailing, and the wind was very cold. We took it in turns to steer and whoever was not on watch had the warm and comfortable cabin to shelter in, books to read and a glowing fire before which to sit. Because of the overcast sky night came even earlier than usual, and at half-past four we had to light the navigation lamps and were soon sailing in such utter darkness that one could not even see the horizon. The port light cast a blood red glow on the lee bow-wave, and the wake was alight with the pale green gleam of phosphorescence ; those little patches of illumination which we carried with us only served to intensify the blackness of the night.

By 8 p.m. I was growing anxious, for according to my reckoning Berry Head should be a bare 8 miles distant, but there was no sign of the flashing light upon it. I knew that visibility had grown poor, for the stern light of a steamer, which only slowly had overtaken us, vanished when she had drawn but a short distance ahead. Also the wind was increasing, and as it had veered almost to E. I thought that neither Brixham nor Torquay would offer us a comfortable anchorage.

But half an hour later, faint and orange through the mist, we made out the double flash of Berry Head light bearing W. by S. and we decided to make for Dartmouth. Then, in a sudden savage squall, the wind hardened, and without delay I worked my way forward along the slippery deck and pulled down the first reef. That had to be done by the sense of feel alone, and once again I blessed the foolproof simplicity of reefing in the old-fashioned way. Easing down the throat I got the cliphook (which I use for the tack instead of a lashing) into the reef cringle ; then, hauling on the reef tackle, which is always kept ready rove along the boom, I had the reef down in a few seconds, and was able to tie the points at my leisure, for as the sail is loose-footed the points do not take any strain and are only needed to tidy up the bag of hanging canvas at the foot of the sail.

As soon as that was done we gybed and headed S.W. by W. for the still invisible Start. The sea was surprisingly steep, and each crest made a great fuss as it came foaming up on the quarter with a phosphorescent gleam ; one of them tumbled into the cockpit on top of the helmsman and convinced me that we were still running a little too fast for comfort, so I handed the staysail.

Dartmouth is a safe harbour to make for in any weather provided the dead reckoning has been kept accurately. Nothing could be seen of the land, now drawing close under our lee, as we stormed along, but faintly in the sky we could just make out the loom of the town lights ; they spoke invitingly of peace and warmth.

Presently we picked up the welcome flash of the Castle Ledge buoy off the entrance, seen through the gap between the mainland and the Mewstone, but we continued on our course until it was on a safe bearing, then gybed with great care, for there was a lot of weight in the wind, and headed for it. At 10.30 p.m., in a welter of confused seas and flying spray, we rounded the buoy, at once got the leading lights in line, and steered for them.

I have entered that difficult harbour on many occasions, and I have learnt to expect that unless the wind has any south in it, it will blow straight out in squalls between exasperating patches of calm, and on one of her previous visits *Wanderer II* actually took 8 hours to get inside. But this night, by some strange fluke we carried a fair wind right up the first reach ; it came in strong squalls and we made the most of them. Then for a while we lost the wind completely, and we worked in turns at the sweep while the swell boomed and echoed uncannily on the rocks each side of us until we reached the Kingswear pier, where we found some wind again and were soon inside sailing through pools of golden light which the street lamps and lighted windows of the houses threw across the water. But the Kingswear side, where we wished to bring up, was very dark, and large mooring buoys there caused us some anxiety for the ebb was running by then. However, we found a clear berth at last, and just as though the noise of our chain, as the anchor went plunging to the bottom, was a pre-arranged signal, all the street lamps of the town went out. It was exactly midnight.

A strong south-easter held us in port for several days while the scud flew fast and low overhead ; some swell found its persistent way round the double bend into our anchorage, and we realised that the month was November and that we were a long way from our home port in a very small boat. But we were anchored close to *Nettle*, a fine old 21-ton yawl in which Hugh Ruttledge of Everest fame and his wife and daughter were living. Their kindness to us was something rare, the memory of which we shall treasure for many a day, and we soon felt that we had known them for years as we visited each other's yachts to talk of the mountains, the sea and other things.

On the fourth day of our stay at Dartmouth the wind had drawn round to the north, and the river was looking its very best as we set all sail to topsail, said goodbye to the Ruttledges who had rowed across to wish us *bon voyage* and ran swiftly out of the river. Just as we reached the narrows by the castle a hard squall came upon us with a quick darkening of the water, and we had to get the topsail down in a hurry, but as soon as we had got clear out to sea we found only a moderate N.W. wind. To port the Devon landscape looked soft and colourful in the thin autumn sunshine as we fetched pleasantly up the coast to Berry Head and from there we had a delightful turn to windward in smooth water to Torquay, where we picked up a harbour mooring at teatime. During our short cruise that was the only passage we managed to complete in daylight.

Of all the small walled harbours into which *Wanderer* has poked her inquiring bow at one time or another, I know of none cleaner or more convenient for the visiting yachtsman than Torquay, though I understand that S.E. winds send in a heavy swell and that in the summer it becomes overcrowded. It was a Sunday night that we spent there, a night with faint N.W. airs and brilliant starlight, and as one by one the twinkling lights of the town sprang up on the twin hills, a peal of church bells rang magnificently across the still harbour.

After lunch the following day we slipped from our buoy, sailed out of the harbour and along the north shore of the bay.

At 1.45 p.m. we took our departure from the Oar Stone on a course to clear the Bill of Portland by 6 miles. With eleven Brixham fishing boats out trawling under a cloud of gulls, and the distant hills of Dartmoor rising against the pale blue sky, the bay looked really beautiful as we left it quickly astern.

The N.W. wind was of just the right strength for comfortable sailing, and it served us well until 6 p.m. when it veered to N.E. and we had to harden in the sheets with a consequent reduction of speed. Later in the evening it freshened, the topsail had to come in, and at 11 p.m., when Portland light bore N. by E., very faint and some distance away, the wind came ahead, the tide was against us and we made very little progress. In Susan's watch, from midnight until 3 a.m., the wind moderated, and on the offshore tack she lost sight of Portland light, so when I went on deck to relieve her we put about, set the topsail and headed between N. and N.N.E.

Progress was wearisomely slow as we plugged on against a short tidal sea which again and again knocked all way off the yacht, and it was cold in the cockpit in spite of the riding light placed between the helmsman's knees. We were also troubled by steamers. One came very close, circling round to investigate, but apparently satisfied with what she saw, she winked twice with her Aldis lamp and went off on her proper business. But the helmsman of another seemed to be as sleepy as I was, for he steered such an uncertain course that a dozen times or more he showed me first his starboard then his port light. We were moving so slowly that I was undecided whether to go about to clear him on the other tack or to continue as I went. I shone the electric torch at him and on to our sails, but not until he had got uncomfortably close did he sheer off on a more definite course.

Dawn came reluctantly and no land was visible, but the wind increased again and once more we crashed along with the topsail handed. At 8.30 a.m. we could just make out the Bill about 4 miles away, and it was soon obvious that we could not hope to beat on and round St. Albans Head on that tide ; it therefore seemed wise to make Portland harbour for a rest, and we bore away accordingly. By the time we reached the harbour entrance the wind was blowing quite hard from E. with a clear sky, and I wondered where we would find shelter, for one is not allowed to bring up close under the lee of the breakwater. No shelter could be expected in Castle Cove, but away in the S.W. corner of the harbour we spied a row of concrete Mulberries, so we ran down to them and found a well-protected anchorage under their lee.

For two nights we lay there while the E. wind blew hard. The harbour was speckled with whitecaps, and the naval launches plying between the ships and the shore drove to and fro in a deluge of wind-whipped spray, but on the third morning the wind hauled round to N.E.—a slant for us—and moderated. We wasted no time in making use of it and sailed quickly along past the Dorset coast a point free, but at 3 p.m., when Anvil Point bore N., the tide turned against us and the wind veered to head us off. On the port tack *Wanderer* had the hollow little seas almost dead ahead, for they were not running true with the wind, and again and again she lost steerage way as she plunged. On the other tack she did better, so we decided to make for Poole, but we soaked away to leeward so much on the tide that it took us 6½ hours to cover the 5 miles to Poole Bar, and having navigated the entrance channel, without any difficulty that time, we came-to in our old berth in South Deep.

The last short sail of our little autumn cruise was a grand one with a fresh S.S.W. wind, a considerable swell and a lumpy sea. From Poole to Hurst we averaged 5½ knots under lower sail, but in the Solent the wind by degrees died away, so we set the topsail and replaced the small jib with the large one, and shortly afterwards we had to set the yankee. Very slowly the old familiar landmarks slipped astern as we ghosted on past Calshot Spit to the mouth of the Hamble. In the river there were only the faintest of airs, not strong enough even to ruffle the water, and night had fallen when at last we let the anchor go off Bursledon in a clear space between the shadowy shapes of the yachts waiting there to be laid up for the winter.

After we had stowed the sails and made all snug, we stood on deck for a few minutes enjoying the peaceful scene. The moon was up but she was blurred and only faintly visible for a thin sea mist had drifted in with the flood. Away in the distance a train clattered through a cutting, while nearer to us a curlew cried on the marshlands, and there was an occasional deep rumble as the tide moved the anchor chain gently along the bottom of the creek. Except for those small sounds all was completely still. With her mast and rigging hazily silhouetted against the silvery vapour, *Wanderer* lay silently above her own reflection. We had one last look round, then with great content we went below to the warm cabin where the firelight was dancing cosily on the deckhead and the polished woodwork.

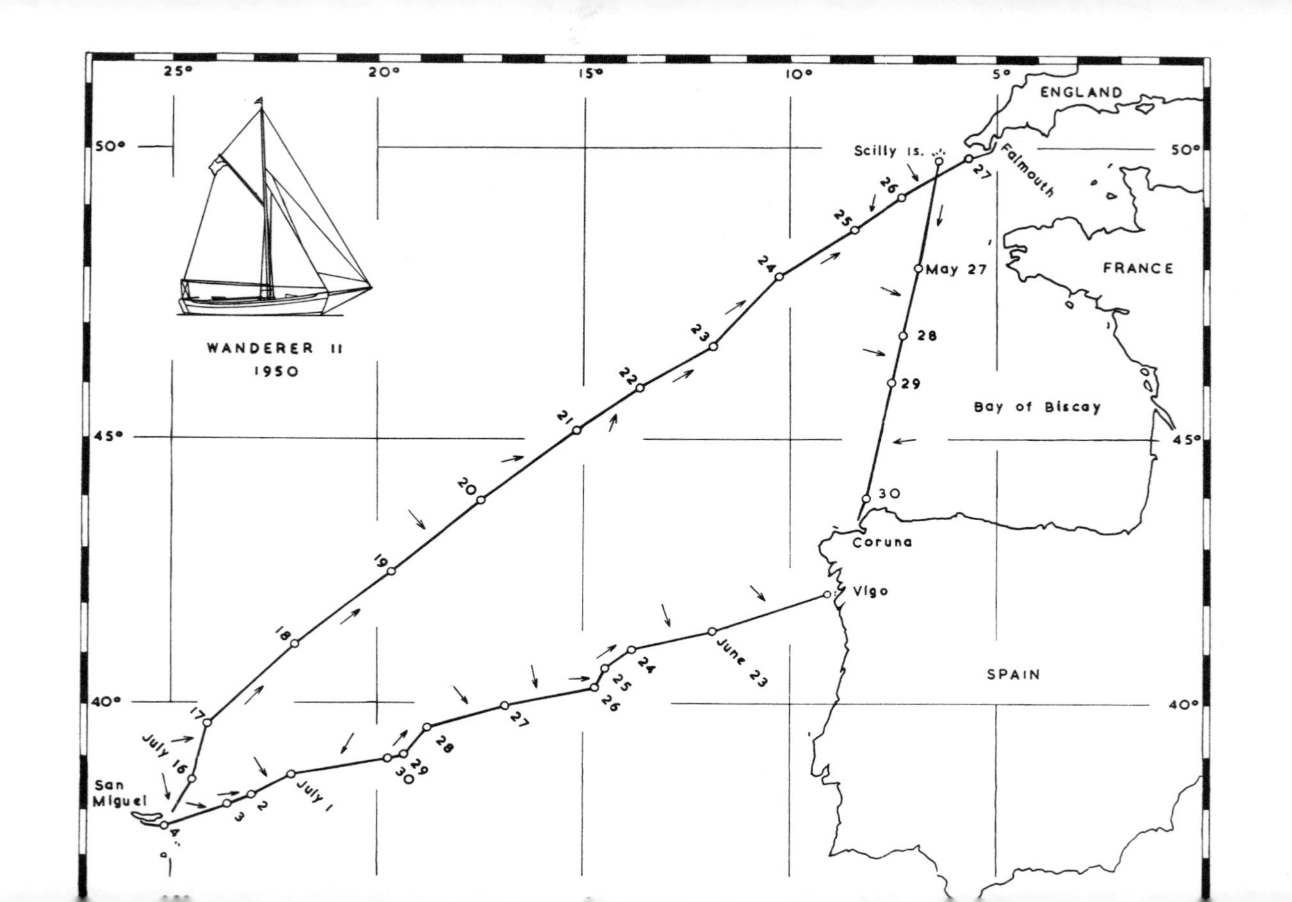
WANDERER II
1950
ENGLAND
FRANCE
SPAIN
Bay of Biscay
Falmouth
Scilly Is.
Coruna
Vigo
San Miguel
May 27
28
29
30
June 23
24
25
26
27
28
29
30
July 1
2
3
4
July 16
17
18
19
20
21
22
23
24
25
26
27
25°
20°
15°
10°
5°
50°
45°
40°

CHAPTER XVI

TO SPAIN AND SAN MIGUEL, AZORES

WITH the idea in our minds that one day we might go voyaging far afield to see something of the world, Susan and I thought it would be wise to make an experimental ocean voyage. As an objective San Miguel, the largest and most important island of the Azores situated 1,200 miles W.S.W. of the Lizard, was suitable and convenient, and finding it would put my newly-learnt navigation to the test. We proposed to go there by way of the north-west coast of Spain, but we felt we ought to be prepared to make the passage out direct in case the winds dictated such a course, and in any event the homeward passage would be made without putting in anywhere; therefore, acting on the assumption that we might be at sea for 20 days we planned to take on food and water enough for 40 days so as to provide a safety margin should continued adverse weather or damage to the gear seriously delay us.

During the winter we made our preparations with some care. We overhauled all the sails and gear, had a new mainsail and topsail made, re-built the sea-anchor, and moved the bilge pump from the cockpit to the oilskin locker so that in bad weather one could sit and pump in comfort down below; as the cockpit drains into the bilge we made for it a portable canvas lining to be shipped in bad weather. *Wanderer II*'s normal fresh water supply was 20 gallons; this we doubled by fitting eight 2½-gallon cans in the fireplace recess just forward of the mast. To allow for the extra weight of water we sacrificed the fire-place, the 2-burner cooker (leaving a single Primus slung in gimbals) and the 7-foot pram dinghy, replacing the latter with a Titcraft folding boat of ply and canvas; the total saving in weight was 310 lb. As the extra water trimmed the yacht a little by the head, we moved 15 of the 30 fathoms of chain out of the chain-locker and stowed it in the bilge farther aft.

During the voyage I used *Astronomical Navigation Tables* with

Reed's Nautical Almanac for obtaining position lines from observations of sun and stars, and for a chronometer made do with the cabin clock checked daily by time signals from the B.B.C., but these grew very faint as distance increased and when nearing the Azores were obtainable only during the hours of darkness. I kept the dead reckoning by plotting on the chart when that was on a sufficiently large scale, otherwise on a plotting diagram, and thus avoided the use of the traverse tables. Instead of entering the barometer readings in the log we marked them on a barograph chart at the change of watch, or more often when we remembered. I did the navigation and Susan did the cooking, which was often a much more difficult and less rewarding occupation.

Having wintered at Yarmouth, I.O.W., we left on 8th May, 1950 and sailed to Newtown Creek where we intended to remain for some days to complete our fitting-out and then to stretch our new mainsail and topsail in the Solent, for we did not wish to leave the country until nearer the end of the month and were therefore in no immediate hurry to get to the westward. But the next day was warm and sunny with a light E. wind, conditions which we could not ignore, so we spent the forenoon sail stretching and in the evening slipped out past the Needles and arrived at Fowey 30 hours later.

The passage down Channel revealed considerable deviation of the steering compass, perhaps due to the altered position of the bilge pump, so after spending one night at Fowey we ran rapidly round to Falmouth with a fresh E. wind to get the compass adjusted; but although we brought up as close under the lee of the dock wall as possible, our berth was an uncomfortable one, and when I asked Mr. Cousins, the adjuster, to come aboard and attend to our compass he replied that he would have nothing to do with us until the wind moderated or changed direction. So we beat wetly across to St. Mawes where we found a quiet berth near the little harbour, and there remained for several days attending to the many things that still needed doing to make the yacht ready for sea. Our attempt to check the steering compass with the hand bearing-compass was not a success; so we fixed our position on the chart by means of horizontal sextant angles between Pendennis and

St. Mawes castles and the end of the harbour wall (all these were clearly shown on the large-scale harbour chart), made a pelorus out of an old course-setting protractor (as the compass was placed in the bridge deck it could not be used for taking bearings direct), then swung the yacht taking bearings of Black Rock beacon, and made out a deviation card which showed that we had a whole point ($11\frac{1}{4}°$) of deviation on westerly courses. We also made a detailed list of the contents of every shelf and locker (27 in all) so that we might be able to find anything we needed without undue delay. The stowing of so much food in so small a vessel had been no mean undertaking. There was, for example, no possibility of stowing all the tins of one kind together; each space had to be packed to capacity, using every corner and the spaces between the frames to the best advantage and stowing there such things as could be made to fit. The result would have been chaos without our lists. We removed the paper label from every tin, marked each tin with a code letter or number and then varnished it; no tin rusted through, though at times some of them were submerged in bilge water.

When at last the little vessel was ready so that she could, if necessary, be independent of the shore for 40 days, there was no visible sign of that fact in her cabin, nothing to suggest to the chance visitor that she was just about to start on a longish voyage. The chance visitor was, therefore, not likely to ask awkward questions unless he noticed our lack of freeboard.

On 20th May we left St. Mawes under all sail to topsail and yankee jib with a light N.N.W. air which died as we approached the Lizard; as the west-going stream was setting us towards the headland we used the sweep a little anxiously for half an hour until a breeze made from W. by S., and soon after lunch we took our departure, heading S.S.W. close-hauled. In the evening the wind backed and started to freshen, so we tacked and reduced sail bit by bit until soon after midnight we were sailing under staysail only. A large, regular sea was building up, but when in the afternoon the wind veered suddenly to the S.W. and strengthened to force 8 it was no longer possible to continue sailing; so we handed the staysail and went below, leaving the boat to look after herself with the helm lashed down.

But the motion was wild and we got little rest. In the evening *Eugene Marie*, a large, French diesel trawler, called us on deck with her siren, and as she passed slowly very close to windward of us her skipper hailed and asked: " Do you want for anything? " The trawler made a grand picture; at one moment she was perched high up above us on top of a crested sea against the sky, and the next was deep in the trough so that we could look down upon her deck and the top of her wheelhouse. At dusk the wind eased a little, so we re-set the staysail, gybed, and a couple of hours later were able to get the reefed mainsail on her; but she headed little better than S.E. and, deeply laden as she was, was very wet. Neither of us got any sleep that night, and when the morning forecast promised us further strong winds from a southerly quarter we decided that it was scarcely worthwhile to persist in so futile an attempt to work to windward in such conditions, and after breakfast we bore away for the Isles of Scilly which lay some 55 miles to the N.N.E.

Owing to the various courses steered and the time spent lying-to, I did not feel very confident of my dead reckoning, but during the run to the Scillies, which had it not been such a retrograde step we would much have enjoyed, I was able to get observations of the sun, and the position obtained agreed within a few miles with the D.R. position. We made a good landfall just before heavy rain obscured everything, and in a squall the reef which had only recently been shaken out had to be tucked in again in a hurry. We entered through St. Mary's Sound and came-to in the pool off Hugh Town in time for supper, having sailed 206 miles to make good only 62.

We were fortunate to be in, for a gale blew from S.E. and was followed by a day of heavy rain, after which we were able to get away and take our departure for Cape Prior in N.W. Spain, allowing quarter of a point (3°) for the inset into the Bay of Biscay, and reached, then ran, with topsail and spinnaker set, swiftly on our way; but during the night we had to reduce sail as the wind freshened. Our first day's run was 119 miles, but the second was only 75 miles, for the greater part of it was spent under staysail only in a strong beam wind. Every half hour or so a strong squall, heralded by a darkening of the overcast sky to windward bore down on us and for a few minutes

Susan steers as in worsening weather we run back for the Scillies

the sea smoked; for some of those squalls we handed the staysail.

The total inset into the bay during the first two days amounted to 30 miles, considerably more than I had expected, and an adjustment was made to the course accordingly. During the third day the weather improved and we were able to make all sail, yet by midnight there was not a breath of wind and we lay becalmed for 12 hours. Although we had to keep a watch, for we were by then on the Ushant–Finisterre shipping lane, we made up much of our lost sleep and enjoyed our meals, for we were getting our sea legs.

When at last the wind made it came from N.E., quickly freshening and veering to E. and by dusk we were reduced to staysail and single-reefed mainsail. The night's sail proved to be one of the wettest but most exhilarating that either of us had ever experienced as *Wanderer* hurried along with a strong wind from just abaft the beam. The sea was short, steep and crested, and often heavy deluges of spray came in over the weather quarter and drove across the cockpit to the discomfort of the helmsman; from down below these dollops sounded much worse than they really were. Ragged black clouds hurried across the sky, but between them the moon shone brilliantly so that one could then read the patent log without a torch, and every hour saw us $5\frac{3}{4}$ sea miles farther on our way.

By daybreak the sky was overcast with low, damp cloud and visibility was reduced to about 3 miles. All too early I began to fuss about our landfall, but in mid-morning was able to get a snap shot of the sun when the cloud thinned, and on plotting the resulting position line on the chart found that by a happy chance it agreed almost exactly with our course and cleared Cape Prior by 2 miles. Crossing that line later by a noon latitude fixed us 23 miles from the invisible cape and showed our day's run to be 127 miles. Soon after we sighted high land on the weather bow; we could not identify it but presumed it to be in the neighbourhood of Cape Ortegal. The wind then backed a little and we ran on fast before a steep following sea, but now with dry decks, while slowly the magnificent coastline of Spain unfolded itself, basking in hot sunshine with Cape Prior now clear off the bowsprit end. We rounded it in the evening and with only 13 more miles to go to La Coruña felt confident of being at anchor before dark; but close to the land the wind fell light and variable. In turn we set the yankee and the masthead spinnaker to make the best use of every air. Soon, however, there was no wind at all and we got out the sweep to scull for a couple of hours. But we were tired, for with all the excitement of making the land neither of us had slept since dawn, so we anchored with the kedge in 11 fathoms outside the harbour. Almost at once a breeze came in from seaward to put us on a lee shore; so wearily we weighed and sailed into port, but another hour's work was needed with the sweep before we were able to reach an anchorage off San Anton castle amidst the brilliant lights, loud noises and strange smells of our first Spanish harbour.

We were awakened a few hours later by a boat bumping alongside. It contained a party of men and youths who apparently had nothing better to do than gape at us, and as we were unable to get rid of them and it was too hot to ship the washboards in the companionway, they could look right down into our cabin. That embarrassed us a bit, but as we had to endure similar curiosity at most Spanish anchorages we eventually got accustomed to it. After breakfast, eaten in public, we moved to a more convenient berth off the Real Club Nautico and remained there for two hot and windless days. We were entered without formality, the officials not even wanting to come aboard; they asked us to write our names on a scrap of paper, looked at our signatures with evident relief, smiled and said: " Ah, matrimonial. Two's two! ", gave us each a cigarette and went away.

But at every other place we went to in Spain the civil guard complete with firearms always came aboard no matter how isolated our anchorage might be; we thought this was out of curiosity, not a sense of duty, and sometimes they stayed over-long, but all were courteous.

We like bustling, virile Coruña with its glass-fronted buildings sparkling round the curve of the bay, but so fouled by the inhabitants were its landing places and so thickly coated with oil was the water of the harbour that we were glad when a light breeze enabled us to sail the 9 miles to the best natural harbour on that part of the coast, the Ria de El Ferrol. We found a quiet, clean berth on the south side just within the entrance where we cleaned the filth off the topsides and the dinghy, and using it as a base made several day sails and explored the countryside on foot. Eventually we were asked to move as some fishermen wished to cast their nets where we lay. We then had an exhilarating sail along the coast to the west and south to the Ria de Camariñas which lies just beyond Cape Villano; this headland, incidentally, bears little resemblance to the sketch in the *Pilot*, being a fine, jagged promontory with a conspicuous rock close N. of it, the whole a warm, red-brown colour; and its lighthouse, like so many in Spain, is perched so high as frequently to be obscured by cloud. There we gybed and stood in towards the shore a little apprehensively, for the approach to the Ria has some unmarked dangers in it. We soon spied the long, white hermitage on Monte Farelo, which is the key to the situation, and smoothed our water rapidly as we came under the lee of the land. There was no easing of the wind as we entered the Ria, which is a delightful place with a mountainous background, wooded slopes and little sandy beaches, and two slashing tacks took us up to the village off which we anchored, having averaged 5.7 knots for the 57-mile trip.

Camariñas, with its gaily coloured cottages jumbled picturesquely round the walled harbour, was typical of the small coastal villages in that part of Spain; it was isolated and primitive and its inhabitants made a living by fishing and exporting timber grown in the surrounding forest. We saw no motor vehicles; the bullock cart, often with a high basketwork affair added to enable a large load to be carried, was the usual form of land transport except, of course, for the heads of the women on which tubs of water or baskets of market produce were often balanced, while trade with Vigo and other ports was carried on by able-looking coasters, gaff-cutter or ketch rigged, many of them without auxiliary power.

In Spain fiestas, religious holidays during which rockets are let off and church bells are rung, are frequent. Camariñas was having one the day we remained there, and we thought it must have been a special one for children, for in the evening when we returned to the village from a walk out to Villano lighthouse, some two hundred children all dressed in their Sunday best were dancing to a small band. At our approach the band stopped playing and the children crowded round us touching us and fingering our clothes while they escorted us to our dinghy, and as we embarked and rowed away they shouted "Adios" and cheered and cheered again. Maybe they thought we had sailed in specially for their fiesta.

The day was overcast and gloomy as we ran down the coast towards Cape Finisterre. To seaward the shipping lane was busy, and inshore of us some crabbers were tending their pots; the crew of one which passed close blew kisses to Susan. Because of the considerable swell we took good care to avoid Muniz rock ($2\frac{1}{4}$ fathoms) and La Carroca shoal (1 fathom) by taking a number of bearings and vertical sextant angles, but saw no breakers on either of them. We rounded the famous headland in early afternoon and were at once in smooth water. For a little while the sun came out, the deck steamed and then became too hot for bare feet, the wind dropped to a light air and soon we lay becalmed, while the sky clouded over again, a fine rain fell, and a thunderstorm brewed and rumbled among the hills. Corcubion, the port we wished to reach, lay 6 miles away, and we had to scull the whole way to an anchorage there which we barely reached before dark.

We remained for a day in torrid heat, not willingly, for the place was disappointing, but because there was no wind. We found the village dirty, squalid, and poverty-stricken; not only was the church bell cracked but the face of the clock also. The only sign of industry came from a factory on the opposite shore; its chimney belched thick orange smoke which hung low and heavy on the hills, and every few minutes there was a loud crash as though a thousand tin trays laden with crockery were being dropped on a concrete floor.

We left that sad little place, which is set in such lovely surroundings, as soon as we got some wind, and beat down the coast to Muros Bay and anchored in crystal-clear water in a beautiful bay on the southern shore; as the chart gave it no name we christened it Ensenada de Wanderer Dos. Ashore we found healthy-looking men and women tilling the fertile coastal plain, and many vines trained across the mountain streams. It was a good place to be just then for the weather became bad, and instead of the N. and N.E. winds which usually prevail at that time of year the wind blew hard from S., sometimes with gale force and often accompanied by rain. Twice we made abortive attempts to get away to the south; on the first we could not weather Cape Corrubedo 20 miles from our anchorage, so turned and ran back to our old berth; and on the second off Muros village the wind died, so we sculled to the anchorage just outside the small walled harbour which was packed with open, double-ended fishing boats preparing for sea. A few of them were lateen rigged, but the majority carried a single, square-headed lug, the luff of which was tautened for windward work by a spar thrust out from the mast. In the evening the boats came out and anchored all around us while their crews, usually six to a boat and many of them quite young men, cooked and ate their evening meal.

At dusk the fleet of little black boats numbering about a hundred weighed their grapnels and put to sea under oars, for there was still no wind and none of them had engines. Each spoke a greeting as she passed, and the place seemed strangely empty when this floating village had vanished round the headland. But later a party of eight young men came out from the harbour in a boat they paddled along with their hands, and for half an hour or so sang beautifully in the starlight. They did not speak to us, but were still singing as they paddled away, their voices fading gently in the distance.

In the morning we got a fair wind at last and were able to continue on our way, and stopping only for the hours of darkness in an open anchorage, reached Vigo Bay without further incident, and sailing right to its head brought up off San Adrian. A fiesta was in progress, and two loudspeakers playing the same tune, but situated at different distances from us, produced the oddest echoing effect.

We woke to find the place enveloped in mist, and without a breath of wind we sculled the 4 miles to the town of Vigo, which was to be our last stop in Spain, and managed to insert ourselves into the small basin right alongside the Real Club Nautico. It was congested with small craft and swimming race pens, and at her owner's invitation we tied up alongside *Atruxo*, the only Spanish crusing yacht we saw while in Spain. There we remained conveniently and comfortably (except for the wash caused by people using the high diving board less than a boat's length from us) for three days, obtaining everything we needed in the town and receiving much kindness from the President and members of the club.

We crept out of the basin before breakfast on 22nd June, found a light E. wind to carry us down the bay to the Islas Cies, and by noon were clear of the land. At sea the wind was N.N.W. and it freshened nicely so that we were sailing at 5½ knots when we took our departure for Armel Point (the east end of the island of San Miguel) 820 miles away. As the mountains of Spain faded into the distance astern and I unshackled the

: A typical
gged Spanish
g boat

: Under oars a
g boat from
s puts to sea
e night's
g

anchor chain, lashed the anchor securely and plugged the navel pipe with a large cork, I realised that our ocean passage now really had begun, and I wondered what the North Atlantic had in store for us; *Wanderer II* seemed to me just then to be very small. I do not believe that Susan gave the matter a moment's thought, and she sang to herself as she got the lunch. She told me afterwards that she was not worried as she had complete confidence in *Wanderer* and me, so it was just as well I did not mention my misgivings at that time.

While we were at sea Susan prepared and cooked all the meals except breakfast, which was got by whoever had taken the last of the night watches, while I did the navigation and the sail shifting. That was hardly a fair division of labour, for the cook has a hard time of it in any small vessel at sea. What is more, the cook had to steer while I navigated, and therefore often got more than her fair share of steering during the day.

When planning the cruise in the winter in our armchairs before the fire we had decided to take 4-hour watches; but when the time came we found that at night we could not keep awake at the helm for more than three hours and often less than that. So we usually divided the night into two 2-hour and two 2½-hour watches. It was a bad arrangement, for far too much of one's short spell below was spent in struggling out of and into oilskins and damp clothes, or in getting a hot drink or a bite of food. The need to set or take in sail also frequently interfered with one's watch below.

Much of the pleasure and satisfaction of an ocean passage is obtained, we find, by getting the best performance out of the yacht, and although we never drove her to the extent of risking damage we kept her going properly day and night, always setting more sail as soon as she could carry it and hanging on to it as long as possible. We hoped that as we settled into sea routine we might be able to take longer night watches, but that was not so, and on both the outward and homeward passages we had to keep to our 2- and 2½-hour watches with the result that we were usually short of sleep.

By dusk the wind had freshened a lot, the seas were growing steeper, and we were reduced to the single-reefed mainsail and the staysail. The evening meal consisted of scrambled eggs eaten straight from the saucepan, a dish which has the merit of being easy to prepare and to eat when one is feeling squeamish; as I said at the time after mine had parted company with me, " Easy come, easy go ". I should, however, point out that we did not make a habit of eating out of saucepans except when the motion was particularly violent; normally we ate with knives and forks off china plates in a civilised manner, and washed up immediately afterwards.

A large passenger ship crossed our bows in my first night watch, and so close was she that through binoculars I could make out the figures of men and women in evening dress on her brightly lighted decks. Her steady, ordered progress seemed in strange contrast to our wild, wet rush through the night, and again, but I believe for the last time, I felt that our little ship was rather small. We continued to sail fast throughout the night and made a day's run of 127 miles. By " day " I mean, of course, from ship's noon to ship's noon, a matter of a little more than 24 hours when sailing to the west, and a little less than 24 hours when sailing east.

Having gone as far south as Vigo before leaving for the Azores we could look forward to a large proportion of N. and N.E. wind, for in summer the Portuguese "trade" commences in that latitude, and according to meteorological statistics we might expect 81 per cent of such winds. You can then imagine our disappointment when on our third day at sea the wind backed to west, dead ahead for our purpose, and we had to start beating to windward. On that outward passage we had all told 5 days of headwinds, and they tried us sorely, for they were accompanied by a short, steep little sea which again and again knocked the way off the yacht and made her motion very uncomfortable.

However, we could count ourselves fortunate in some respects; for the most part the headwinds were light so that we were able to carry the yankee jib-topsail, and as *Wanderer* can always be persuaded to sail herself when close-hauled, we were both able to turn in and make up lost sleep on those occasions. We find that it does not pay to lash the helm, for then if the wind freshens the yacht luffs, while if it eases she bears away, and it never did remain constant in strength for very long. Therefore we trimmed the sheets in such a manner that the forward sails balanced the after ones, and although a little speed was sacrificed the helm required no attention. There were some days when we never touched the helm except when putting about on to the more favourable tack when the wind changed direction. When the wind was dead ahead we kept on the starboard tack for two reasons: the swell was almost always from N.W. no matter from what direction the wind might blow, and on the beam it interfered with us less than when on the bow; also the farther to the south we went the greater should be our chance of finding a fair wind.

Sometimes the sun shone brilliantly from a clear sky and then the sea became a wonderful vivid blue, an indescribably beautiful colour about which we had often read but had not previously seen. More often, however, the sky was veiled with thin cloud or haze which made observations of the celestial bodies awkward, but only on two days was the sky so heavily overcast as to prevent sights being taken. During the crossing the Portuguese and Azores currents ran at about their maximum speed, setting us each day some 25 miles south of the course; to counteract this we made an alteration of half a point to the course steered.

On our sixth day at sea we sighted a tanker nearly hull-down and heading about W.N.W., bound from Gibraltar to some Canadian port, perhaps. She was the first vessel we had seen since leaving the shipping lane off the Spanish coast, and somehow her presence seemed to intensify the emptiness of the great ocean. Yet we never did feel lonely, for no sooner had the land dropped out of sight than we were accompanied by storm petrels and fulmars; they never left us for long, seemed to enjoy our company, often flew inside the topmast stay, and sometimes tried unsuccessfully to land on the gaff or crosstrees. They were good companions, and when the weather looked threatening one could hardly feel scared while surrounded by such small and fearless creatures.

The flight of the fulmar is remarkable for its ease and grace; occasionally a few strokes are taken, but mostly it is sailing with wings quite steady while the bird sweeps round in great arcs, swooping down into the trough of the sea, then up to the crest with one wing-tip only just clearing the water. On several occasions we met turtles measuring about 18 inches across the shell. They appeared not to notice us until we were close aboard, and then submerged only a little way. They did not strike us as being particularly seaworthy or of a very efficient shape, but they must be both for we met them several hundred miles from land, and I believe they go ashore only to lay their eggs.

Sometimes we were followed by sharks though we did nothing to encourage them, but the most awe-inspiring visitation was by two whales with an estimated waterline length of 40 feet. They surfaced one morning to blow and circled closely round *Wanderer*, inspecting her from every angle, and then, much to our relief, lost interest in a thing so slow and uncomfortable, and made off.

By noon of the 29th we had been at sea for a week and our days' runs had been 127, 78, 48, 25, 103, 96 and 34 miles, a mixed bunch; but we were progressing and Armel Point was 290 miles distant.

Early the following morning heavy rain set in, and after a short calm the wind suddenly came away strong from N.E., the first time it had been abaft the beam since leaving Spain. We shortened sail, but there must have been considerable weight in that wind, for the lee deck was often buried and the washing-up bowl, which had inadvertently been left on the stern deck, was swept overboard. By breakfast time the wind had reached fresh gale strength, a heavy, crested sea was building up, and rain was still driving from a leaden sky. We handed the mainsail and got the boom into its crutch and continued running fast under staysail only. But the sea continued to rise and the wind to strengthen, and fearing that the staysail would flog itself to bits as it gybed repeatedly from side to side in spite of its hardened sheets, I put a lifeline round my waist, crawled forward and took it off, bending on in its place, but not setting, the tiny storm staysail. By then every sea was capped by a heavily breaking crest, and I thought it was no longer prudent to persist in steering the course, so we bore away a bit and ran before them.

With no sail set *Wanderer* rolled fast and far, dipping her rails in turn in the sea. Steering required concentration, so we took spells at the helm of only one hour each. We were interested and reassured to see that instead of causing the overtaking seas to become steeper and more threatening immediately astern, the wake appeared to create a slick, smoothing them to some extent so that provided the helmsman took them exactly stern-on they passed harmlessly by; but away off each quarter and abeam the crests broke angrily with a roar which vied with the shrilling of the gale in the rigging.

I take it that only a fine-lined vessel whose passage through the water makes very little disturbance could continue to run safely in such weather; one of another type might well cause an overtaking sea to break aboard with serious consequences. I am timid by nature, but when eventually I realised how well our little vessel was behaving and that she was not going to drown us, I derived some pleasure from our swooping progress, and indeed it was heartening after days of headwinds to be moving at a good speed in the right direction (more or less) even though we were under bare poles. Nevertheless I dread bad weather and have no wish to repeat that experience.

By late afternoon the rain had stopped and some patches of blue sky appeared. The scene was magnificent. As each large overtaking sea approached one could look back on either quarter at its overhanging crest blown forward in a curve and just about to break and fall, and, through the crest in that brief moment while it was still solid water, the light shone pale green and beautiful. Then the stern lifted, and quickly the yacht rose until she was perched right on top of that sea, commanding a panoramic view of blue, wind-tossed water spread out all round her before she dropped down into the following trough.

In the evening the gale, having blown for ten hours, began to moderate. At first the easing of the wind was almost imperceptible, and we could scarcely believe that it was moderating. But as the lulls between the squalls grew longer and more frequent the change in the note of the wind became obvious, dropping from a high-pitched shrilling to a lower, less angry note, and I felt as though a weight had been lifted from me. We had not eaten much since breakfast, so I set the storm staysail and sheeted it flat to help steady us while Susan went below and prepared a meal of tinned steak with boiled potatoes and onions and a treacle pudding, followed by coffee. After we had eaten we tied in the second reef and set the close-reefed mainsail and got back on the correct course, but still bore away again now and then when a succession of two or three particularly steep and heavily crested seas overtook us.

The night was bright, often with the nearly full moon shining clearly, and steering was exhilarating. We were moving fast, our tiny sails being almost a press of canvas, and if the helmsman dozed for a moment and let *Wanderer* luff a point or so, she at once woke him to his duty by shipping a dollop over the weather side. A leak in the deck above the blanket locker had soaked our sleeping bags, most of our clothes were wet, and the cabin smelt like the inside of a bus on a warm, wet day. But such small discomforts did not bother us much for we were light-hearted at having weathered that short and not too violent gale and made such good use of it, and there was the cheering prospect of having a decent run to prick off on the chart at noon. Steadily the wind continued to take off, but we did not let the speed drop. At dawn we shook out one reef and changed staysails; after breakfast we set No. 2 jib; in mid forenoon we shook out the final reef and soon after set No. 1 jib and topsail. The day's run was 119 miles and Armel Point was only 155 miles away.

There followed 24 hours of light headwind with an overcast sky, a falling glass and a day's run of only 52 miles, but by noon on 2nd July the wind had veered to N.W. and was up to force 6. Progress close-hauled was no longer possible, so we hove-to on the starboard tack under single-reefed main and staysail, but as we fore-reached too much we had to change staysails and tuck in the second reef; then, with the helm lashed down about 20°, we lay fairly quietly and shipped little water. The wind reached its peak (probably no more than force 7) soon after midnight, and to prevent fore-reaching we had to lash the helm hard down and sheet the mainsail as near amidships as we could get it. In the harder squalls the leech vibrated to such a degree that it almost seemed as though we had a badly balanced engine running.

Although that blow did not reach the strength of the N.E. gale, it was more tiring to us mentally for it hindered our progress and it lasted longer. The noise of the wind in the rigging and of the crests against the weather side and on deck was trying during our 26 hours of inactivity. For the first time in our married life I gave Susan her breakfast in bed that day, and though it consisted of nothing more elaborate than boiled eggs, crispbread, marmalade and coffee, it took quite a time to get ready, for so wild was the motion and so steep the angle of heel that the simplest little action such as drawing a saucepan of water from the tap or pre-heating the Primus, was a major undertaking which in my weary mental and physical state was only to be attempted after careful thought and planning. One's bunk was certainly the best place on board just then, and thanks to the canvas bunkboards with which each is fitted even the weather one could be used safely.

In the afternoon the sky began to clear again and the wind to ease, and with some difficulty owing to the motion I was able to get some observations of the sun, but in such conditions I found that the sextant soon grew heavy in the hand. In the afternoon we let draw and proceeded cautiously on our way—the seas still being of a size and shape that called for some respect when taken on the bow—close-hauled on the starboard tack, but the wind gradually backed and headed us off.

The next day was gloriously bright and sunny with a vivid blue sea and sky and a sharp horizon; visibility I guessed must be 40 miles or more. As San Miguel rises to a height of 3,600 feet towards its eastern end we expected to sight it during the morning. At 0700 Armel Point bore by account N. by W. 36 miles, so we put about to head for it. Excitedly we scanned the horizon, but though terns visited us, and Susan, who is a non-smoker, could smell pines and sweet-scented flowers, there was no sight of land nor any cloud in the sky to suggest the proximity of land. I began to have doubts about my sights of the previous day, but an observation at 0900 gave a position line passing only 10 miles east of the island, so at least our longitude was correct.

By observation the noon position was 21 miles S. by E. of Armel Point. I had scarcely finished working out my sums when Susan shouted that she could see land fine on the lee bow, and there, faint but sure enough, was the outline of Armel Point rising steeply from the sea—a perfect landfall. That was indeed a wonderfully satisfying moment for both of us, and the little worries and discomforts we had endured in order to achieve it seemed a very small price to have paid for such a thrill. The rest of the island, which has a length from W. to E. of 35 miles, was still invisible, wrapped in a pale blue mist the same colour as the sky.

Wanderer seemed to be in as great a hurry as we were to investigate her landfall, and close-hauled on the port tack she forged towards it, her lee bow-wave sparkling in the almost tropical sunshine, and water running in her scuppers. But not until we were within 10 miles of it did we realise what a magnificent island we had found out there in mid-Atlantic: high volcanic peaks reached skywards, some of them still softly clad in mist, and as we drew closer we could make out large areas of dark trees, a patchwork of small fields, and here and there tiny clusters of whitewashed dwellings hanging on the steep slopes.

By 1800 we were within a mile of the southern shore. There we put about and commenced the 17-mile beat along the coast past Villa Franca (the old capital which has twice been destroyed by earthquakes) to the present capital and port of Ponta Delgada; but it was slow work against the fresh W. wind with no lee to be had from the island, and we did not come to the harbour until early next morning. There under the lee of the great breakwater we lost the wind and ghosted to an anchorage on the north side close to the illuminated clock tower of the cathedral where we let go at 0300. We were 12 days 20 hours out from Vigo, a direct distance of 847 miles.

All seemed curiously still and silent after we had turned into our bunks, and accustomed as we then were to broken sleep we were astir soon after dawn, when we hoisted international flag "Q" and had breakfast. Scarcely was the meal finished when the pilot, Sr. Courtinho, who proved to be a good friend to us during our stay, came alongside; he gave us pratique without formality, not even glancing at the bill of health we had obtained at Vigo, and towed us to the best berth in the harbour right up in the western corner close to the landing place. The harbour is an artificial one formed by a breakwater nearly a mile long and is protected from all winds except those from S.E.,

which send in some sea, but is said to be safe even then. There is no inner harbour or basin.

No sooner had we anchored in our new berth than a longshoreman whisked away all our dirty, salt-stiffened clothes and returned them 24 hours later clean and crisp and even with the holes repaired. He served us well in other ways, acting as watchman when we were ashore, and ferrying off water, provisions and visitors, and was reluctant to accept payment. In the forenoon we called on Commander Davis, the British Vice-Consul. He said he felt he already knew us quite well, for the longshoreman's wife, who did our laundry, had taken all our dirty clothes to the consulate to be identified against our list which, being in English, she could not understand. He lent us his chauffeur-driven car and an interpreter so that we might change our traveller's cheques and do our shopping with ease, and that evening he and Mrs. Davis gave a party to which they invited everyone they thought might be of interest or assistance to us. That was a foretaste of the kindness, hospitality and entertainment we were to enjoy throughout our 10-day stay at Ponta Delgada. Not only were the five British on the island extremely kind but the Portuguese also, and the latter were not inclined to forget that Britain was Portugal's oldest ally.

We were driven luxuriously to see the sights of the island along roads hedged for mile after mile with blue hydrangeas; we saw oranges, bananas, pineapples, tobacco and tea growing in profusion, for it is a warm and fertile land; we were shown the hot springs at Furnas, which are said to be a safety valve to this volcanic place, and the blue and green crater lakes of the Seven Cities. We attended parties in the hillside homes of the pineapple planters (these started at about teatime and continued until midnight), were made honorary life members of the Clube Naval, and were guests of honour at a succession of splendid lunches and dinners.

During the short periods we spent in *Wanderer*, where the cabin temperature was 82°, a stream of visitors flocked aboard and showed much interest in her; I think they had not before seen so small a seagoing vessel, and they could not understand how she had managed to come so far. No harbour or pilotage dues were charged, and the Captain of the Port, seeing us one day rowing about in our 7-foot folding dinghy, placed his motor launch with her crew of four bluejackets and a petty officer entirely at our disposal.

We could well have spent a month there without a dull moment, but we had to be back in England early in August. So, having turned end for end the peak and throat halyards which showed some signs of chafe, and given all the brightwork a coat of varnish, we filled up with water and fresh provisions, notably pineapples and bananas, all of which were gifts, and at 0845 on 15th July left the harbour where our many friends waved to us, bound for Falmouth.

The wind was N.W., and in the lee of the island we were at times almost becalmed, but as we approached its eastern end the wind drew ahead, and not until the evening did it become more certain and back enough to allow us to lay N.E. by E. close-hauled on the port tack. The lovely, hospitable island of San Miguel, still thinly clad in its cloak of pale blue mist, looked remote and a little mysterious as we drew away from it; the last we saw of it was the flash of the lighthouse at Armel Point dipping on the horizon, and we felt sad.

The wind was variable in force and direction on the second day, and we used it to make some northing, for it was likely that the N.E. wind which should prevail at that time of year (though we had seen nothing of it during our stay) might set in, and the farther we got to the north the greater would be the chance of finding W. or S.W. winds. That day we saw some more turtles industriously swimming towards Spain, and storm petrels and fulmars joined company with us once more and did not leave us until we reached soundings.

Early the next morning the wind backed to W. and put the mainsail properly to sleep at last. We set the small spinnaker, took in the headsails and started to move along well. The noon position by observation showed that the S.-running current was still operating, but now only to the extent of 15 miles a day. In the afternoon the wind backed to S.W. and freshened nicely, so, as it seemed that the expected nor'-easter might not put in an appearance after all, we took a chance and altered course to E.N.E. on the first leg of the great circle course for the Lizard. On this passage there is a difference of only 25 miles between the rhumb line and the great circle course, but it would add to the interest to keep to the latter if we could.

All through the night and the day of the 18th we continued running fast and covered 129 miles. The sky was clear and blue and the sun so hot that the helmsman covered his shoulders with a towel and wore a wide-brimmed straw hat, and to keep the sun off the watch below we covered the decklights and hatchway. The night was fine and starlit, and as *Wanderer* hurried on her way she was couched on a great cushion of phosphorescence, while the full length of the 70-foot logline with the rotator at its end was a streak of silver light which was lifted and dropped by the overtaking seas. During my second watch and just as I was growing sleepy an aircraft droned overhead; I got some satisfaction from knowing that I was not the only one to have to keep awake, and I thought that the pilot must feel rather isolated and precarious up there in the night sky; I did not envy him.

Again the day was brilliantly blue with a large but regular sea and blazing sunshine. This was the kind of sailing weather for which one buys a boat but so rarely gets in home waters, and although the helm could not be left for more than a moment we enjoyed our spells of steering. There was great excitement in the forenoon as it appeared from log readings that *Wanderer* might make her record run. She certainly seemed to have got the right idea and during the two hours preceding noon achieved 6½ knots, her maximum speed which is usually reached only in smooth water and with a beam wind. It was almost too much of a good thing, for there was a lot of wind by then and there were moments when I felt we were " carrying on " and would have been happier with less sail. However, with the small spinnaker partly balancing the mainsail she steered fairly easily but rolled heavily, especially when travelling on the crests of the seas and the roaring of the bow-wave was impressive. We were not disappointed, for the observed position at noon showed the day's run to be 134 miles, an average of 5.6 knots, which is fast going on a waterline length of 21 feet, and was the best she had ever made.

We had got our sea-legs again by then (we always lose them after a few days in port) and enjoyed our meals. The bananas, of which we had two large stems, were ripening so rapidly that we had to eat fourteen a day to keep pace with them; the pineapples were also doing well in the hot weather and we ate one every second day. We always had a cold lunch as soon as I had worked out the noon position and written up the log, and as we had run out of salad dressing Susan made some with the olive oil from the tinned sardines, the vinegar from the pickled onions, and sugar, mustard and pepper. Life indeed was very pleasant as our little vessel drove swiftly onward, but in the afternoon a large black cloud came up over the west horizon, and a short period of rain was followed by a shift of wind from S.W. to N.N.W., and for the first time in 56 hours we had to take in the spinnaker and set the working headsails. But next morning after a high, yellow dawn the wind shifted back to its old quarter so that we could re-set the spinnaker. Instantly *Wanderer* gathered up her skirts, threw a bucketful of spray at Susan who was steering, playfully tossed some potatoes and tomatoes off the galley bench into the bilge, and settled down in her stride once more, managing a run of 120 miles. Again it was splendid sailing, mostly in hot sunshine, for although a succession of small, puffy, white clouds hurried in formation across the sky, they were widely spaced and rarely came between us and the sun. But the wind was freshening and there was more sea than of late; one crest tumbled aboard and fell through the open hatch upon the watch below.

As it had not been possible to leave the helm during the past few days we had only managed to get about 4 hours' sleep each in every 24 hours, so were feeling tired. That evening, therefore, we handed all fore-and-aft sail and then set the other small spinnaker so that we were under twins; we took their guys through blocks at the quarters and hitched them to the tiller thus enabling the yacht to steer herself, but the rolling was so violent that after all we got little sleep. On a short-handed trade wind passage I suppose that special self-steering twins might be worthwhile, but I doubt if they are worth bothering with in the variables. Of necessity they are small for they will sometimes be used in strong winds, and ours totalled only 220 square feet as against a total of 340 square feet when mainsail, topsail, and one of the twins are set; so unless we urgently need sleep or the wind is very strong, we prefer to carry more sail even if we must then steer. Our twin spinnakers also have the disadvantage that they will not work properly when the wind is more than 1½ points out on the quarter. That was the only occasion during the whole of that cruise that we used the twins and then they were only set for 10 hours after which a change in direction of the wind called for fore-and-aft sails again. The day's run was 124 miles, making a total of 507 miles in 4 days; but it was the last of the really good runs to be made on that passage, and only once thereafter did we manage to make good 100.

Early on the 22nd the glass began to fall and the wind to freshen, and when Susan called me at 0330 the yacht was heavily pressed, and we had to reduce sail. At dawn rain commenced and continued without a break until evening when with a rising glass the wind veered and freshened even more, so that we had to tuck in the second reef. Having had no sights for two days due to the overcast sky, I particularly wanted a check on the latitude so as to find out what the current had been doing with us, and was fortunate enough to get an observation of Polaris in a temporary clearing of the sky at dusk.

That night we passed a number of stationary vessels, which at dawn proved to be French tunnymen, now, alas, nearly all power-driven. We came across more of them during the day, and some altered course alarmingly to have a close look at us and only narrowly missed our log-line. They were more inclined to do this when Susan was on deck alone (no doubt a solitary, auburn-haired woman out there in the wide Atlantic piqued their curiosity) and then came so close that the tips of their great fishing rods almost stroked our sails. Fortunately wind and sea had moderated by then.

We had now reached latitude 46° 40′ N. and had expected before then to have received some help from a favourable current, but the set was still more southerly than easterly and averaged about 12 miles a day. Again there was much rain with poor visibility during the night of the 24th, when we passed through another fleet of fishing vessels, using our navigation lights for the first time on that passage. Throughout the day the wind varied between light and fresh, and there was so much sail drill I almost wished *Wanderer* possessed a snug stemhead bermudian rig with roller reefing gear.

The following night there was again almost constant rain, some of it torrential, and the glass, having recovered from its previous low was falling once more. At 0430, at about which time we crossed the 100-fathom line, we had to take in the topsail and tuck in a reef, but a few hours later were able to make all sail again. The rain stopped in the forenoon, the sky cleared, the wind veered, and by noon we could only just lay the course close-hauled on the port tack. The day's run was 86 miles and the Lizard was only 145 miles away. We felt a little depressed that the fair wind should have deserted us so near home and towards the end of a passage which until then had looked as though it was going to be a fast one. However, we persuaded the yacht to steer herself, sometimes laying the course, sometimes not, and were able to make up some of our lost sleep, for in our bunks we found pitching less disturbing than heavy rolling. As there were some trawlers about after dark only one of us slept at a time, the other sat and read and looked out often to see that all was well.

We did not have to steer again until breakfast time on the 26th, when the wind fell light and became variable. In turn we set the yankee and the masthead spinnaker (the first time we had used that huge sail since we were in Spanish waters) to make the most of every faint air until evening, when we got a fine breeze from N. by E. and got moving properly again. The run was only 52 miles, the poorest of the passage. The night was fine and clear with a nearly full moon, but after our cruise in southern waters we found it cold, and the thick clothes which we had not worn since we were in the Bay of Biscay were very welcome. At 0100 on the 27th at the change of watch, I picked up the loom of the Bishop light just where it should be a little forward of the port beam, and a few minutes later Susan saw the loom of the Lizard light right ahead—a good landfall, and after 11 days out of sight of land that was indeed a satisfying moment, one I believe that both of us will treasure for a very long time.

If the wind continued to blow at its present strength we could be at anchor in Falmouth harbour that day, and although we had greatly enjoyed the passage, the thought of an unbroken night's sleep in a still bunk, and a new, crusty loaf with fresh butter and a crisp lettuce to eat, had a strong appeal just then, and now we wanted to be done with the sea and the vigilance for a little while; but a couple of hours later the wind fell light.

Shortly before sunrise the *Queen Elizabeth* bound east passed 2 miles to the north of us. As the sun rose clear and undistorted, and just as its lower limb was touching the eastern horizon, the *Queen Elizabeth* passed across its face. To me the sun looked like a highly-polished copper tray on a mantelpiece, and the black silhouette of the great ship like a tiny model placed before it. The illusion was over within a few seconds, for the ship moved fast, as did the sun.

But we moved slowly with tantalisingly light airs, while the Cornish coast crept up over the horizon. We had made such small inroads into our fresh-water supply that we were able to have a great personal clean-up, washing ourselves all over and even shampooing our hair. After that we tidied up below, scrubbed the deck and cleaned the brass, and we thought that *Wanderer* looked quite smart with nothing to tell she had just made an ocean voyage except for the whiteness of her salt-scoured rigging and faded sails. Thanks to a little baggywrinkle fitted to the after lower shrouds there was no sign of chafe on the mainsail. The only part of her gear to have carried away was the iron tie between the lower throat block and the gaff jaws; that had snapped one morning when I was swigging up the throat and was quickly replaced with a shackle which made a much stronger job. Throat, peak, and staysail halyards, all of hemp, showed signs of chafe although they had received frequent applications of grease, and the dressing was chafed completely off the seats and elbows of our oilskins.

At noon cross bearings of Land's End and the Lizard fixed our position 17 miles W. by S. of the latter and showed a day's run of 78 miles. We got a better breeze in the afternoon which enabled us to reach the Lizard before dark. There in the lee of the headland we at last lost the ocean swell and crept peacefully up towards Falmouth, but because of a very faint headwind we did not come to an anchorage off the town until 3 o'clock next morning. The direct distance from Ponta Delgada to Falmouth is 1,185 miles, and we had taken 12 days 18 hours over it.

. . . . .

In 1951 Susan and I decided to have a larger yacht built for more extended voyaging. We sold *Wanderer II* to Bill Howell, an Australian dentist at that time working in London, and he with another Australian, Frank McNulty, made a fast and seamanlike voyage in her to Tahiti. Bill then continued single-handed to Seattle, where he sold her. She has since changed hands several times and is based in Hawaii.

NOTES

1. *Mercury* was an old wooden sailing vessel used as a school ship for boys, and for many years was moored in the river just above Hamble village.
2. Roger Pinckney is an architect closely associated with the design of Liverpool Cathedral, and subsequently was elected Commodore of the Royal Cruising Club.
3. Mrs. Pinckney continued to cruise with her son Roger in the new *Dyarchy* until her death at the age of 91.
4. Since those early days the working of observations to obtain position lines has been much simplified for use in aircraft, first with *Astronomical Navigation Tables*, now out of print, and then with *Sight Reduction Tables* which most cruising people use today.
5. Schooner sets are no longer made, but there is a large choice of dry-battery-operated radio sets with short-wave bands suitable for obtaining time signals in all parts of the world.
6. In common with most yachts of her time *Tern II* had no electric supply, and her navigation, riding, and cabin lights burned paraffin.
7. Under new ownership *Tern II* made several fine cruises and successfully completed a voyage from England to New Zealand.
8. At about that time *Andrillot*, first of the famous Vertue class, was being built. The waterlines of the Vertue are a little fuller at the ends than those of *Wanderer II*, and although the draught was less the hull was stiffer; it is also slightly larger.
9. Today I am not so sure of the merits of point (or slab as it is sometimes called now) reefing, and would prefer to have roller gear because of its ease of operation. All the work can be done from a safe position at the mast, and the boom does not have to be brought inboard.
10. Having now had considerable experience of both rigs I have rather reluctantly come to the conclusion that gaff rig is not for me, partly because of the extra weight and windage, partly because of the difficulty of preventing chafe, but chiefly because it is a poor performer to windward when well reefed.
11. I chose to set up the rigging with old-fashioned deadeyes and lanyards in preference to more easily adjusted rigging screws because of the saving in cost; I also felt they were more in keeping with gaff rig.
12. For leeboards read bunkboards.
13. These systems of buoyage are now known as Cardinal and Lateral respectively.
14. Since vane gears were perfected, largely for the single-handed Atlantic races, I consider there is no longer any need for twin sails, the more so

as a well designed and built gear will steer a yacht on any point of sailing, while twin sails will only steer downwind.

15. The Irish Cruising Club now publishes in two volumes sailing directions for the whole of Ireland, and these are available to everyone. My own little book covering the south-west coast has long been out of print.
16. This I was fortunate enough to do after the war on two occasions with my wife in *Wanderer III.*
17. Frank Carr, C.B., C.B.E., was later appointed Director of the National Maritime Museum at Greenwich, 1947–66.
18. Continuous revision of the book has been carried on since then and it has been reprinted several times; annual corrections are provided.
19. In this he was successful and was able to complete his great voyage.
20. I do not understand why with no sail on her and the helm lashed down *Wanderer II* would not lie a-hull, i.e., stopped with wind and sea abeam, as her successor of similar profile did on many occasions. I suspect I was a poor observer during this my first real gale.
21. Puffers were small coal-burning steam-driven vessels which in those days did most of Scotland's coastal trade and often went farther afield.
22. I cannot now believe that any yacht owner would remove the silencer from his outboard, and can only conclude that some of those motors were badly silenced by their makers.
23. Pneumatic fenders are better still and now are widely used.
24. The two excellent volumes of sailing directions by Adlard Coles (*Biscay Harbours and Anchorages*) now cover the whole coast.
25. Susan Sclater, and we got married two years later.
26. Now Rear Admiral McMullen, C.B., O.B.E.
27. After Roger Pinckney had sold *Dyarchy* to W. H. Batten she made several fine cruises in European waters, and in 1975 voyaged out to the West Indies.

INDEX